LITERARY CELEBRITY AND
PUBLIC LIFE IN THE
NINETEENTH-CENTURY
UNITED STATES

BONNIE CARR O'NEILL

LITERARY CELEBRITY AND PUBLIC LIFE IN THE NINETEENTH-CENTURY UNITED STATES

THE UNIVERSITY OF
GEORGIA PRESS
ATHENS

Paperback edition, 2023
Published by the University of Georgia Press
Athens, Georgia 30602
www.ugapress.org
© 2017 by the University of Georgia Press
All rights reserved
Designed by Kaelin Chappell Broaddus
Set in 11/13.5 Fournier MT Pro by Graphic Composition, Inc.

Printed digitally

Library of Congress Cataloging-in-Publication Data

Names: O'Neill, Bonnie Carr, author.
Title: Literary celebrity and public life in the nineteenth-century United States / Bonnie Carr O'Neill.
Description: Athens : The University of Georgia Press, 2017. | Includes bibliographical references and index.
Identifiers: LCCN 2017003987 | ISBN 9780820351568 (hardback : alk. paper) | ISBN 9780820351575 (ebook)
Subjects: LCSH: American literature—19th century—History and criticism. | Authors, American—19th century—History—19th century. | Celebrities—United States—History—19th century. | Popular culture—United States—History—19th century.
Classification: LCC PS201 .O54 2017 | DDC 810.9/003—dc23
LC record available at https://lccn.loc.gov/2017003987

Paperback ISBN 978-0-8203-6486-5

CONTENTS

Acknowledgments vii

INTRODUCTION
Celebrity Culture in the Public Sphere
1

CHAPTER ONE
P. T. Barnum
Commercial Pleasure and the Creation of a Mass Audience
21

CHAPTER TWO
Walt Whitman
Mediation, Affect, and Authority in Celebrity Culture
51

CHAPTER THREE
Ralph Waldo Emerson
The Impersonal in the Personal Public Sphere
87

CHAPTER FOUR
Frederick Douglass
Celebrity, Privacy, and the Embodied Self
118

CHAPTER FIVE
Fanny Fern
Celebrity's Revolutionary Power
154

Notes 193

Bibliography 211

Index 225

ACKNOWLEDGMENTS

Although most of this book contains new work, it also expands essays published several years ago. I am therefore called now to acknowledge professional debts that my creditors may have forgotten—or, worse, think I have forgotten. It is a great pleasure to finally and formally say thanks. I could not have written this book without the resources of numerous libraries. In particular, I wish to thank the librarians at the American Antiquarian Society, the Houghton Library at Harvard University, the Concord (Massachusetts) Free Public Library, Washington University's Olin Library, and Wake Forest University's Z. Smith Reynolds Library. At Mitchell Memorial Library of Mississippi State University, I thank Hillary Hamblen Richardson, as well as librarians in the departments of Interlibrary Loan and Special Collections and the Ulysses S. Grant Presidential Collection.

The ideas for this book germinated at Washington University in Saint Louis, and I remain deeply grateful for the support of the English Department there, especially Vivian Pollak. At Wake Forest University, I benefited from a grant from the Archie Fund for Research in the Arts and Humanities. I wish to thank Eric Wilson, who was then the chair of the English Department, for his support. In 2005 I participated in an NEH summer seminar at the University of New Mexico titled "Reading Emerson's Essays." I am indebted to Russell Goodman for including me in that seminar, which profoundly influenced my thinking about both Emerson and the work of scholarship. I am grateful to my seminar group at the Futures of American Studies Institute in 2013, who gave me generous feedback on chapter 4 and encouraged me to write more fully about Barnum, a figure I find myself unable to elude. Here at Mississippi State University, I am fortunate to work in a department renowned for its collegiality. Warm thanks go to former department head Richard Raymond for fostering such a supportive environment, not to mention his professional guidance and continued support of my work.

Numerous people read and commented on individual chapters or portions of the manuscript. Their help was instrumental to helping me clarify and develop my ideas, and the book would be better if I had the insight to take even more of their good advice. I owe thanks particularly to Branka Arsić, David H. Blake, Kris Boudreau, Rian Bowie, Pete Degabriele, David Dowling, Stacy Kastner, Salah Khan, Kelly Marsh, Jason Phillips, and Ashley Reed. Tommy Anderson has been an indispensible guide to the publishing process and a great cheerleader. As I note above, portions of this book were published in different forms, and I am grateful for the guidance and feedback I received from editors and readers. An earlier version of my chapter on Emerson appeared in *American Literature*; I thank Priscilla Wald for helping a then-young professor navigate the review process. I also thank Sharon M. Harris and Theresa Strouth Gaul, who included an early version of the Fanny Fern chapter in their volume *Letters and Cultural Transformations in the United States, 1760–1860* (Ashgate, 2008). Donald E. Pease wrote a signed review of my article on Whitman's early journalism, which was subsequently included in a special issue of *PMLA*; I am grateful to him, as well as to a second anonymous reviewer at *PMLA*, who helped me improve that essay. Wes Mott invited me to contribute an essay, "Fame," to his collection *Emerson in Context* (Cambridge University Press, 2014), and in doing so he helped me refine my thinking about Emerson's relationship to mass culture.

I wish to thank the three readers who reviewed my manuscript for the University of Georgia Press, especially one who read it more than once and supported the project at every stage. Thanks to Sydney Dupre for bringing me and my project through the transitions at the Press. Hearty thanks to Walter Biggins, acquisitions editor at Georgia. Walter first expressed interest in this project several years before I was ready to send it out, when he was at another press. It was some kind of kismet to have landed at Georgia together. Thank you also to Thomas Roche at the press and to Lori Rider for their attentive editing.

Finally, I thank my family, especially my parents, Doug and Jo-Anne Carr; my siblings, Heather, Ian, and Meagan; and their families for their unflagging confidence. My son, Rex, arrived in the middle of everything, and he brought so much energy, curiosity, and fun. My husband, Bryan, has done everything possible to give me space and time to do my work, thereby ensuring our partnership will outlast this project. I cannot thank him enough. This book is dedicated to these two, Bryan and Rex, the heart of my own private sphere.

LITERARY CELEBRITY AND
PUBLIC LIFE IN THE
NINETEENTH-CENTURY
UNITED STATES

INTRODUCTION

CELEBRITY CULTURE IN THE PUBLIC SPHERE

In an essay occasioned by his reading of James Eliot Cabot's *A Memoir of Ralph Waldo Emerson*, Henry James reflects on the reputation and literary merits of the Concord Sage. For James, Emerson's great contribution, the reason "that indeed we cannot afford to drop him," is that "he did something better than any one else; he had a particular faculty, which has not been surpassed, for speaking to the soul in a voice of direction and authority." Emerson's success lies less in his message than in his manner, his ability to communicate with his audiences. In James's rendering, Emerson is himself a representative man in his fitness to his time and place: "In what other country, on sleety winter nights, would provincial and bucolic populations have gone forth in hundreds for the cold comfort of a literary discourse?" This "cold comfort" is Emerson's gift to his countrymen, the sense of improvement and insight that comes with attending the public lecture outside of one's regular vocation. Looking to Emerson's potential fame, James concludes that "if Emerson goes his way"—if he continues to appeal to audiences in the future—"on the strength of his message alone, the case will be rare, the exception striking, and the honor great." Writing less than a decade after Emerson's death, James wonders whether Emerson's legacy will transform from celebrity, a temporary appeal to a mass audience of his contemporaries, into fame, the durable reputation for greatness.[1]

Both Emerson's celebrity and his fame depend, however precariously, on his association with transcendentalism. James addresses Emerson's discomfort with the transcendentalist label, quoting a letter Emerson wrote to his wife Lidian in 1842:

> He liked to explain the transcendentalists but did not care at all to be explained by them: a doctrine "whereof you know I am wholly guiltless," he says to his wife in 1842, "and which is spoken of as a known and fixed element, like salt or meal. So that I have to begin with endless disclaimers and explanations: 'I am not the man you take me for.'" He was never the man any one took him for, for the simple reason that no one could possibly take him for the elusive, irreducible, merely gustatory spirit for which he took himself.[2]

In James's reading, Emerson's rejection of the term "transcendentalist" manifests his characteristic aloofness; that same tendency caused him to withdraw from Margaret Fuller's enthusiastic friendship and tack away from Brook Farm. Leon Edel notes that the essay traces "the exquisite qualities of Emerson's mind and its expression in his writings."[3] But although James provides some excerpts from Emerson's works and discusses his ideal of the scholar, James is ultimately not interested in Emerson's philosophy or even style, which he dismisses: "it is hardly too much, or too little, to say of Emerson's writings in general that they were not composed at all."[4] The "felicities" and occasional "eloquence" of Emerson's writings barely make up for his inability to achieve a form. Of more interest to me, in this passage James puts his finger on the great challenge of publicity and celebrity more specifically: the public figure's understanding of himself cannot be reconciled with his audience's view of him. Under these circumstances, what can Emerson, or any other public figure, do? Throughout the essay, James attempts to interpret Emerson's character, identify and analyze the qualities of the self that appealed to the popular mind, and thereby justify that appeal.

James asks the same question many of Emerson's early critics asked, that some still ask, and that, indeed, first attracted my own interest years ago: what made Emerson so appealing to his audiences? How do we account for his popularity? Relocating interest in Emerson from his works—his ideas—to his personality, James is not unlike Cabot or the other early biographers whose works I explore more fully in chapter 2. James's essay strikes me as a strong example of the influence of the celebrity culture that was just getting started as Emerson began his lecturing career. The interest in the character of public figures, the effort to personalize them, is a defining element of celebrity culture.

In this book, I study the emergence of celebrities and celebrity culture in the mid-nineteenth-century United States. I am especially interested in the personalization of public life that I see as inherent in celebrity culture, and, looking at Emerson and others, I explore the cultural, literary, and discursive effects of such personalization on both public figures and their audiences. Emerson's letter to Lidian exposes a central problem of the mass publicity that comes with celebrity, the disjunction between an author's ideas about himself and the audience's ideas about him. As readers and as scholars, we may be tempted to do as James does: to mark that distance and implicitly trust Emerson as the best judge of his own character—to dismiss contemporary audiences as mistaken in their collective judgment and privilege the authority of authorship. In this work I resist that urge. Instead, I ask that we credit audiences' judgments, acknowledge the authority they claim as interpreters of public men and women, and recognize that authority as constitutive of the celebrity culture in which both audiences and authors participate, for better or for worse. In taking these positions, we come to a new set of critical questions. Instead of asking only what it is about this man or woman that audiences find so appealing, or how audiences could be so wrong in their judgments, we now ask also about the significance of audience authority, the strategies authors developed in response to it, and the relevance of both to other social concerns, such as majoritarianism, social inclusiveness, and participation.

At the outset, I wish to distinguish celebrity from celebrity culture and establish certain key terms and concepts that run through this book. "Celebrity" is a form of heightened publicity experienced by relatively few people in a society. It is a condition in which a public figure is recognized—is "known"—by far more people than she can herself know. To the celebrity, the audience is composed almost entirely of strangers; to the audience, the celebrity is familiar, even, presumably, intimately so. As the example of Emerson shows, however, that presumption of knowledge and familiarity, while authoritative, may not be correct or definitive, as it is based on impressions, feelings, and ideas of the celebrity as encountered through media. Audiences' interpretations of the celebrity are unsettled and lack consensus.

Both individual celebrities and their observers participate in celebrity culture. In this book, I use the phrase "celebrity culture" comprehensively to include the organization of a host of popular media—mechanisms for the production and distribution of texts; lectures and other kinds of performance—that put authors and others before a public audience, as well as the various responses to this heightened publicity. Promoting an image of the public figure, these media encourage audiences to respond to the public figure as a text, to "read" and interpret her image. In referring to the celebrity image, I acknowledge that, despite audiences' presumptions of familiarity with the celebrity, they never encounter her directly. Instead, audiences encounter representations of the celebrity disseminated through mass media. The representations I discuss are not visual artifacts; indeed, my work deals only tangentially with photography (see my discussion of Whitman and Lincoln in chapter 3). In calling the celebrity an image, I follow celebrity theorists such as Richard Dyer: "By 'image' here, I do not understand an exclusively visual sign, but rather a complex configuration of visual, verbal, and aural signs."[5] The images I discuss are artifacts of language, disseminated to a mass audience via organs of the period's flourishing print industry. These images often do retain visual characteristics: time and again, we see journalists, biographers, and even the celebrities themselves attempt to account for a public figure's appearance, to create in language an approximation of her physical form, personal traits, and moral character. By design and in effect, these visual images render the celebrity recognizable and encourage audiences to associate her body with the ideas or traits she is understood to represent.

My emphasis on the celebrity image, audience authority, and print culture signals my methodology, which brings together celebrity theory and public-sphere scholarship. Celebrity theorists such as Dyer and P. David Marshall are interested in the ways audiences view celebrities as representatives of specific ideas or values. The celebrity's meaning is in the eye of the beholder; nonetheless, "audiences cannot make media images mean anything they want to, but they can select from the complexity of the image the meanings and feelings, the variations, inflections and contradictions, that work for them."[6] Although public figures may attempt to shape audiences' interpretations of them, they are ultimately limited. The audiences' authority to interpret the celebrity or "media image" resembles the interpretive power of readers in classic reader-response theory, wherein, Jane Tompkins explains, "The text's intentions may be manifold, they may even be infinite, but they are always present embryonically in the work itself, implied by it, circumscribed by it, and finally traceable to it."[7] Taking seriously audiences' interest in celebrities, moreover, we attempt to understand the cultural work of celebrities and the popular discourses they elicit. In her seminal reading of popular novels, Tompkins explains they do cultural work: they "offer powerful examples of the way a culture thinks about itself, articulating and proposing solutions for the problems that shape a particular historical moment."[8] The same could be said about celebrities. In popular responses to them, their persons and works, celebrities reveal how "a culture thinks about itself."

Examining celebrities and celebrity culture, moreover, enables me to look closely at one specific element of the material culture of democracy.[9] Insofar as celebrities are representative figures, their significance is more or less political, and their elevation to popular notice seems to some like a vernacular style of election.[10] But of course celebrity culture is not part of the political process, nor is it an institution of the state. As they seek to understand or interpret the celebrity figure's meaning and significance, audiences participate in discursive practices that resemble those of the civic public sphere. More specifically, celebrity culture personalizes the discourses over civic, political, and social issues that go forward in the public sphere. Unlike the idealized public sphere associated with the Enlightenment era, which valued reason and impersonal expression, celebrity culture supports what I call here a personal public sphere, in which participants do not seek, claim, or value anonymity as a means to cultural authority. But the personal public sphere does not shed its value for abstraction like an old shirt. The public sphere that emerges with celebrity culture is rife with contradiction and paradox. Celebrities themselves are both representative and exceptional, and insofar as they stand for values and ideas that matter to their observers, they may be regarded impersonally. At the same time, audiences' scrutiny of celebrities' bodies, lives, and personal qualities relocates selfhood from abstract qualities such as virtue to circumstantial and embodied traits. This tension between impersonality or abstract selfhood and personality or embodied selfhood is not just a feature of celebrity culture; it lies at the heart of contemporary debates over citizenship and national identity.

THE TENDENCY TO PERSONALIZE PUBLIC FIGURES PREDATES THE onset of celebrity and mass culture as a component of fame that enshrines heroic or virtuous individuals. In his comprehensive history of fame, Leo Braudy traces this personal interest into antiquity. Of Alexander the Great, Braudy writes, "the crucial question is less who he *was* than who he was *like*, how he explained himself to his own times and therefore how he wanted to be seen. Only then might we know in part how he saw himself." Fame, for Alexander and for Braudy, is a form of self-publication or "self-naming."[11] Braudy's history of fame is a history of the individual—or, at least, of the discursive use of the individual. If one names oneself with actions, those actions are always aspirational, seeking a heroism that itself bespeaks a noble character. For this reason, Braudy says, fame is linked to honor, and it is strongly associated with figures of cultural authority.

As the forms of cultural authority shift, the uses and forms of fame do as well. Specifically, with the rise of democracy, the concentration of cultural authority in monarchs and aristocratic elites weakens; similarly, the church's social and political influence declines over time. For Braudy, this definitive shift occurs in the eighteenth century and, along with "the expanded powers of media" in the period, gives rise to a "fame culture." In short, the expanded newspaper and periodical press provides a pathway to fame without the patronage of traditional elites, and as a result, fame is no longer associated with social rank or public exertion—heroism in battle, for instance—but with individual identity. Referencing Enlightenment figures including Rousseau, Voltaire, Johnson, Laurence Sterne, and Benjamin Franklin, Braudy claims that fame "becomes . . . an attribute of the self, a justification of the individual in opposition to traditional standards of identity, a spiritual essence that is on view for the world." The fame Braudy describes is related but not yet identical to celebrity. His evocation of self as a "spiritual essence" marks a cultural shift in understanding virtue: "the concepts of both honor and fame are by the eighteenth century firmly along the way to losing the exclusively public definition from which they had been inseparable through the ages."[12] As a result, fame may celebrate or remark on the oppositional relationship between the virtuous and "the world." But the idea that the famous person exhibits abstract qualities of virtue or honor remains compelling.

In addition, fame is always approbatory and fixed, a stable public reputation for virtuous achievement. Celebrity, by contrast, is an unsettled public identity, and it flourishes in controversy, scandal, and debate. Finally, although an expanded press contributes to Braudy's fame culture, in general fame is not linked to a specific economic and cultural infrastructure as celebrity is. In short, fame lifts the public figure out of this world to the ideal plane, whereas celebrity recognizes his worldliness.

A product of mass culture, celebrity is inextricably linked with capitalism. As Tom Mole explains, "Celebrity is a cultural apparatus consisting of three elements: an individual, an industry, and an audience. Modern celebrity culture begins when these three components routinely work together to render an individual personally fascinating." The convergence of these three elements occurs in the romantic period, Mole says, when the industrialization of printing renders the celebrity image available to an audience that is "massive, anonymous, socially diverse, [and] geographically distributed."[13] Mole's history maintains the thematic connection to individualism but puts it through a romantic filter: "On the one hand, by connecting the Romantic conception of a deep, privatized, developmental, self-actualizing selfhood to an industrial infrastructure of promotion and distribution, celebrity culture constituted a powerful engine for normalizing Romantic understandings of subjectivity. On the other hand, studying celebrity culture reveals the extent to which the attitudes of high Romanticism were elaborated in opposition to that culture."[14] Mole's analysis acknowledges the complex links between culture and economy, the push and pull of ideology and philosophy, and the artistic revolt against the economic structures that both limit expression and, paradoxically, make expression possible.

In my study, I focus on the interrelations of celebrity culture and the public sphere of civic discourse. Nevertheless, Mole's association of celebrity's origins with romanticism and industrial print culture helps shape my own understanding of celebrity's emergence in the United States. The industrialization of the publishing industry in the 1830s and 1840s gave rise to a mass culture that in turn elevated some authors to unprecedented celebrity. Studies of the changing profession of authorship in the period tend to note the ways a newly commercial printing and publishing industry changes authorship from a gentlemanly—that is, leisured and self-funded—pursuit to a professional and even "entrepreneurial" one.[15] The rise of the best-seller in the same period is a dramatic example of the changing literary profession; these books benefit from a commercial publishing industry that combines its technical achievements in production and distribution with savvy promotional strategies to reach a mass market of readers.[16] If these practices made stars of some authors who were able to command massive sales, the periodical press's practices of reprinting tended to decentralize publishing and diminish authors' claims to social authority. That diminishment of the authorial power ironically contributes to the development of celebrity authors. As Meredith McGill explains, "In rejecting authorship as a governing principle for the production and distribution of literary texts, the culture of reprinting does not eliminate authors so much as suspend, reconfigure, and intensify their authority, placing a premium on texts that circulate with the names of authors attached."[17] Fanny Fern is an example of a writer whose work was reprinted under her familiar pseudonym, enhancing her fame and ensuring that her savvily marketed books became best-sellers. Reprinting culture helps demonstrate just how mass culture contributed to the creation of both individual celebrities, such as Fern, and celebrity culture. As McGill's study shows, mass culture is linked to technologies of mass production, specifically the print industry, and systems of distribution, such as postal exchanges, railroads, and canal networks. These developments made it possible for nineteenth-century readers to share in cultural events and conversations through the press and across vast geographical spaces.

Celebrity's historical development parallels a theoretical consideration of authorship. I have claimed that celebrity makes the author a text, by which I mean, following Roland Barthes, a field of interpretive practice and plural signification. Such a claim seems to excise authorship since, for Barthes, "to give a text an Author is to impose a limit on that text, to furnish it with a final signified, to close the writing."[18] For nineteenth-century audiences, however, the concept of authorship in the sense Barthes evokes here remains present as a positive value. Authors maintain their appeal as authoritative, even prophetic figures in the mid-nineteenth-century United States. Cultural anxiety over the popular success of authors who do not fit conventional ideals of authorship—of black people and women in particular—simply reveals the entrenchment of the traditional association of authorship with social authority. But while the concept of authorship retains its traditional appeal, the interpretive practice with which audiences approach their subjects is undergoing transformation. Committed to the idea of works and authors, audiences nevertheless approached authors as texts, and in doing so subverted and democratized a traditional model of cultural authority. Put another way, I do not see contemporary audiences' obsession with authors as "tyrannical" insofar as it prompts an examination of and challenge to potentially tyrannical cultural authority.[19]

Audiences express their interest in authors—and in public figures more generally—in largely affective terms borne of the illusion of their constant presence to one another. This important transformation of civic discourse follows directly from the structural changes to the print industry sharply illustrated by the penny press. As I discuss in chapter 2, the penny press gives rise to a personal journalistic style that comes to dominate civic discourse. Editor-driven newspapers cultivated a first-person vernacular style and encouraged audiences to respond in kind. Newspapers thereby promoted an attitude of familiarity among their readers that pervades public life. In addition, penny papers took part in a carnivalesque print culture that "allowed the body to be omnipresent" to readers.[20] In its insistence on physical presence, nineteenth-century print culture emboldened an audience seeking sensational pleasure and challenged the impersonal authority of print. The impersonal public sphere, Michael Warner reminds us, is characteristic of an eighteenth-century print discourse in which the subject claims reasonableness via "an identification with a disembodied public subject that he can imagine as parallel to his private person."[21] But in the carnivalesque, personal public sphere I describe, these assumptions are pressured if not abandoned altogether, subsumed by a cultural ideal of proximity and presence. The literary models for these social relations are rooted in oratory, not print;[22] hence, they are especially evident in the public lecture halls, where audiences felt themselves to be with the speaker, when the successful orator stimulated the "electric" spark of sympathy among the assembly. And public figures certainly were more available to the public than they are now, with open access even to a sitting president, which so fatigued John Quincy Adams and Abraham Lincoln, and which Andrew Jackson encouraged. Such accessibility inspired Charles Dickens's horror at the seemingly endless, painful series of handshaking receptions he endured during his American tour.[23] The assumption of openness contributes to a sense of social equality between observer and observed and facilitates a celebrity culture in which discussions and debates over the public figure's meaning have both personal and public resonance.

In their assumptions of familiarity with and access to public persons, mass audiences do not fully recognize the degree to which their experience of the celebrity is mediated or the ways that mediation may limit their understanding of the celebrity. Jonathan Elmer argues that mass culture as a whole is tasked with "mediating the contradictory demands of middle-class sensibilities," specifically, desires for pleasure on the one hand and social order or discipline on the other.[24] In the case of celebrity culture, mediation may regulate affective responses of all kinds, including the pleasure in interpreting the public figure's true self, which remains unknowable, or the erotic desire for the public figure, who remains physically inaccessible. That inaccessibility or social distance between celebrity and audience is at odds with the audiences' presumption of familiarity. Even so, audiences' scrutiny of celebrity authors themselves rather than their works can be invasive, and it can also overshadow interest in the work the author produces. This tendency toward exposure is not just inconvenient or irritating; it is philosophically significant as it undermines the presumed barrier between private and public life that generates self-unity in the classical public sphere. Hence,

Michael Warner argues, the consumption of "branded" or commercialized public identities makes individual observers' desires—their selves, in a sense—"recognizable through their display in the media."[25] In this way, consumption of the celebrity image makes the consuming subject visible to herself even as it integrates her into the public sphere. The observing subject, seeking knowledge of or familiarity with the celebrity, gains access to her own mediated self through the mediation of public life. Extrapolating further, the study of individual celebrities provides insight into the "public" in all its contradictions and conflicts.

Critical distrust of mediation has generated powerful critiques of celebrity and mass culture particularly as they are manifest in the twentieth century. First, Max Horkheimer and Theodor Adorno argue that the celebrity is the product of a mechanistic "culture industry" that takes advantage of a credulous public to serve its own commercial and cultural interests.[26] And Daniel Boorstin argues that because of "a passion for human equality," democracy creates "a suspicion of individual heroic greatness." To him, the celebrity is pure illusion: he offers no substance or value but instead is a "human pseudo-event," "*a person who is well known for his well-knownness.*"[27] These influential interpretations of celebrity and mass culture share a skepticism about the public's ability to apprehend public life, the corruptive tendencies of marketplace capitalism, and even the value of democratic equality. In their worry that celebrity and mass culture generate discourse based on illusions and empty signifiers, critical condemnations of celebrity culture both distrust the commodification of pleasure—a position that deserves consideration—and fail to recognize the other functions of mass culture. As a result, they offer jeremiads against a public sphere that seems to have traded its social and political authority for the ephemeral satisfactions of the marketplace. They are jeremiads, that is, against the passing of a model of public life and, with it, the apparent abandonment of enlightened citizenship.

But the era this work addresses was a time of intense political engagement—engagement with the very definition of citizenship, in many cases. Critiques of Habermas's public-sphere theory hinge on this notion that the public sphere is "enlightened"—that participants engaged in reasoned debate. Emphasizing reason creates an understanding of the public sphere that is both exclusive and historically inaccurate. Tracing a history of the concept of the self, Sidonie Smith shows that the notion of a metaphysical self is distinctly masculine: "the architecture of the 'self of essences' rests upon and reinforces the specularization of 'woman' as the Other through whom 'man' constructs his stature, status, and significance."[28] This binary construction sees female selfhood as inextricable from the body and biology and lacking the unity of self that governs male agency. Similar constructions shape cultural assumptions about people of color. As Carolyn Sorisio demonstrates, contemporary science plays a considerable role in essentializing the identities of women and people of color.[29] These strategies for othering women and nonwhites have a double effect: on the one hand, they attest to the constant and significant presence of nonnormative bodies in the public sphere;[30] on the other hand, they reinforce the norms of white masculinity that legitimate participation in the public sphere. Michael Warner captures the public sphere's contradictions as a space that promises inclusion while privileging certain types of participation—certain participants—over others: "The bourgeois public sphere is a frame of reference in which it is supposed that all particularities have the same status as mere particularity. But the ability to establish that frame of reference is a feature of some particularities." Therefore, the privileges of the bourgeois public sphere are associated with "unmarked identities: the male, the white, the middle class, the normal."[31] In practical terms, this thinking justifies women's and nonwhites' exclusion from full citizenship and delegitimizes their contributions to the debates of the public sphere even though they are active in public life.[32] Indeed, Dana Nelson argues that the public presence and increasing influence of women and people of color motivate efforts to reify "national manhood," the ideology that a fraternal bond connects white, middle-class men who collectively and individually embody the national identity. This ideology forms in part through "altero-referential articulation" of shared values—that is, through the observation of differences that distinguish the white male national subject from his gender and racial Other.[33]

National manhood dominates efforts to define the national identity, and hence the public, in a period of nationalist efforts to do just that. It extends the cultural preference for reason, understood in gendered and racial terms, into the raucous antebellum public sphere. Like the presence of women and people of color, that raucousness defies associations of the public sphere with enlightenment: however well reasoned the arguments, the discourse of the antebellum public sphere is seldom dispassionate. Social reform movements illustrate especially well the heterogeneity of nineteenth-century public life, the passionate rhetoric it gives rise to, and the limitations of the Enlightenment public-sphere model in understanding it. In contrast to idealizations of a rational-critical public sphere, T. Gregory Garvey sees the public sphere as a site of dissent and transgression, noting that political factionalism and acts of civil disobedience characterize the democratic life of the early republic.[34] Taking a different approach, Christopher Castiglia abandons the term "public sphere," preferring "civil sphere" to describe "locations where subjectivity and state interest blend into affective hybrids that create both the possibilities for independent critique and forms of self-management that limit those possibilities."[35] Castiglia is interested in the ways political ideals are internalized by the individual and how, in turn, that political consciousness affects not just politics itself but social actions. His model of the civic sphere as a site where affect resonates politically is very close to my own understanding of the public life celebrity culture makes possible. While celebrity culture is not directly involved in critiques of state action, it gives opportunities for affective expression regarding persons and subjects that are politically relevant. Moreover, celebrity culture's attention to bodies extends to the popular debates about race and gender that inform ideologies of selfhood and citizenship. These ideas come together in Nelson's concept of "presidentialism," wherein "the singular body of the President ... stands as a guarantee of manly constitution *qua* national accord."[36] At the risk of oversimplifying Nelson's argument, presidentialism makes a kind of celebrity of the political man—it reads his body and character as a sign for shared values and desires and thus marries the model of detached or abstract selfhood to celebrity culture's acceptance of embodiment.

Likewise, individual celebrities, in Jason Goldsmith's words, act as "mechanisms through which national sentiments were fostered among a diverse and heterogeneous populace." That nationalism is expressed through sentiments is crucial: "vectors of emotional identification, celebrities elaborate nations and national identities," Goldsmith clarifies.[37] Indeed, celebrity culture is sentimental. It accepts feeling as a reliable guide to truth, but that feeling is processed through the commercial marketplace. As Chris Rojek explains, the commercialization that makes celebrity possible assures that "celebrity culture has emerged as a central mechanism in structuring the market of human sentiments. Celebrities are commodities in the sense that consumers desire to possess them."[38] That desire may ostensibly be satisfied by purchase of the celebrity's image, such as buying his book or a newspaper reviewing his lecture. That said, consuming an author's image ultimately is not the same as consuming the author himself, and even if we see his work as a metonym for himself, his self is not a piece of property in the same way that a book is. For audiences, the sense of ownership, the satisfaction of possession, comes not from the economic exchange but from the work of interpretation by which the spectator claims a hold on the celebrity figure, a hold most often expressed in affective, not intellectual or reasoned, terms.

The coincidence of celebrity culture's emergence with the rise of nationalism does not mean that celebrity is always nationalistic in its orientation. Rather, as Goldsmith indicates, it suggests that celebrities and the debates they mediate may be read in reference to ongoing debates over national identity. While it is true that democracy is a precondition of celebrity, it is also the case that both celebrities and celebrity culture register the uncertainties that come with democracy: what is the significance of personal fame or greatness under conditions of political equality? In the absence of traditional social hierarchies, by what benchmarks are we to measure individual achievement and moral behavior? Debates over individual celebrities' meanings participate in these larger discussions and reveal the range of answers at play in the moment. But celebrity culture does more than respond to an already existing epistemological construct; it changes the culture, shifts the terms on which the judgments of individualism and social and political relationships are made. The rise of mass culture makes it not just possible but inevitable that individuals regard themselves and others in a public context. This is the basis for the rise of nationalism as Benedict Anderson describes it,[39] and as it engages the public sphere, celebrity culture registers concerns about acceptance and belonging that shape national identity. The celebrity's relationship to national identity is therefore more complicated than that of the traditional hero, who is understood to represent the national body synecdochically. In the age of celebrity, the positive association of publicity with national belonging is less assured because the public figure's meaning is always contested.

The celebrity stands out from the crowd. She is the exceptional figure who is distinguished from the mass by her achievements and personal qualities, yet who nevertheless represents popular tastes and interests. In their exceptionalism, celebrities seem to affirm the Jacksonian ethos of individualism and self-making. As they compel the affective responses of a mass audience, however, celebrities and celebrity culture incite long-standing anxieties over democracy and majority power. In a democracy, the voices of individual persons are presumed to harmonize into the voice of the people, resolving individual interests with pluralistic national identity. This is exactly the kind of rational union that Jefferson calls for in his first inaugural address: "All too will bear in mind this sacred principle, that though the will of the majority is in all cases to prevail, that will, to be rightful, must be reasonable; that the minority possess their equal rights, which equal laws must protect, and to violate would be oppression."[40] In this appeal to reason and love of liberty, Jefferson attempts to assuage his political adversaries and avoid what Tocqueville famously termed "the tyranny of the majority." In contrast with Jefferson's vision of a polity united by reason and respect, if not for persons then for principles, Tocqueville construes public opinion as the will of the majority that brooks no opposition. In a democracy, Tocqueville notes, "the majority possess a power which is physical and moral at the same time, which acts upon the will as much as the actions and represses not only all contest, but all controversy." For Tocqueville, majority power is especially fearsome in its reach, as it "acts upon the will" and controls the very desires of the individuals it includes. This affective power cannot be regulated; it is called extralegal in that it can discipline those who exercise their legally protected civil liberties to speak out against the majority. Majority power controls and limits public discourse, Tocqueville warns, and as a result "the soul is enslaved."[41] And majority opinion is not expressed only through politics. Jennifer Greiman argues that in popular culture, public spectacles engage crowds of spectators in performances of popular sovereignty that limit individual agency.[42] The seemingly neutral act of spectatorship compels one's complicity with dominant ideologies at the expense of personal liberty and conscience.

Insofar as individual celebrities are themselves spectacles compelling popular or majority response, they affirm these concerns about popular opinion. But although celebrity requires a mass audience, that audience need not be, and rarely is, unified in its response to the public figure. Indeed, celebrity is defined more by the act of interpretation than by any consensus among the audience. P. David Marshall explains, "At any given moment, there may be a governing consensus about what the celebrity represents, but this representation may be from a variety of positions and perspectives." Conceived in this way, the celebrity signifies only in relation to observers, whose identification of and with the celebrity-sign renders the celebrity meaningful. As Marshall writes, "The celebrity's power is derived from the collective configuration of its meaning. . . . Celebrities represent subject positions that audiences can adopt or adapt in their formation of social identities." In Marshall's analysis, the audience's interpretation of the celebrity is a means to establishing individual identity. When these individual responses are aggregated in a mass audience, they form a "discursive battleground": "Each celebrity represents a complex form of audience-subjectivity that, when placed within a system of celebrities, provides the ground on which distinctions, differences, and oppositions are played out. The celebrity, then, is an embodiment of a discursive battleground on the norms of individuality and personality within a culture."[43] Marshall's understanding of the multivalent celebrity sign diverges from theories that celebrities represent recognizable and stable identities. In this way, Marshall implicitly rejects a Lockean understanding of self as "the sameness of rational being" and favors a poststructuralist understanding of identity as socially constructed.[44] Celebrity's function in the creation of identity for the individual observers is a facet of the work of mass culture more generally, as defined by Jonathan Elmer. The work of critical observation that is characteristic of everyone who participates in mass culture enables the observer to reach an understanding of the larger society to which he belongs: "Mass culture is the figure produced by society's reflection-into-itself."[45] In celebrity culture, the individual public figure is objectified by a mass audience, whereas in mass culture as Elmer describes, the observer objectifies the mass. These patterns of observation are inversions and mirrors of one another, yet the result is the same: a reflection of the observer, as revealed through the vagaries, contradictions, and controversies commonly understood as popular opinion. Seen in this way, Marshall and other celebrity theorists reject the assumption that audiences are passive consumers or homogeneous masses. They claim that audience members engage with celebrities not just actively but critically, albeit in vernacular forms. That critical engagement, moreover, attends to matters of social significance. Insofar as celebrity culture mediates these discourses through public figures whom audiences regard personally, celebrity culture widens the public sphere of civic exchange. It provides avenues through which those who are traditionally excluded from the public sphere may enter it, even as they are still politically disenfranchised.

IN GENERAL, MY WORK IN THIS BOOK IS MOTIVATED BY THE EFFORT TO show how celebrity culture is both politically and aesthetically generative in the period. Undeniably, the public sphere is transformed by mass culture, and celebrity provides clear, detailed examples of that transformational process. I do not mean to suggest that the rise of mass culture and celebrity were the only agents of change in the period, or that they were wholly positive. They were instrumental, however, and they are part of the context for other transformative events and developments. One might say that the problem of the nineteenth century is the problem of union. On the one hand, individual celebrities provide an answer to that crisis: as the objects of public debate, they embody a variety of responses to the issues and concentrate the plurality of responses to it into a single, singular individual. On the other hand, as it democratizes cultural authority, celebrity culture highlights the impossibility of consensus. Controversies over celebrities' meanings and significances indicate the lines of disagreement that divide a society on given issues. I make the case that the debates over celebrities' meanings help widen the public sphere by providing a new mechanism for participation in civic debate even as those debates are refracted through the celebrity personality. In addition, these debates over celebrities' meanings affirm the fictive nature of the "public" and reveal its character as a composite of ever-shifting constituencies and counterpublics vying with one another for legitimacy and authority. Unlike democratic politics, however, which demands the antagonistic demands of differing constituencies be reconciled in rational consensus, celebrity culture is motivated by difference. It thrives in a personal public sphere governed not by reason but by sentiment. Too frequently, the sentimental style of the personal public sphere veers to insult and invective. But, considering celebrity's shadowing of politics—the celebrity assumes an authority parallel to the political leader's—this shift from a civic discourse that encompasses pluralities and eschews consensus is politically significant. It resembles the agonistic pluralism that Chantal Mouffe advocates in that celebrity culture "provid[es] channels through which collective passions will be given ways to express themselves over issues which, while allowing enough possibility for identification, will not construct the opponent as an enemy but as an adversary."[46]

Having said that, in the following pages we will see that some responses to public figures in the personal public sphere seem more antagonistic than adversarial. Whitman's calling Rev. John Sullivan a "serpent-tongued priest" or William Moulton's efforts to wreck Fanny Fern's reputation and thus career are undoubtedly antagonistic, destructive acts. But these individual utterances demonstrate celebrity culture's functioning and significance: in the personal public sphere, everyone is an interpreter of public lives, and no one judgment claims ascendancy over others. Its ability to embrace plurality and democratize authority is the source of both the triumph and the banality of celebrity culture. The examples I discuss here likewise acknowledge both these qualities as they alternately reject or embrace their own celebrity or the personal public sphere.

Given my claim that the personalization of public life is pervasive in the period, some might think my choice of authors arbitrary and incomplete. Likewise, because I focus on celebrity culture in its earliest phases, my historical and geographical focus on the middle decades of the century and the major publishing hubs of New York and Boston may seem limited. It is my hope that this book demonstrates methods that may be employed in other literary and cultural instances to make sense of mass publicity in the period. More specifically, these five case studies all demonstrate the ways that celebrity culture informs and shapes the debates over national identity and belonging that are particularly acute in this moment. The selection of authors reveals different facets of these debates, from the perspective of individuals, such as Barnum and Emerson, whose privileged position in the society is assured, and those, such as Fern and Douglass, whose status is precarious. The book opens with Barnum, who established key practices of nineteenth-century popular culture and in whose works I see all the major themes of this book. Scholars have demonstrated Barnum's almost uncanny ability to capitalize on popular discourses about subjects such as national identity, race, gender, confidence, and even science and the production of knowledge, but few have given much attention to his participation in celebrity culture. I examine three areas of Barnum's career in particular: his exhibits of human beings in racially themed freak shows, his use of "humbug" or deceptive promotional practices, and his efforts to control his public identity in response to his celebrity. Neil Harris's influential discussion of Barnum's "operational aesthetic" portrays Barnum's practices as reflections of Jacksonian individualism. But when these methods are directed toward the objectification of nonwhite human bodies, Barnum's promotional practices engage his white audiences in the deception of nonwhite others who are objectified as grotesques and savages. Barnum's humbugs and racially themed human exhibits are essential to celebrity culture in part because they cultivate habits of objectification and confer on audience members the assurances of their own authority, and they do so as part of a commercial marketplace for paid amusements. In Barnum's racial exhibits, be they the 1835 Joice Heth tour or the 1863 exhibit of Cheyenne and Kiowa leaders, pleasure is a commodity and politics is made pleasurable. In other words, Barnum shows how mass culture can and does engage with matters of political and ideological import through the medium of a particular human body and in a context where the political stakes are low and the personal rewards of pleasure are, for some, quite high.

Of course, Barnum was also a celebrity in his own right. As a result of his public stature, he found himself the object of public scrutiny. Barnum carefully controlled the public's access to his private life, so much so that he has been accused of lacking a private self. I address this issue by considering his palatial home, Iranistan, as an ostentatious presentation of a privacy inaccessible to all but his most intimate family and friends. As a colossal advertisement of selfhood, Iranistan is central to Barnum's claim of personhood. His privacy differentiates this famous man from the many people he puts on display. Barnum's methods as a showman and an autobiographer reveal celebrity culture as it takes shape, and he provides a unique vantage point on how industry, individual, and audience can be brought together to create something that is calculated for profit and at the same time speaks to political and philosophical questions about such matters as identity, memory, race, money, and national belonging.

As a showman, Barnum excelled at crafting exhibits that tapped into America's fascination with itself. His entertainments contribute directly to the formation of the personal public sphere that privileges affect over reason. Turning to Walt Whitman in chapter 2, I consider the ways these characteristics of celebrity culture play out for a poet who is deeply invested in popular success. Whitman's consciousness of the personal nature of public life in the period begins with his early journalism and therefore forms an essential part of the "foreground" for *Leaves of Grass*. An editor at the *New York Aurora*, Whitman flung himself into the volatile newspaper scene where individual editors wrote in a highly personal, even inflammatory style that invited readers' responses. Whitman's struggles at the *Aurora* indicate the limits of editorial authority: any claim to authority is inevitably contested in a personal public sphere. The combative persona he uses in the *Aurora* gives way eventually to the compassionate one he assumes in his poetry. As the poet Whitman recommends love as the best response to public figures—strangers in public as well as recognizable figures such as Lincoln—he abandons the divisive emotionalism of the journalism but retains the commitment to personality and sentiment that characterize the personal public sphere. In a discussion of the 1860 "Calamus" cluster, I show that Whitman confronts the challenges of achieving that intimate and loving response in a personal public sphere where individuals encounter others as highly mediated images. Using Lacan's theory of the gaze, I show that Whitman puts his own image before his readers in the effort to make himself the object of readers' desire. Whitman's drive for public intimacy among strangers attempts to make use of celebrity's ability to mobilize desire among a mass audience. Turning to "When Lilacs Last in the Dooryard Bloom'd," I argue that Lincoln's death forces him to confront the challenges of this loving response in his absence. "O how shall I warble myself for the dead one there I loved?" the poem asks. If love, and even desire, is indeed the best response to public figures, how can that love be expressed when its object is no longer present? The poem struggles with a condition that is common to celebrity culture, in which desire is constantly arising but impossible to satisfy or adequately express.

Whitman's work as a journalist and poet might be said to reflect on the practical effects of the personal public sphere—how it shapes an individual's engagement with public life, and the extent to which it fosters participation in civic discourse. Emerson's resistance to celebrity culture, the subject of chapter 3, is part of his ongoing negotiations with capitalism and mass culture that figure into his thinking about individualism and self-reliance. Unlike Whitman, who acquiesced to and even embraced mediated public relations, Emerson sought immediacy and genuineness in his expression and his relations with nature and men. The ethos of the personal public sphere challenged Emerson's impersonal philosophy, and Emerson's celebrity put him in the conflicted position of arguing for impersonality even as audiences came to regard him in increasingly personal terms. Audience responses to his lectures focused heavily on physical and personal traits, such as his appearance and deportment and his style of delivery. Emerson himself deplored the culture's turn toward Barnumesque spectacle, entertainments that elicited affective rather than intellectual responses. The tension between popular response to Emerson and Emerson's response to popular culture highlights the anxieties about affect and intellectual seriousness that are central to mass culture. In addition, audience's attempts to "read" Emerson and gain access to his physical presence, perhaps by attending a lecture or reading a description of him, raise questions about the availability of the public person in a highly mediated environment. Emerson's celebrity illustrates the ways celebrity culture empowers audiences, who "read" public figures as though they are texts and, in so doing, upend the public figure's claims to cultural authority. At the same time, popular focus on Emerson's physical presence on the lecture platform reinforces his exceptional status as a "genius." Of course, these readings of Emerson, which his first biographers also promulgate, defy Emerson's own understanding of genius as an impersonal power more or less available to all. Emerson's celebrity therefore contributes to the "gulf" Emerson perceives between himself and his audiences, and contributes to the rift between high and low or elite and popular culture that Emerson himself sought to overcome as a lecturer.

The popular fascination with the physical person contradicted Emerson's identification of the self with the impersonal currents of moral power. This understanding of an abstract or transcendent self is the basis for personhood, but the racial ideology of nineteenth-century America associates it strictly with white men. Chapter 4, on Frederick Douglass, considers Douglass's deliberate use of his celebrity in response to his own disenfranchisement. Douglass is a public figure in a society that denies him entry into the public sphere; moreover, his celebrity reveals how publicity—the specific publicity of black people, who are denied the privileges of privacy—ironically bars his claim to personhood. Like Barnum, Douglass manages his public self-presentation in his autobiographies in such a manner as to conceal his private life—his family life, his friendships—from public view. At the same time, he stages in print "family reunions" with his former master, Thomas Auld, and his children. The effects of these gestures are far-reaching. First and foremost, Douglass confronts and challenges his culture's inability to recognize black privacy and, by extension, black selfhood. At the same time, he redirects his observers' gazes onto scenes that reveal the flaws in their racial assumptions: he stages scenes that display himself on display, as it were, effectively turning on itself the logic of exhibition as a means of forming cultural identity. By representing scenes of reunion with his master's family, Douglass opens the plantation home to public view. If in his early career, Douglass represents Thomas Auld as a monster, by the end of Auld's life he rehumanizes his old master, casting him as a man redeemed by his regrets over slavery. In this manner Douglass imagines a way forward through Reconstruction, provided that white America can, like Thomas Auld, acknowledge and embrace its black sons and daughters.

As a black man, Douglass faced obstacles to personhood—namely, the ideological assumption that he lacked abstract selfhood. As a woman, Fanny Fern faced a similar bar to participation in the public sphere, yet, as I discuss in chapter 5, she spoke out anyway. Both Douglass and Fern show how the personal public sphere allows alternative means of participating in civic discourse and claiming personhood. Perhaps more than any of the other writers I discuss, Fern made ample use of the personal public sphere's embrace of affect, vernacular expression, and idiosyncrasy. Fern reveled in her difference—that is, her noncompliance with expectations of women's expression and her rejection of sentimental womanhood. But she also claimed to be a representative figure in that she presented her own extraordinary experience as a woman in public as an amplified version of all women's experiences, notwithstanding their consignment to the domestic scene. Fern made her visibility a platform from which to display all women's experiences, thus using the techniques of exhibition and spectacle inherent in mass culture to draw out observers, who identified themselves ideologically through their responses to her work. This strategy emerged early on, in Fern's first publications in Boston's *Olive Branch* newspaper. The paper reproduced a set of correspondence between Fern and her first readers that chronicles Fern's celebrity as it took shape. These letters demonstrate in especially dramatic fashion how celebrity and celebrity culture contribute to the work of self-making for individual audience members. Readers' praise and censure of Fern employ highly sentimental language and focus on perceptions of her moral character in gendered terms. In response, Fern redirects the conversation. She generates ironic self-portraits that attempt to redefine selfhood, releasing it from the ideological confines of social class and gender.

These same debates over Fern's identity get replayed in *Ruth Hall*—both in the narrative itself and in responses to the book. Of particular interest, William Moulton's *Life and Beauties of Fanny Fern* exposes the autobiographical details of the novel in order to humiliate Fern. Moulton failed in his attempt to ruin Fern; indeed, his book fueled popular interest in her. Though it came at a high personal cost, Fern's celebrity gave her cultural power that she used to critique and subvert gender ideology. Not only did she capitalize on her affective appeal— she literally converted audiences' desire for her into personal wealth—but she recognized those affective ties to her vast readership as affirmation of her that licensed her public speech. If Whitman promotes love as the most fitting response to public figures, Fern shows that sympathy can radically transform social relationships.

Reflecting on the times, Emerson considers the affective power of certain public figures: "What is the reason to be given for the extreme attraction which *persons* have for us, but that they are the Age? they are the results of the Past; they are the heralds of the Future."[47] The lines carry Emerson's reverence for the great figures whose words and deeds shape historical movements and in whom the zeitgeist is best expressed. But while Emerson espouses a theory of how certain individuals contribute to the progressive development of human civilization, he remains skeptical of any tendency to put too much stock in personality. Ultimately, Emerson tolerated and even profited from the cultural fascination with "persons," as do the other writers I examine in this volume. Taken together, these writers illuminate the contours of the complicated, changing public sphere that they share with their audiences. The celebrity culture that makes affect discursively meaningful and economically potent gives readers new ways of participating in public life and in turn reshapes cultural identity. Exposing authors to public scrutiny, celebrity reallocates moral, intellectual, and emotional authority to readers. Reading becomes a mode of civic participation that transcends social divisions. Celebrity culture not only reflects the democratization of public life but also reveals the agonism of and indeed divisions within the democratic public sphere, the tensions over meaning formation and cultural authority that result when the public sphere becomes more inclusive but perhaps no more unified.

CHAPTER I

P. T. BARNUM
Commercial Pleasure and the Creation of a Mass Audience

IN THE NINETEENTH-CENTURY UNITED STATES, P. T. BARNUM'S NAME evoked the most wonderful, bizarre, and extravagant exhibits that could be devised by art or nature. "Barnum" was a byword for the new form of commodified pleasure that drew on the nation's economic and geopolitical ambitions. More specifically, Barnum built an entertainment empire out of the raw materials of the national obsessions with race, gender, and cultural identity, obsessions he both shared and apparently embodied. His success hinged on his associating his enterprises with himself, and in creating those associations he pioneered modern advertising practices and generated a new discourse of self-referentiality.[1] He also managed to attract considerable attention to himself as the man behind Barnum's American Museum, Jenny Lind's American tour, and many other popular attractions. Celebrity enlarges Barnum's public presence, so that he finds himself in the unequal position of being known by those he does not know. He demonstrates this experience in an episode from his autobiography *Struggles and Triumphs* (1855):

> If I showed myself about the Museum or wherever else I was known, I found eyes peering and fingers pointing at me, and could frequently overhear the remark, "There's Barnum." On one occasion soon after my return, I was sitting in the ticket-office reading a newspaper. A man came and purchased a ticket of admission. "Is Mr. Barnum in the Museum?" he asked. The ticket-seller, pointing to me, answered, "This is Mr. Barnum." Supposing the gentleman had business with me, I looked up from the paper. "Is this Mr. Barnum?" he asked. "It is," I replied. He stared at me for a moment, and then, throwing down his ticket, exclaimed, "It's all right; I have got the worth of my money"; and away he went, without going into the Museum at all!.[2]

The purveyor of so many human curiosities became a curiosity himself, on par with the dwarves, plate spinners, "savage Indians," and other human oddities and freaks he puts on display. Barnum is unable to set the terms of his own display as he does with his exhibits, however, and it is not clear exactly what the observer sees when he stares at Barnum.

Barnum's reputation owed as much to his promotional strategies as to the entertainments he produced, and he was often criticized for the extravagantly misleading advertising claims that earned him the epithet "humbug." He was especially proficient in generating newspaper puffs. As with most of his business endeavors, Barnum did not invent the puff, but he pressed the limits of the form. He defends his work as "the world's way":

> If my "puffing" was more persistent, my advertising more audacious, my posters more glaring, my pictures more exaggerated, my flags more patriotic and my transparencies more brilliant than they would have been under the management of my neighbors, it is not because I had less scruple than they, but more energy, far more ingenuity, and a better foundation for such promises. In all this, if I cannot be justified, I at least find palliation in the fact that I presented a wilderness of wonderful, instructive and amusing realities of such evident and marked merit that I have yet to learn of a single instance where a visitor went away from the Museum complaining that he had been defrauded of his money. (*ST* 43)

The key word in this passage is "more": Barnum represents himself as a man whose tendencies to excess reveal the characteristics of his times. He conveys the "go-ahead" spirit of the Jacksonian free market. As Bluford Adams notes, "Barnum was well aware of his own symbolic importance to middle-class masculinity."[3] Is this what the visitor saw when he gazed up at Barnum—the living embodiment of the zeitgeist? or did he regard Barnum as he would all of the showman's exhibits, as a curiosity or freak of nature? In any case, the encounter between the observer and his object is defined in purely economic terms, as satisfaction for money well spent. The observer experiences the celebrity as a product of the marketplace. Through monetary exchange the observer "consumes" the celebrity figure in the sense that he obtains proximity to the celebrity that enables him to satisfy certain personal desires for and about Barnum.

Who is Barnum? Seeking the answer to this question, the museum visitor is assured of insight into Barnum through the observation of his physical features. In this effort, he engages the very practices of spectatorship that Barnum's museum and other enterprises promote. But the visitor's assurance is misguided, and not simply because Barnum's physical presence communicates so little. The visitor surely recognizes, as all Barnum's patrons do, that Barnum is a humbug: he habitually deceives his audiences to attract their notice. He ought not to be trusted. In claiming he had gotten his money's worth, the visitor asserts a judgment independent of Barnum's persona and claims an authority based on evidence Barnum does not knowingly present. But Barnum collects the admission fee in any case, so the transaction is mutually beneficial even if it is not enlightening.

Although Barnum's career thrives in this epistemological murk, he offers a crystal-clear explanation of his aims as a showman: he provides wholesome amusements for hardworking people. Barnum thus helps invent popular culture by transforming affect—here, amusement—into a commodity. This fact is significant in itself, but it is further complicated by Barnum's methods, specifically his use of deceptive practices or humbug, and his exhibitions of human beings as objects for visual consumption. From his first success as a showman, the 1836 Joice Heth exhibit, Barnum regularly displayed human beings in a manner that emphasized their physical and racial differences from their white audiences.[4] Thus shaping popular culture at the moment of its emergence, Barnum contributes to ideologies of racial identity and cultural belonging. That he does so through carefully stage-managed acts of deception suggests not simply the fiction of race—its constructedness—but, more potently, the assurances of superiority and mastery that accompany white subjectivity.

But what happens when Barnum is himself the subject of the white gaze? The opening anecdote is remarkable not only because it portrays Barnum as the object of public curiosity but also because, in relating the incident, Barnum attempts to claim it, repackage it, and extend it into the public sphere as an object of the gaze of a mass public. In this manner, he subsumes his individual spectator into the enlarged cultural object, the text of his autobiography. As a writer, Barnum constantly does this kind of repackaging: he recounts the details of his many exhibits, then explains his promotional strategies and public reaction to them. Recognizing public attraction to himself as a personality, he attempts to craft that public image in a manner that shows off and exercises his mastery as the impresario of his own celebrity. In doing so, he attempts to protect his private life from public exposure. Having promoted a culture in which spectatorship and authority are conjoined, however, the outcome is not assured. Landmark works of public relations, Barnum's writings represent their author as a public figure, and they preserve the private Barnum from public view. This method would also separate the acts of deceit or humbug from the private person—Barnum implies that a separate set of moral values attains to the man in his public and private spheres of action, even as his exhibitions of persons of color deny them the same privilege. In these efforts, Barnum establishes precedents and practices that shape popular culture in the period, but he does not insulate himself against popular judgment. Barnum shows the incredible, inevitably frustrated effort of public relations and image making in the nascent celebrity culture, and he demonstrates as well why the limits of such self-authorship are politically resonant.

Interpreting Barnum, the man at the ticket window subjects him to the same analytical process that patrons used to understand Barnum's exhibits. Barnum was notorious for making false claims about his entertainments, and he invited audience members to determine the authenticity of the acts to their own satisfaction. At the same time, Barnum's growing celebrity made his own authenticity suspect as many impostors flooded the marketplace. Bluford Adams explains, "By the late 1840s, Barnum had taken his place alongside Jack Downing and Davy Crockett as a universally recognizable persona that could be donned by anyone with access to a printing press."[5] The line emphasizes Barnum's relationship to the American traditions of folk humor and tall tales, which he adapts and embodies in a popular culture of paid amusements. These antecedents indicate Barnum's debts to American oral and literary traditions.[6] He owes his self-presentation to the typical representations of the Yankee wag, and as an autobiographer he crafts himself as a Franklinian figure of his own self-making. But the proliferation of Barnums to which Adams alludes denotes the mechanistic character of Barnum's project. He is a self-made man for the industrial age, in which self is not fashioned so much as manufactured.

Barnum's promotional methods generate the Barnum image. More than a persona or projected, rhetorical identity, the image is assembled from a variety of visual and verbal signs circulated through mass media. Images are "polysemus," according to Roland Barthes. "They imply, underlying their signifiers, a 'floating chain' of signifieds, the reader able to choose some and ignore others." The meaning of the image is therefore not fixed, despite the author's efforts to effect "an *anchorage*," a limitation on the possible meanings for an image.[7] In celebrity culture, the individual celebrity is the image's author and text in one, as Barnum illustrates: as an autobiographer, he literally authors his own image in deliberate effort to shape or even counter popular interpretations of him. Indeed, the inevitable tension between audiences' claims to interpretive authority and the celebrity's claims to authorial control are complicated by the shared assumption that the image is finally limited by the celebrity's identity or self. Barnum's astute consumer must determine whether the image is really Barnum's—a hopeless quest, in that the image by definition is a representation, not the man nor the self that animates him. Curiously, the museum patron who confronts Barnum in the ticket office presumes to sidestep this interpretive confusion altogether, but as a spectator, he objectifies the man and converts flesh to image. Relating the incident, Barnum returns the favor. Similarly, in his autobiography, Barnum relishes anecdotes in which strangers share their knowledge of Barnum, unaware that they address the man himself (see *ST* 229–32). In such moments, Barnum encounters his own image, the representation of him that circulates beyond the physical person in the culture at large. He recognizes that image as his greatest hoax; audiences presume to understand what they do not see—to know Barnum in an essential way—even as they fail to identify the man in the flesh.

Such false encounters and false assurances are central to Barnum's work, which relied on exaggerations and deceptions to attract public attention. Neil Harris calls Barnum's playful use of fraud the "operational aesthetic" and associates it with other frauds and hoaxes popular at the time, such as the Great Moon Hoax of 1835, and confidence games, often called "diddles" in the popular lexicon. In Barnum's use of the operational aesthetic, audiences took as a given that his explanations for his exhibits were incomplete or deceptive. As viewers, their job was to solve the puzzle of the exhibit using practical knowledge and common sense. This technique empowers audiences to assume an authoritative role in generating knowledge and undermines the influence of institutions and experts in the age when intellectual authority was increasingly concentrated in academic institutions and specialized professions.[8] Barnum's earliest exhibit tells the story: in 1835 he toured the country with Joice Heth, an aged slave whom he claimed was 161 years old and the former nurse to the infant George Washington. Audiences lined up to hear her tell stories of baby George and sing hymns. Barnum skillfully orchestrated newspaper coverage that drew attention to Heth's backstory and her physical characteristics, including her black skin and arthritic body. Unable to straighten her legs, she sat with them drawn up; her left arm was also bent at the elbow and immobile. The fingernails of her left hand were four inches long. Readers saw her likeness in illustrated advertisements, and newspaper reviews corroborated the grotesque images: several compared her appearance to "an animated mummy" or "an Egyptian mummy just escaped from a sarcophagus"; another associated her longevity with stereotypes of women's behavior: "The dear old lady, after carrying on a desperate flirtation with Death, has finally jilted him."[9] When crowds began to thin, Barnum altered his strategy. Taking a hint from European impresario Johann Maelzel, Barnum placed newspaper puffs claiming that Heth was not a human being at all but "a curiously constructed automaton, made up of whalebone, india-rubber, and numberless springs ingeniously put together" (*Life* 157). The repackaging of Heth as an automaton was a turning point for Barnum: whereas he first claimed he was himself taken in by the improbable story of Heth's past, he now advertised claims about her that he knew to be untrue. In a final twist, on Heth's death Barnum staged an autopsy to determine if in fact she were human and, if so, how old she really was. Judging by the ossification of her arteries, the chief examiner, Dr. David L. Rogers, determined Heth's age to be no more than eighty years.

Richard Adams Locke, the editor of the *New-York Sun* and perpetrator of the Moon Hoax, was present at the autopsy—he claimed to have been hidden behind a curtain—and published an exposé of the "dissection" that identifies Heth as "one of the most precious humbugs that ever was imposed upon a credulous community" (*Life* 172). Locke's exposure of the Heth hoax might have brought it to an end and publicly discredited Barnum. Instead, the affair escalated further when Barnum's assistant, Levi Lyman, managed to convince *New York Herald* editor James Gordon Bennett that the autopsy was itself a humbug—the autopsy of "an old negress who had recently died at Harlem"—and that Heth was alive and well, still meeting crowds in Connecticut (*Life* 173). This final hoax won Barnum even more publicity, though it cost him the goodwill of Bennett, who never forgave Barnum for the humiliation of humbugging him and his paper.

Barnum's manipulations of Heth's story invite audiences into speculations about the exhibit's composition and meaning. In her first incarnation, Heth offers a window into America's founding. As Benjamin Reiss explains, she gave audiences a way to talk about serious social issues of race and northern attitudes toward slavery: "The Barnum-Heth tour was a traveling, shape-shifting, improvised forum for public discussion—and just as often, public avoidance—of the racial issues that were coming to dominate political and social discourse, and which were newly shaping nineteenth-century America's self-perceptions."[10] But this conversation is carefully framed by the terms of her display as a freak or grotesque. Rosemarie Garland Thomson links the freak show to Jacksonian ideologies of equality that in fact accentuate bodily difference of race and physical ability: "This black, disabled woman commodified as a freakish amusement testifies to America's need to ratify a dominant, normative identity by ritually displaying in public those perceived as the embodiment of what collective America took itself *not* to be."[11] Hence Heth is doubly objectified, both by her public display and also by her transformation into a commodity for visual consumption—a transformation, moreover, that replicates her commodification as a chattel under slavery. Like all freak shows, the Heth exhibit participates in the process of shaping a cultural identity by defining physical characteristics that exclude one from the civic body.

What I find most extraordinary about the Heth exhibit and Barnum's other displays of human beings is their fraudulence—the efforts Barnum exerts to fabricate and sell the body as a spectacle. Over and over again, Barnum rehearses the stages of his deceptions, acknowledging and indeed reveling in the falsehoods he generated to promote his exhibits. Viewers already suspected they were being lied to—the advertising claims stretched credulity—and took pleasure in discerning the truth of the exhibit. James Cook argues that the operational aesthetic is intrinsic to the commercial marketplace. The uncertainty or built-in perceptual "fuzziness" of Barnum's advertisements and exhibits underscores the risks inherent to all commercial transactions, and it requires consumers to approach transactions prudently.[12] Barnum's own experience as a businessman bears out this advice: as he relates in his autobiographies, he encountered many business schemes that were little more than scams. He presents his career as a difficult effort to get ahead in an economic world beset with "sharp trades, especially dishonest tricks and unprincipled deceptions" (*Life* 39). His own tricks are innocuous by contrast because they offer something in return for the deception—the pleasure of figuring out the trick or the fun of being bested by a worthy humbug. But the exhibits were not just puzzles for viewers to solve. Barnum's active presence in managing and presenting the exhibits made them contests between him and his patrons, who attempted not just to figure out the puzzle but, in doing so, to beat Barnum at his own game.[13] The Heth exhibit establishes the techniques that Barnum returned to throughout his career as a purveyor of what James Cook calls "artful deceptions." As Cook explains, the artful deception is not simply a lie, because the audience knows it is being lied to. The artful deception is "a calculated intermixing of the genuine and the fake, enchantment and disenchantment, energetic public exposé and momentary suspension of disbelief." Cook extends Harris's idea of the operational aesthetic to better account for Barnum's agency in creating the terms of the fraud. He notes that the artful deception draws attention to "the act of fooling."[14] This distinguishes the artful deception from the swindle, con, or fraud—and it also makes it pleasurable. As both Cook and Harris argue, Barnum effected his hoaxes in the midst of a society preoccupied with its own gullibility and eager to avoid falling prey to confidence men and other urban tricksters.[15]

"Operational aesthetic," "artful deception": these are alternatives for "humbug," Barnum's term of art for himself and his works. Proclaiming himself the "Prince of Humbugs," Barnum embraces his reputation for jiggery-pokery and sharp dealing, but he infuses into that image the good humor of the Yankee wag, a practical joker who achieves social status by besting others with his wit. Such is the cornerstone of Barnum's self-portrait in *The Life of P. T. Barnum, Written by Himself* (1855). If the title echoes that of Frederick Douglass's popular slave narrative, Barnum aims for familiarity rather than homage to the heroic fugitive. Barnum's *Life* traces his career in show business to his childhood and youth in rural Connecticut, where he was raised in a culture distinguished by its penchants for practical joking and financial acuity. Everyone in Barnum's Bethel attempts to get the better of someone else, whether in a contest of wits or in trade. Barnum's youthful experience running a country store demonstrates how the two types of competition are related—a valuable lesson:

> Many is the time I cut open bundles of rags, brought to the store by country women in exchange for goods, and declared to be all linen and cotton, that contained quantities of worthless woolen trash in the interior, and sometimes stones, gravel, ashes, etc. And sometimes, too, have I (contrary to our usual practice) measured the load of oats, corn, or rye which our farmer-customer assured us contained a specified number of bushels, perhaps sixty, and found it four or five bushels short. . . . These were exceptions to the general rule of honesty, but they occurred with sufficient frequency to make us watchful of our customers, and to teach me the truth of the adage, "There's cheating in all trades but ours" (*Life* 39–40).

The passage lays the foundation for Barnum's defense of his own humbugs: deception and sharp dealing are the way of the world. The book continues to detail Barnum's significant enterprises, including the Joice Heth episode and the Feejee Mermaid exhibit and culminating in his triumphant management of Jenny Lind's American tour. Throughout, Barnum exposes his own humbugs. Like an 1850s version of Donald Trump's *The Art of the Deal*, the book provides an inside look at the makings of a business empire, and it links business success with certain traits of insight into the market and great personal energy.

In exposing his work in this way, Barnum attempts to enlarge both the jokes and his audience. He invites readers to relive the Joice Heth episode and other amusements. To some extent, his method works. One reviewer calls *The Life* "a very amusing book, which everyone will read, half the world will abuse, and nobody can help laughing at and with."[16] The half who disliked the book may be said to act on Barnum's own lessons. Barnum's fundamental assumption that dishonesty rules the marketplace, combined with his own willingness to use deceptive promotional tactics, invites distrust. As another reviewer explains, Barnum's book and the liberties with truth that he takes in it "[prove] that he did not consider deception, when for the sake of gain, fun, or cuteness, as any wrong. . . . His life and history ignore the essential importance of truth." The reviewer concludes by sketching a path forward for the showman. He acknowledges that Barnum "has been an unscrupulous and successful manipulator of public gullibility; but he has some redeeming traits of character. If he had not, he would be a monster. If he would now be a reformer, let him go and make restitution of his ill-gotten gains." In the terms of this review, Barnum's methods risk making him into a freak or grotesque such as he puts on display in his museum. Seen this way, Barnum is unfit for a society that prizes "honor, industry, economy, perseverance, and earnestness."[17] Barnum needs to show that his self-interest is checked by moral conscience, and in doing so he renders a self-portrait in which audiences recognize the same virtues they seek in themselves.

The review encapsulates the criticisms that drove Barnum's revisions of his autobiography. In *Struggles and Triumphs*, he continues to defend his business practices as consistent with those of others in the marketplace. He explains his humbugs in the effort to show that they are instruments of amusement, not deception. In Barnum's hands, humbug is a synonym for hype, a form of advertising that uses technologies of mass production and distribution to deploy aggressive rhetoric. Hype aims to reach as large an audience as possible and create the sense of the commercial enterprise as a cultural event.[18] Barnum uses puffs, advertisements, and other promotional devices to incite desire in the audience for the object. Then the humbug substitutes the desired object for something else, leaving the spectator only partially satisfied: he may have gotten the worth of his money, but he has not gotten exactly what he has paid for. Barnum's infamous Feejee Mermaid exhibit exemplifies this phenomenon: advertisements for the curiosity featured detailed images of seductive female creatures with bare breasts and shapely tails, but the curious spectator encountered instead a grotesque, the preserved bodies of a monkey and a fish conjoined. If for Barnum the mermaid hype served as indirect advertising for his museum (*ST* 111), the effort succeeded by appealing to his audiences' desires. In lieu of the erotic pleasure of observing the mermaid Barnum advertised, the spectator gets "amusement"—the pleasurable or humorous or chagrined self-recognition that comes from seeing his fantasy revealed as a grotesque.

Barnum's humbugs mobilize a variety of desires among the mass public. In particular, he trades in curiosity, a desire for knowledge, and erotic desire, such as that prompted by his ads for exotics such as the mermaid and the Circassian Beauty.[19] Sometimes he promotes a fantasy of fulfilled ideology, as in his management of Jenny Lind, which successfully linked her to the ideal of true womanhood.[20] Above all, Barnum promoted a desire for amusement, which is to say pleasure purchased as a commodity and consumed in public. To be sure, mid-century New York offered nearly unlimited pleasures such as the various gambling dens, pool halls, and houses of prostitution vividly described in sensational works such as George Foster's *New York by Gaslight*. Located on the corner of Broadway and Ann Street, Barnum's America Museum was a fixture in the rough Bowery neighborhood Foster's work exposed, but Barnum claimed "to furnish healthful entertainment to the American people" (*ST* 45), satisfying the public's desire for amusement without corrupting their morals. Barnum's career and methods attest to the relocation of pleasure from the private sphere to the public sphere. He succeeds by making the satisfaction of desire in public a respectable activity, and he makes it respectable by conjoining it to dominant ideologies of individualism, gender, and race.

Barnum's most strenuous, most methodical, and least examined effort to redeem his methods comes in his 1866 book, *Humbugs of the World*. Here, Barnum acts as an authority on humbugs. The book is meant as a comprehensive guide to great scams of the day. It is also a defense of Barnum and his own works. In the book's introductory chapters, Barnum takes exception to the standard definition of "humbug" as an imposture or deception. He defends the humbug, who uses deception and hype to attract business and then provides a valuable service or commodity: "'humbug' consists in putting on glittering appearances—outside show—novel expedients, by which to suddenly arrest public attention, and attract the public eye and ear."[21] For Barnum, the key to the humbug is the means of publicizing it: the person who makes promises he fails to fulfill is not a humbug but a swindler. He seeks to differentiate the art of humbug from the more conventional scams that permeate the marketplace. "My doctrine," Barnum avers, is "that a man may, by common usage, be termed a 'humbug,' without by any means impeaching his integrity" (*HW* 24). The remainder of the book details the variety of scams and impostures that proliferate: forms of witchcraft and spiritualism, varieties of literature, public hoaxes, quack medicine, and adulterations of prepared foods. Barnum singles out some hoaxes that affect the understanding rather than the pocketbook; he dismisses Mormonism and Islam, for instance, as religious hoaxes, linking the Mormon Bible and the Koran as works that "sounded two strings of humbug together—the literary and the religious" (*HW* 13). But the majority of the humbugs Barnum examines are commercial in nature, and as such they reinforce the idea that Barnum's worldview is intimately tied up in the marketplace.

Indeed, *Humbugs* articulates a worldview in which humbug is an ever-present feature. The "universal humbug," as he calls it, pervades all areas of society across history. But if Barnum acknowledges that self-interest drives individuals to dishonesty, he does not despair that human beings are inherently or irreversibly immoral, and in fact he cautions against such a judgment: "The greatest humbug of all is the man who believes—or pretends to believe—that everything and everybody are humbugs. We sometimes meet a person who professes that there is no virtue; that every man has his price, and every woman hers. . . . He thinks himself philosophic and practical, a man of the world; he thinks to show knowledge and wisdom, penetration, deep acquaintance with men and things. Poor fellow! he has exposed his own nakedness. Instead of showing that others are rotten inside, he has proved that he is. He claims that it is not safe to believe others—it is perfectly safe to disbelieve him" (*HW* 16–17). Barnum represents here a self-trust so extreme that it turns the individualist into a cranky, corrupted loner. As Neil Harris points out, the passage supports Barnum's "notion of humbug as social therapy," the antidote to a humorless practicality.[22] He proposes a healthier alternative to a life of skepticism: good judgment borne of conscious, responsible participation in the world as it is, rather than sanctimonious withdrawal.

Articulating his philosophy of universal humbug, Barnum takes aim at the sensualist who, distrusting others, indulges himself and his appetites. This is the man with "a hog's mind in a man's body—sensual, greedy, selfish, cruel, cunning, sly, coarse, yet stupid, short-sighted, unreasoning, unable to comprehend anything except what concerns the flesh" (*HW* 16–17). Such unchecked self-interest, Barnum argues, follows from a too-great distrust. The individual loses confidence in everyone else, focuses only on self, and is thereby corrupted. Moreover, Barnum's philosophy of humbug challenges prevailing ideas of self-trust that emerge in the Jacksonian period and that are given most memorable expression by transcendentalist writers. Barnum's idea of the universal humbug counters the ideal of a universal moral law that is the cornerstone of the philosophy of self-reliance associated with transcendentalism. Acknowledging the prevalence of humbugs in the marketplace, Barnum advocates everyday vigilance and celebrates the "wide-awake" American spirit. But when vigilance flags, he cheekily suggests that the marketplace itself can supply aid: "It would be a wonderful thing for mankind if some philosophic Yankee would contrive some kind of 'ometer' that would measure the infusion of humbug in anything. A 'Humbugometer' he might call it. I would warrant him a good sale" (*HW* 159). The passage ironically parallels another by Thoreau, who in *Walden* imagines a "Realometer": "Let us settle ourselves, and work and wedge our feet downward through the mud and slush of opinion, and prejudice, and tradition, and delusion, and appearance, that alluvion which covers the globe, ... till we come to a hard bottom and rocks in place, which we can call *reality*, and say, This is, and no mistake; and then begin, having a *point d'appui*, below freshet and frost and fire, a place where you might found a wall or a state, or set a lamp-post safely, or perhaps a gauge, not a Nilometer, but a Realometer, that future ages might know how deep a freshet of shams and appearances had gathered from time to time."[23]

In light of Barnum's practical worldview, it is not the showman but the philosopher who is overly dramatic. Individual judgment, not reality itself, is at issue, Barnum claims. One need not be so indignant about "shams and appearances" if he or she can judge them as such, and Barnum offers his own experience in *Humbugs* as a guide. In contrast with Thoreau's retreat to Walden Pond, Barnum suggests a method for living with and in a society driven by commercial interests without becoming its victim.

Barnum's *Humbugs of the World* is not the first of its kind; like all of his productions, it revisits, revises, and enlarges something that already existed in the wider culture. As a guidebook to practical scams and humbugs, Barnum's book takes up a subject previously treated by David Meredith Reese's more overtly political book *Humbugs of New-York* (1838). Reese denounces as humbugs several forms of "ultraism," including "Ultra-Temperance," "Ultra-Abolitionism," "Ultra-Protestantism," and "Ultra-Sectarianism." Reese defines "ultraism" as any philosophy that goes beyond the Bible, and he traces the ways in which the "ultras" exceed biblical mandates. This technique enables him to both support less extreme versions of these philosophies and condemn those he views as overly zealous. For instance, he acknowledges the benefits of a gradualist approach to abolition—the approach favored by the Founders, he notes—but he rejects the argument that "'*the act of holding a slave is sin,*' or as they often express it, 'to claim "*property in man,*" *under any circumstances, is sin.*' We maintain that this position is *ultra*, or that it goes beyond the Bible" (emphasis in original).[24] Reese supports his argument not with references to biblical examples of or support for slavery but by arguing that slaveholding is not always unrighteous or sinful. Circumstances may show the slaveholder does his slaves a greater good by keeping them in bondage than by setting them free in a hostile world for which they are unprepared and from which they have been sheltered.

Barnum, himself a temperance advocate, does not dismiss reform movements as humbugs.[25] But he does share Reese's assumption that humbug is something that requires explanation. And both books share the understanding that humbugs are a problematic form of mass public opinion, the effects of which may be both individual and collective. As generally used, the term "humbug" is elastic, encompassing a range of untruths, hoaxes, and outright frauds as well as points of religious and political doctrine; hence, humbug may hurt the individual's pocketbook, or it may lead to political corruptions that influence an entire population. Moreover, the political and religious discussions in Reese's book lend significance to Barnum's treatment of miscegenation in *Humbugs of the World*. In a chapter focused on hoaxes, Barnum includes a short section relating the history of the "Miscegenation Hoax." Without naming it, Barnum refers to a pamphlet written by David G. Croly and published anonymously in 1864, *Miscegenation: The Theory of the Blending of the Races, Applied to the White Man and Negro*. This work coins the term "miscegenation," which came to replace the more conventional term "amalgamation" to refer to interracial couplings. Posing as Republicans, Croly argues that the inevitable and socially desirable goal of emancipation is the union of black and white: "Providence has kindly placed on the American soil for his own wise purposes, four millions of colored people. They are our brothers, our sisters. By mingling with them we become powerful, prosperous, and progressive; by refusing to do so we become feeble, unhealthy, narrow-minded, unfit for the nobler offices of freedom, and certain of early decay."[26] The pamphlet caused a furor, as parties on either side of the slavery issue publicly embraced or condemned its arguments until the hoax was revealed in November 1864. The author was not a Republican supporter of Lincoln and miscegenation but a Democrat promoting a satirical vision of Republicans' embrace of emancipated black men and women. In *Humbugs* Barnum revels in the Miscegenation Hoax. He juxtaposes his discussion of it with a discussion of the Great Moon Hoax of 1836; each, he claims, is a fine example of the literary hoax, putting scientific (or pseudoscientific) discourse to use in gulling an eager and inflamed public.

Barnum's chuckling over the Miscegenation Hoax ought to be a mere footnote in his long and varied career, but I consider it a fascinating counterpart to his other works that play on and with race. Whereas Barnum's contemporaries criticized him for the Feejee Mermaid and his puffing, modern observers are likely to view his racial humbugs as his most transgressive and offensive works. What is so funny about the Miscegenation Hoax, and what does it reveal about Barnum and the popular culture in which he participated? On a basic level, Barnum enjoyed the Miscegenation Hoax simply because it worked so well, and he appreciated the hoax's sophistication. From the vantage point of a professional hoaxer, the Miscegenation Hoax was a tremendous technical achievement in that it mimicked Republican abolitionist rhetoric and arguments so successfully as to be accepted as the work of one of the party's ranks. Yet once the hoax was revealed, the work demanded a complete reconsideration as a parody of abolitionist discourse that condemned the very people who accepted it at face value—people such as Horace Greeley, Wendell Phillips, and Theodore Tilton, whom the pamphlet cites as examples of the natural "love of the blonde for the black." According to this argument, individuals are inevitably attracted to those whose physical traits are opposite their own: "The sympathy Mr. Greeley, Mr. Phillips, and Mr. Tilton feel for the negro is the love which the blonde bears for the black; it is a love of race, a sympathy stronger to them than the love they bear to woman. It is founded upon natural law."[27] Read under the assumption that, like Greeley, Phillips, and Tilton, the author supports racial equality, these lines hold up the well-known abolitionists as role models. Read in full awareness of the hoax, he makes Greeley, Phillips, and Tilton the butts of an elaborate racist joke that goes so far as to impugn their masculine love of women.

But at the heart of Barnum's regard for the Miscegenation Hoax is the joke of interracial coupling. Nineteenth-century anxiety over miscegenation was premised on the fear that whiteness might disappear as a distinctive and superior social category.[28] This view is evident in Croly's vision of the "absorption" of the Negro into white society, which assumes a darker complexion over time through miscegenation. He argues that the white race cannot rule America without the infusion of color: "All that is needed to make us the finest race on earth is to engraft upon our stock the negro element which providence has placed by our side on this continent."[29] Of course, Croly means nothing of the sort, and once the hoax is exposed, his claims must be read as a satire of Republican and abolitionist arguments for racial equality. In his irony, Croly evokes the "repugnance" to interracial coupling that contemporary race science justifies with its theories of polygenesis. In his appreciation of the hoax, Barnum signals his own support for polygenesis and racial separation, as well as his disbelief that white and black could share in a mutual erotic preference for one another.[30] Hence, just as Barnum's humbugs succeed by inciting desire in his audience, he appreciates the Miscegenation Hoax as a humbug that first acknowledges and then cuts off desire, specifically the desire "of the blonde for the black."

A similar logic is evident in Barnum's exhibitions of human beings. Freak shows were standard fare at Barnum's American Museum, where he constantly featured "gipsies, Albinoes, fat boys, giants, dwarfs, rope-dancers, live 'Yankees,' . . . [and] American Indians, who enacted their warlike and religious ceremonies on the stage" (*ST* 103). These exhibits are themselves characterized by their racial, ethnic, and physiological traits. These exhibits' success speaks to the white audience's complete acceptance of its racial superiority as expressed by casual objectification of nonwhite bodies. Barnum's museum exhibits help generate and perpetuate a normative white gaze by which all bodies in the personal public sphere are objectified and interpreted. Barnum's presentation of his human grotesques emphasizes that they cross categories of race, gender, and even species—the Bearded Lady, for instance, appears to be both man and woman in one body. In the case of Barnum's racially ambiguous freaks, these transgressive bodies speak to concerns about racial identity and miscegenation rampant in the culture. The especially notorious example of "What Is It?" illustrates the particular combination of racial ideology and humbug that built Barnum's human exhibits. "What Is It?" consisted of a black man dressed in skins, jumping about the stage. Several actors played the character over the years. In Britain, where Barnum originated "What Is It?" at the Egyptian Hall in 1846, he was portrayed by Hervey Leach, a British performer who darkened his skin for the role. In the American Museum in the 1860s, the part was played by William Henry Johnson, known as "Zip," a black man from New Jersey. Labeled a conehead, Johnson may have suffered from microcephaly. These details reveal the degree to which "freaks were/are always constructed" through acts of framing and presentation.[31] In this case, those frameworks draw heavily from blackface minstrelsy and, Linda Frost shows, the rhetoric of savagery in popular discourse.[32] In a private letter to his friend and colleague Moses Kimball in 1846, Barnum acknowledges the fraudulence at the heart of "What Is It?": "I half fear that it will not only be exposed, but that *I* shall be *found out* in the matter. However, I go it, live or die." Barnum goes on in the letter to explain the nature of the fraud: "The thing is not to be called *anything* by the exhibitor. We know not & therefore do not assert whether it is human or animal. We leave all that to the sagacious public to decide."[33] Thus the exhibit shifts intellectual authority away from experts and onto audience members, just as Barnum's other humbugs purport to do. As one advertisement for the Feejee Mermaid famously asked, "Who is to decide when *doctors* disagree?"[34] Advertisements for the 1860s version were true to this formula: "Is it a man? Is it a monkey? Or is it both?"[35] Barnum billed "What Is It?" as a "wild man" and a "nondescript," prompting his white audiences to attempt to define the creature they observed. Note how Barnum manages to have it both ways: even as he credits audience authority over expert judgment, he presents "What Is It?" in a manner that draws on contemporary race science. He juxtaposes the savagery of the "wild man" with the presumed civility of his white audience, and his questions about the origins of "What Is It?" suggest the likelihood that black and white, exhibit and spectator, are completely different species. Adams situates "What Is It?" in its context in Barnum's Lecture Room, where it shared the stage with a production of Dion Boucicault's play *The Octoroon* and a waxwork representation of John Brown. Together, these exhibits create a triptych of the racial preoccupations of Civil War–era white society. "In a culture obsessed with the line between blacks and whites, Barnum used the 'What Is It?' to help fortify the racist tradition of a line between blacks and animals,"[36] thus affirming the theory of polygenesis that Darwin's recent work brought into doubt.

Ultimately, though, Barnum is not sincere in his construction and presentation of freaks such as "What Is It?" He is not seeking authoritative answers to the questions of identity that he poses, and he does not in fact respect individual spectators' conclusions about them. His aim is commercial, not intellectual. Despite Barnum's reputation for humbug, however, his human exhibits invited serious consideration. The suggested connection between "What Is It?" and evolutionary theory is especially prominent in a passage from George Templeton Strong's diary, reflecting on "What Is It?" in light of his reading in the recently published *Origin of Species*: "Some say it's an advanced chimpanzee, others that it's a cross between nigger and baboon. But it seems to me clearly an idiotic negro dwarf. . . . But his anatomical details are fearfully simian, and he's a great fact for Darwin." Strong's comment is as curious for its earnestness as it is for its racism. Strong was a sophisticated, educated observer of the world around him, who fit in his visit to Barnum's museum amid social calls, committee meetings, and trips to the Philharmonic. While he acknowledges some elements of fraud in "What Is It?"—Barnum's story about its origins is "probably bosh," he writes—the exhibit demonstrates for him evidence of Darwin's theories and seems to uphold the notion of the nondescript as a "missing link" in the evolutionary chain.[37] Strong recognizes Barnum's role in constructing "What Is It?" but nevertheless uses the exhibit to uphold assumptions of racial difference that are rooted in personal conjecture and scientific amateurism. Strong's diaries provide an unguarded portrait of the racism among privileged white society of the period. While Strong supports Union efforts in the Civil War, his brief comments on "What Is It?" provide a window into a world where white supremacy is unquestioned and racial difference is a puzzle of natural history. Barnum's racial exhibits do not promote these views so much as they exploit them for profit, all the while repaying the viewer with the assurances of their ascendancy in the face of nagging doubt disguised as curiosity.

Strong's comments about "What Is It?" support Thomson's arguments that freak shows allowed their audiences release from and reification of ideologies of selfhood and individualism in nineteenth-century America. Emphasizing the tensions between individualism and mass culture in the period, Thomson claims that freaks and freak shows offered ways of acknowledging difference without abandoning the social and economic structures that promised unity and positive national identity.[38] Like other displays of nonnormative, nonwhite bodies, "What Is It?" contained the threat of racial difference. Moreover, the implication that "What Is It?" and similar nondescripts represent a "missing link" in human evolution evokes the specter of interspecies breeding and, by extension, miscegenation. Barnum's nondescript underlines the unnatural outcomes of such genetic mixing. James Cook argues that Barnum's exhibit of "What Is It?" as a nondescript "provided [Barnum's] white viewers with a public forum to talk openly and confidently about the boundaries of racial distinction, often in brutally dehumanizing ways."[39] While this is undoubtedly true, the discussion of the Miscegenation Hoax indicates that forums for such discussion were not wanting in the 1860s United States, even if those conversations were not promoted in good faith. Like the Miscegenation Hoax, Barnum's "What Is It?" appeals to white Americans' curiosity and anxiety about blackness, humbugging them into questioning the possibilities for their kinship with the nondescript other, fulfilling their desire to maintain racial and social distinctions.

If "What Is It?" seems less than subtle, Barnum could be even blunter. In 1863 he exhibited a group of Native Americans at his American Museum, and he wrote of the episode in *Struggles and Triumphs*. Although Barnum exhibited Indians frequently in both the United States and Europe over the years, this is his only public account of such events. Privately, Barnum confessed Indian exhibits were a managerial headache: "Damn Indians *anyhow*," he wrote to Moses Kimball in 1843, "they are a lazy, shiftless set of brutes—though they will *draw*."[40] The "draw" or profitability of Indian exhibits encouraged Barnum to book a delegation of western Indian leaders who had traveled east to meet President Lincoln at the White House. The 1863 exhibit included Cheyenne chiefs War Bonnet, Lean Bear, and Hand-in-the-Water; Kiowas Yellow Buffalo and Yellow Bear; Caddo chief Jacob; the Apache White Bull; and interpreter William Simpson Smith.[41] Barnum arranged their New York visit through the assistance of U.S. Indian agent Samuel G. Colley.

Correspondence of Barnum and Colley appeared in the *New-York Tribune* and other New York papers prior to the exhibit's opening. The published exchange offers a glimpse into Barnum's methods as a dealmaker and a promoter: appearing as news correspondence, the letters function here as a puff for Barnum's museum. Read alongside Barnum's account of the exhibit in *Struggles and Triumphs*, the letters reveal that not only was Barnum's partnership with the Indians an exploitative arrangement based on deceit, but also Barnum's audience was fully aware of and condoned the deception. Barnum lays out his offer to host the Indians, showing them "New-York hospitality." He proposes to display the Indians to a curious public, but he also imagines that the Indians will benefit from seeing the city: "I am confident that many of the best citizens of this and the adjacent cities who have traveled in the Indian country, as well as thousands who have not, are anxious to behold these untamed sons of the forest and the prairie, and to shake hands with men who have never seen till recently a steamboat or a railroad car; who have never, till within the last month, become acquainted with the higher developments of civilized life—to whom the telegraph is a novel mystery; and who, could they gaze upon the glorious harbor of New-York, with its fleets of ships—each to them an entirely new object—would certainly go into ecstacies, notwithstanding all the assorted stolidity of the Indian character."[42]

Barnum promises a reciprocal exchange of gazes, as the Indians and the New Yorkers look on one another with mutual wonder. His depiction of the Indians' wonder at "civilized life" participates in a literary discourse that eliminates cultural specificity and depicts the Indian as one-dimensional and primitive. This stereotype is an essential component of the creation of the "myth of open wilderness" that helps justify western expansion by obscuring the complexity and diversity of Indian cultures.[43] Barnum's depiction of Indian primitivism tells audiences what they will see and how to understand it. In characterizing the Indians as "child-like" and ignorant of the white world, Barnum and Colley reinforce audiences' understanding of the Indians as "untamed sons of the forest and prairie." In their naïveté, the Indians perhaps resemble the provincial tourists who travel to New York specifically to see the curiosities on view at Barnum's; but as savages, however noble and brave, they cannot be seen as equal to their audiences. As Colley puts it, "their child-like simplicity, combined with their prowess and their wisdom, offers a curious study to those not acquainted to Indian character."⁴⁴ They are objects of study, not fellow Americans.

Reinforcing this point, Barnum and Colley agree that the Indians ought to be compensated with "presents which ... will convince them that not only their 'Great Father' at Washington, but the whole of the American people, feel friendly toward them." Barnum associates material exchange with the communication of feeling, but in making such an exchange he would not fully incorporate the Indians into the American capitalist system. The presents he offers are material objects, not cash or a wage. Colley assures Barnum that "the presents which you assure me they will receive will be most acceptable to them. Those given to them by the public, as well as by yourself, will please them beyond my power to express. You are most likely aware that in this respect they resemble children." Neither Barnum nor Colley propose to treat the Indians as full partners in their own exhibition; indeed, Colley does not presume to consult with the Indians, and as their agent he does not request anything more for them than "presents"; a floor to sleep on, "as they have never slept in a bed"; "bread, raw beef, and coffee, all of which they will cook in their own rude Indian style"; as well as "some paint and some oil," presumably for their self-adornment.⁴⁵ In her study of Barnum's Indian exhibits, Linda Frost asserts that the showman regarded Indians from the perspective of an employer overseeing his employees; they were, to him, "the less complicitous worker[s]" in his establishment.⁴⁶ But the letters indicate that Barnum's business relationship was not with the Indians but with Agent Colley. Moreover, in his autobiography, Barnum acknowledges that the entire exhibit was made possible by "a pretty liberal outlay of money" paid to William Smith, the Indians' interpreter (*ST* 283). While some readers understand this expense as a bribe for Smith's assistance in duping the Indians, Barnum represents it merely as the cost of business.⁴⁷

Colley reminds Barnum of both the Indians' political stature and their innocence of the ways of civilized society. In response, Barnum made efforts to appear to treat the chiefs and warriors with appropriate respect even as he used them to generate revenue for his museum. He organized excursions around the city, most notably a visit to Public School No. 14 on April 10, 1863, where they observed children performing calisthenics and singing for them. "Before taking leave," the *New York Times* reports, "they stood up in a line, while Mr. SMITH [the interpreter] designated each one by his and her name, and the tribe to which they belonged, and also intimated their dispositions, giving 'Yellow Buffalo' the credit of being the best Indian in the delegation, and 'Little Heart' the discredit of being the worst one."⁴⁸ As a public relations tactic, the school visit is inspired: the childlike savages encounter actual children under the watchful eyes of schoolteachers, government agents, and Barnum himself. The episode asserts the educative value of the Indian exhibit even as it underscores the Indians' status as "children of the forest," unequal to the occasion and environment. But coverage of the Indian visit also emphasized their presumed savagery: the interpreter's identifying the "best" and "worst" Indians among them reflects a cultural tendency to typify Indians as "good" or "bad" as their behavior appears to correspond with the virtues white Americans prize.[49]

To the visiting delegates, these excursions were courtesies appropriate to their rank as leaders of nations, similar to the treatment they had received in Washington, D.C.[50] They were willing to participate in Barnum's exhibits because they thought they were promoting cross-cultural understanding, and, Barnum reports, they did not know he was charging admission. Barnum's hype of the Indian visit hinged on the public's complicity with his and Colley's deception of the delegates. To this end, the press was a valuable asset, as is evident from a promotional squib in the *New York Times*: "The Wild Indians still remain under the cheerful impression that they are the guests of the City, that BARNUM is the Great Mogul, and the Museum his palace. They are the genuine animal, and no mistake. Paint, leathers and trinkets cover their exterior; but their interior is, metaphorically speaking, filled with dead men's bones. They are a hard set, and, if BARNUM is permitted to remain unscalped, he will do well."[51] The item makes light of the Indians' ignorance of New York and pokes fun at their claims to political stature. While the warning that Barnum might be scalped reads as ironic and diffuses any threat the warriors might pose, the characterization of the Indians as killers remains potent. Barnum develops these effects at length in his representation of the exhibit in *Struggles and Triumphs*. Presenting the Indian delegation to the crowd in his Lecture Room, Barnum dismissed William Smith, the interpreter, and addressed the audience himself. His exhibit inverts patterns of representation familiar to readers of the captivity narratives: here, the "savage" is made captive to the whites. Hence Barnum reclaims the captivity narrative as a means of projecting white masculinity and justifying the nation's expansionist ideology.

Barnum's depiction plays up the presumed savagery of his captives even as their incongruity with their institutional surrounding neutralizes their ferocity. He focuses on Yellow Bear, presenting him to Lecture Room audiences as a "sly, treacherous, blood-thirsty savage" whose diplomatic efforts could not be trusted: "But now he was on a mission to the 'Great Father' at Washington, seeking for presents and favors to his tribe, and he pretended to be exceedingly meek and humble," Barnum told the audience (*ST* 286). Barnum, the great humbug, accuses the Kiowa delegate of humbugging the public and Lincoln himself. True to the patterns of humbug, Barnum turns the tables, taking advantage of the Indians' ignorance of English as he addresses the assembly:

> If the blood-thirsty little villain understood what I was saying, he would kill me in a moment; but as he thinks I am complimenting him, I can safely state the truth to you, that he is a lying, thieving, treacherous, murderous monster. He has tortured to death poor, unprotected women, murdered their husbands, brained their helpless little ones; and he would gladly do the same to you or me, if he thought he could escape punishment. This is but a faint description of the character of Yellow Bear." Here I gave him another patronizing pat on the head, and he, with a pleasant smile, bowed to the audience, as much as to say that my words were quite true, and that he thanked me very much for the high encomiums I had so generously heaped upon him. (*ST* 286–87)

This incident reveals the literary complexity of Barnum's performance. His recitation of violent acts Yellow Bear purportedly committed draws on stock images from captivity narratives, which traditionally depict Indians torturing captives. The suggestion that Yellow Bear has "brained" children draws from a motif of Indians' knocking the heads of children and dashing babies' heads into trees.[52] Barnum's account of Yellow Bear's alleged violent history plays into tropes of the violent savage that persisted through the history of contact. As he pats Yellow Bear's head, Barnum both appeases the savage and invites his audience into a further complicity with his deception of Yellow Bear and his brethren, who cannot understand what he says. Barnum's deception of Yellow Bear repays Yellow Bear's own presumed deception of the president, in which Yellow Bear represents himself as acting in good faith and in respect of white authority.[53] Barnum includes first his Lecture Room audience and then his readers in an elaborate practical joke meant to diminish the Indian warrior and diplomat. The outsider is thus kept out—Barnum's joke aligns white audience members in opposition to and ridicule of Yellow Bear and the other delegates.

Barnum's humbug out-tricks the Indian trickster, and Barnum maintains social order and unifies the white audience at the expense of the culturally and racially distinct individual. The joke reinforces the Indian's status as an outsider by drawing attention to differences in values that Barnum suggests are irreconcilable. Indeed, Barnum's depiction of Yellow Bear leaves no possibility that the Indian is guided by values at all; he is completely "savage." In other instances, Barnum depicts the Indians as driven by petty materialism that fails to acknowledge the rights and privileges of personal property that are so important to Barnum and his middle-class audience. In one instance, one of the chiefs, whom Barnum does not identify, insists that Barnum give him a coat of chain mail that he had on display, arguing he needed to wear it into battle against the enemies who killed his child. "I remained inexorable," Barnum insists, "until he finally brought me a new buckskin Indian suit, which he insisted upon exchanging. I felt compelled to accept his proposal; and never did I see a man more delighted. . . . He ran to his lodging room, and soon appeared again with the coveted armor upon his body, and marched down one of the main halls of the Museum, with folded arms, and head erect, occasionally patting his breast with his right hand, as much as to say, 'Now, Mr. Ute, look sharp, for I will soon be on the war path!'" (*ST* 285–86). Such exchanges of objects were commonplace for Barnum, who frequently traded duplicate or overexposed artifacts for items from other museums. Having arranged with Colley to repay the Indians with presents rather than money, Barnum subsequently mocks the Indians for working cheap. This question of recompense is further complicated by the fact that Barnum, Colley, and Smith colluded to conceal from the Indians that Barnum was charging audiences admission to see them. When they learned what was going on, Barnum reports, "their eyes were opened, and no power could induce them to appear again upon the stage. Their dignity had been offended" (*ST* 287). Of course, neither Barnum nor his audience recognizes the Indians' dignity. To have dignity is to possess a self; these Indians are thought to be "filled with dead men's bones."

I find the 1863 Indians episode a striking transformation of the operational aesthetic as defined by Neil Harris. Under the operational aesthetic, Barnum's audiences take for granted that Barnum is attempting to deceive them. But in both his 1863 presentation of the Indians and his recreation of it in *Struggles and Triumphs*, Barnum aligns himself with an audience that participates in deceiving the Indians. By Barnum's own definition, the exhibit is not a humbug, because he never lets the Indians in on it. The entire affair amounts to a swindle and a mockery—the Indians have nothing to gain but humiliation. Barnum and his audience, schooled in the art of humbug, laugh at the Indians' credulity, which signifies their nonbelonging. Barnum's white patrons are united by the pleasure and humor expressed in their examination of persons they understand to be inferior to themselves in both culture and understanding. The scene captures a moment in which a white, national identity is forged in opposition to the "savage" Indian Other. Far from being passive consumers,[54] Barnum's audiences are active participants in Barnum's objectification of the so-called savages. Barnum himself emerges from the episode looking less like the all-controlling master of ceremonies than a collaborator with his audiences, not to mention U.S. government agents who helped arrange the exhibit. Barnum stands before his audience as the embodiment of national manhood, in Dana Nelson's terms, and through his performance he unites the assembly in a shared sense of racial superiority, national belonging, and mutual commitment to the deceptions he stages.

Barnum responds to—capitalizes on—racial discourses in play in the popular media and channels public opinion into amusements that are spectacles of national identity. Jennifer Greiman describes just such spectatorship: "It instituted forms of association and belonging that implicated spectators in what they watched, revealing the intimacy of their involvement with one another, while also exposing the contours of a collective power that was rooted in rituals of sovereignty."[55] The 1863 Indian exhibit is just one of many displays of Indians and other nonwhite persons Barnum managed, including the Joice Heth exhibit and "What Is It?" Altogether, these exhibits affirm a normative white subject position and inculcate practices of objectifying nonwhite bodies as the exceptions to be evaluated and excluded from the civic body. As he relates the details of the 1863 Indian exhibit and other amusements he managed, Barnum reveals the processes of image making. These exhibits involve complex networks of signs disseminated through various media—advertisements, puffs, promotional materials at the museum—that may reach audiences before they attend an exhibit. Those various components of the images may also partake of already existing representations of similar images made familiar by popular literature such as captivity narratives. Barnum cannot be regarded as the sole creative authority in mounting these cultural displays. They require the collaborative participation of an audience that is already engaged in these sign systems and that takes pleasure and power from its masterful spectatorship.

IN THEIR UNIQUE COMBINATION OF HYPE AND HUMBUG, FRAUD AND fun, Barnum's exhibits help establish the conditions of celebrity culture. The audience's efforts to figure out the fraud parallels the work of understanding the celebrity image via an objectifying gaze. In both cases, audience members assume an authority that is never assured. In addition, Barnum's use of the operational aesthetic highlights the ways that entertainment is both commodified and personalized in the period. Putting human beings on display for the amusement of a mass audience, Barnum capitalizes on and encourages celebrity culture's appraising gaze as it is directed at bodies in public. Insofar as he channels values for white superiority into his exhibitions of Indians and other nonwhite bodies, Barnum commercializes an expression of popular sovereignty; moreover, as he becomes a celebrity himself, he assumes a quasi-political, representative role. Barnum's own celebrity is a by-product of his efforts to associate himself with his entertainments. To this end, he made skillful use of print culture. As I will explore more fully in the next chapter, the expansion of print culture in the 1830s and 1840s was instrumental to the development of a personal public sphere. Barnum's early experience as editor of a country newspaper gave him a comprehensive understanding of the business, and he excelled at using the press to promote his enterprises. His promotional strategies, plus his deliberate association of his name with his every venture, extended and replicated his image before a mass public that came to see Barnum himself in his various products. But the inquisitive public gaze cannot pierce Barnum's private life. Deliberately—ostentatiously—shielding his private life from public view, Barnum lays claim to the privileges of abstract selfhood that his representational status implies.

In his writings, Barnum seldom uses the word "celebrity" in reference to himself, and when he does he uses it as a synonym for "fame" or "renown." Nevertheless, he recognized the tendencies of his audience to regard him personally as representative of his public endeavors and to regard his public endeavors as reflecting himself. As an autobiographer, Barnum exploits audiences' willingness to equate the work with the man, not only as a means to sell books but also to influence public perception of his character. Barnum deliberately presents his story in Franklinian terms, representing himself as the typical Yankee who transforms himself through hard work into a successful businessman and political figure. Franklin's most difficult critic was his own conscience, but Barnum faced the condemnation of all America. Whereas Franklin acknowledges the moral "errata" of his early life and reveals his methods of self-improvement, Barnum confronts his audiences' worst judgments of him and turns them to his benefit. Barnum did not control the terms of his own publicity. He worked out his image through rhetorically complicated and career-long negotiations with a judgmental public, and in this sense alone, Barnum was a celebrity. Popular contention over the celebrity's meaning helps overcome the social distance that is a "precondition" of celebrity.[56] Contention over the celebrity's meaning helps overcome that distance: through the work of interpretation, the observer engages a critical practice that puts him or her on similar social and intellectual footing with the celebrity author and in some cases creates an illusion of emotional connection. These interpretive efforts maintain the older belief that the celebrity's public actions represent his self, "an irreducible core of being, the entity that is perceived within the roles and actions, the entity upon which social forces act."[57] Moreover, the negotiations over the celebrity's meaning not only underscore the celebrity's unique individualism but also support the individualism of members of the audience: each judgment of a public figure exposes something of the values and core beliefs that make up the observer's self. Celebrity culture sanctions the authority of each observer's judgment, though it occurs in a context where judgment is multiplied.

The celebrity's meaning is never definitive and is always in flux: P. David Marshall details the processes by which "the celebrity's meaning is constructed by the audience. An exact 'ideological fit' between production of the cultural icon and consumption is rare. Audience members actively work on the presentation of the celebrity in order to make it fit into their everyday lives."[58] Seen in this light, the celebrity figure is much like one of the exhibits Barnum puts on display: individually and collectively, audiences work to figure out the meaning of the objectified public persona, and their judgments reflect their own values and beliefs. Indeed, scholars note the same processes at work among spectators at freak shows such as those Barnum staged. In the cases of human oddities—often persons with physical differences or disabilities or people of non-European origins—such exhibits function to reinforce physical and racial norms. By definition, celebrities are similarly objectified. As a result, "celebrity status always implies a split between a private self and a public self."[59] But this split is not always acknowledged by observers, who recognize the celebrity's public image or persona as coextensive with his or her self. Such confusion may in fact be inherent to celebrity itself: Sheryl N. Hamilton argues convincingly that "the celebrity is a complex hybrid, the always contingent and unstable fusion of person and persona. A celebrity crystallizes when we both desire and recognize a relationship between a persona and a person. This relationship is one that is mutually authenticating."[60] That hybrid cements the celebrity's freakishness: his self is neither fully public nor fully private. In crossing these boundaries, it emerges as a grotesque amalgamation of both.

Barnum's case reveals the significance of these tensions, their potential to reshape both the public sphere and the individual's understanding of selfhood, its development, and its ability to authorize or legitimate public action. The widespread interest in Barnum's person encroaches on his private life, broadly understood as encompassing his familial and personal relationships and his activities and habits that do not bear directly on his public or professional affairs. Barnum acknowledges and even toys with others' curiosity about him. Most characteristic of his efforts is Iranistan, the mansion he built in an elaborate Oriental style in Fairfield, Connecticut. The home captured Barnum's twin passions, business and family life: he built it as a place of retirement, where "I could withdraw from the whirlpool of business excitement and settle down permanently with my family" (*ST* 163). At the same time, he desired a home that was "unique" (*ST* 163): "for I thought that a pile of buildings of a novel order might indirectly serve as an advertisement of my Museum" (*ST* 164). From these motives, Barnum commissioned a mansion built on the model of King George IV's Royal Pavilion in Brighton, England. The result satisfied Barnum's desire for a unique home: "The finished home was like an ethereal dream. Three stories high, pillared and trellised, with its floors opening onto broad piazzas, the mansion was rimmed by satyrlike faces and surmounted by strange Turkish towers and minarets and a grand central dome soaring 90 feet into the sky."[61] Barnum opened the grounds of his estate as a public park, but the hours of admission were strictly regulated, and pleasure seekers were denied access to the mansion itself.

In its grandeur, Iranistan communicated Barnum's success as a businessman; in its unique style, it was a visual synecdoche for his work as a purveyor of amusements and curiosities. As if to drive the point home, Barnum briefly employed an elephant to plow one of Iranistan's fields adjacent to the tracks of the New York and New Haven Railroad. The spectacle soon attracted newspaper coverage, which of course gave Barnum and his museum free publicity (*ST* 215–16). Similarly, Barnum adorned the stationery he used for business correspondence with an engraving of Iranistan. In these elaborate gestures, Barnum married his public life as a showman to his private life, or at least to the edifice in which he conducted his private affairs. Iranistan's glaring ostentation concealed Barnum's private life from the eyes of the curious.

Iranistan therefore reflected the concerns about public life, privacy, work, and leisure that formed the core of Barnum's industry and that resonated with a society in transition. As the agricultural economy, home-based industry, and artisanal production gave way to factory production and the commercial marketplace in the first decades of the nineteenth century, Americans inevitably turned outward from the family and the local community for employment and to supply their day-to-day material needs. The growth of urban centers such as New York City, home to Barnum's American Museum, was one result of this demographic shift; another was the growing market for leisure activities among a class of workers cut off from traditional communities.[62] A variety of institutions arose to fill this need, and Barnum positioned his American Museum as the premier venue for respectable entertainments and an antidote to the demands of workaday life: "This is a trading world, and men, women and children, who cannot live on gravity alone, need something to satisfy their gayer, lighter moods and hours, and he who ministers to this want is in a business established by the Author of our nature. If he worthily fulfills his mission, and amuses without corrupting, he need never feel that he has lived in vain" (*ST* 79–80). Barnum's trade in amusement as a commodity is, on the one hand, an example of the commodification of everyday life. But on the other hand, Barnum represents his labors as a kind of ministry to those who have been weighed down by that same phenomenon. To be sure, Barnum's efforts are controversial. While some view Barnum's populism as the troubling emergence of a culture industry that "[contaminates] high culture with commercialism,"[63] others recognize his work's value in acknowledging and serving America as Barnum finds it. As Bluford Adams argues, Barnum's and others' views of his work are all steeped in assumptions about class and taste. His opening of the grounds at Iranistan should be understood in this context, as a means of enriching the leisure, and thus the quality of life, of working people. In this respect, Iranistan is aspirational, a symbol of the luxuries potentially available to America's hardworking people. Pleasure seekers got a taste of the good life Barnum presumably experienced by dint of personal effort, which he details in his autobiographies.

But at the same time as the public culture was growing wider and richer, private life in America was growing deeper and more entrenched. Barnum's Iranistan symbolizes and, in Barnumesque fashion, aggrandizes this trend: it represents the home as refuge from public life, a site of authentic self-expression controlled by the patriarchal authority figure. From Iranistan's beautiful grounds, the public could see where Barnum lived, but not how. Private life is interiorized—literally walled off from public view. Home architecture reflects and reinforces this development by more clearly delimiting the home's "public" spaces, such as the parlor or the drawing room, from "private" spaces such as the bedroom and the study. No mere home office, Barnum's personal study was "an orange-colored, satin walled library and retreat which connected onto a modernized bathing room with full shower and tubs"; it was "increasingly important to him" in the years he spent in the home.[64] Iranistan reinterprets the middle-class home for what it is: a monument to the private self that is ironically public. More particularly, it reinforces the idea of the male head of household as a lordly patriarch, provider, and master of the domestic comforts the home contains. As his refuge from an active public life—none more active, perhaps, than Barnum's—it is the symbol and indeed the source of authentic, masculine selfhood that is the basis of citizenship.[65]

Barnum and his family lived in Iranistan only a short time, from 1848 to 1856. They were forced to leave the home, which Barnum built with "no desire even to ascertain the entire cost" (ST 164), when Barnum met severe financial reversals in 1856. His failure was widely commented on. Some saw it as a well-deserved comeuppance for the vulgar humbug; Barnum himself regarded it as "a severe and costly discipline," a God-sent "chastening," that "ward[ed] off all temptation to rust in the repose which affluence induces" (*ST* 238). While Barnum worked with renewed purpose to restore his business reputation and to return his family to the shuttered mansion, the structure was burned to the ground in 1858 by a lighted pipe, mislaid by a workman. The home takes on a moral significance for Barnum, bespeaking the fragility of personal economic achievement and the vulnerability of even the greatest triumphs. In this manner, Barnum revises the Calvinistic views of his Connecticut neighbors: in place of an arbitrary God, Barnum sees the capricious forces of a marketplace where fortunes can be made with effort but lost at a stroke.

Iranistan physically represents Barnum's private life as opulent but inaccessible to the masses, and in its grandeur it announces Barnum's preeminence on the national scene not merely as an impresario or businessman but as a male universal subject and arbiter of public life. The publicity of Barnum's identity is enhanced by the heavy shroud of privacy with which he surrounds himself. What Barnum did locally at Iranistan, he did nationally with his autobiographies, particularly *Struggles and Triumphs*, published in 1855 and updated throughout Barnum's later life. An initial sketch of his Connecticut boyhood establishes his entrepreneurial spirit and waggish good humor as part of the cultural and familial inheritance. Of his family life as an adult, Barnum makes only passing reference: he notes his marriage to Charity Hallett and occasionally mentions family events, such as his children's marriages, only as they relate to other events in his professional career. Barnum sequestered his public and private lives so successfully that Neil Harris argues that "one is not even sure that he had a notion of privacy."[66] Seen in this light, Barnum illustrates how the extreme publicity of celebrity culture destabilizes selfhood. As Eric Fretz puts it, "The revisions of Barnum's autobiography demonstrate a malleable self that transforms itself with the passage of time and the continual (re)act of writing. Barnum's notion of a dynamic self, illustrated in each rewriting of the autobiography, exposes the elusiveness of essential self-identity."[67] This analysis would seem to defy the idea of celebrity as a form of publicity that reassures its audience of the self's stability. In fact, Barnum's careful concealment of his personal life suggests just the opposite: it indicates his complicity with the nineteenth-century distinction between home life and work that, particularly for men, suggested the home as the site of authentic selfhood and the public as an arena of near-constant performance. Barnum's celebrity accentuates this cultural development: the self Barnum represents as elaborately public and infinitely malleable is not his own, but a public persona revised and updated with every addendum to *Struggles and Triumphs*.

Coupled with his near silence about his private life, Barnum's revisions to his autobiography indicate the complicated dynamics of publicity and privacy in the context of celebrity culture. Yes, the public persona, and especially the celebrity persona, is a reproducible commodity, manufactured and sold in the marketplace of consumer goods. But Barnum's private self was not for sale. The work of A. H. Saxon confirms the argument that Barnum wished to preserve a purely private space and identity. In his biography of Barnum, Saxon uses letters, memoranda books, and other private documents to recover the private Barnum from his public reputation. Saxon argues that Barnum's inhibitions about disclosing his personal life result from his profound ability to keep his professional and personal activities separate. He points to Barnum's commitment to Universalism as an example. Barnum remained committed to the Universalist faith throughout his life and was a generous benefactor of several parishes. He refused to join any one parish formally, however, for fear of tainting the institution with his reputation as a showman. Barnum even authored a pamphlet, "Why I Am a Universalist," but in his books he rarely mentions the Universalism that is so important to him. Barnum's unwillingness to mention his private faith attests to his awareness that religion and show business cannot be reconciled with one another in a culture still influenced by Puritanism. But he rejects any notion that they cannot be reconciled in himself. In a private letter, Barnum defended his career against accusations that it was inconsistent with his faith: "It is not a vindication but a fact, that men as politicians, sectarians, and lawyers frequently do what they would *not* do as *men*; and the same I suppose is true generally of caterers for public amusement. I do not defend what I here speak of, but I think it is hardly fair to make fish of a lawyer and flesh of a showman."[68] Barnum defends himself with another version of the "way of the world" argument he uses elsewhere.

In Barnum's careful management of his public and private identities, we see the core issues of nineteenth-century celebrity and public life. Barnum's case, moreover, reveals the political dimensions of this complex dynamic of publicity and privacy: because of his public stature and business success, Barnum was invited to serve his community in a variety of roles. In 1865 he was elected to the Connecticut state senate, a position that depended on both his constituents' recognition of his name and their trust in his character and ability. Reflecting on his political life, Barnum strikes a characteristically Franklinian pose: "I was a party man, but not a partisan, nor a wire-puller, and I had never sought or desired office, though it had often been tendered to me. This was notoriously true, among all who knew me, up to the year 1865, when I accepted from the Republican party a nomination to the Connecticut legislature from the town of Fairfield, and I did this because I felt it would be an honor to be permitted to vote for the then proposed amendment to the Constitution of the United States to abolish slavery forever from the land" (*ST* 321). Throughout his career, Barnum shamelessly appealed to both pro- and antislavery interests to attract audiences.[69] Here, however, he uses his Republican affiliation as the public marker of his inner virtue. The passage takes up the older view of fame as a reward for virtue, and it indicates private experience as the forge of enlightened citizenship. I have argued that celebrity culture endorses the idea of selfhood that is central to juridical personhood, and that in doing so, it legitimates claims to personhood by individuals traditionally excluded from the public sphere. But Barnum's efforts to control his privacy expose celebrity culture's limitations as an agent of democracy. In its demand for access to the public figure's person, celebrity culture infringes relentlessly on the privacy that nourishes the self, and in this sense it may indeed be said to "consume" its subjects. In the face of this incursion, Barnum creates an ostentatious privacy—that is, he uses his extraordinary publicity defensively, as a shield for his private life.

A FULL UNDERSTANDING OF NINETEENTH-CENTURY CULTURE REQUIRES some study of Barnum and his career, and for several reasons. Barnum's operational aesthetic, the modus operandi of his museum exhibits and other amusements, aestheticizes and indeed capitalizes on the intensely personal nature of public life in the period. In particular, it captures and exploits, for fun and profit, the subjectivism of nineteenth-century popular culture, its emphasis on what Emerson calls the first-person singular—individual experience that is meaningful and authoritative because it is individual. But Barnum's amusements also suggest the limits of individual judgment: in his appeal to a mass audience, Barnum makes clear that the individual is still one of many, and he gratifies his audiences' paradoxical desires for the assurance of individual, autonomous judgment and social and cultural inclusion. Inclusion also implies its antithesis, and by objectifying certain bodies, Barnum enables his audiences to participate directly in the exclusionary ideologies that marginalized nonwhite persons and women. In my discussion of Barnum's presentations of human beings in freak shows, I join with other scholars who recognize the ways freak shows contribute to the creation of a white gaze that subjugates nonnormative, nonwhite persons. Barnum's exhibits participate in and develop the same ideologies that justify westward expansion, the dislocation and decimation of Indian cultures, slavery, and the continued subjugation of black people after emancipation. Looking at these issues in the context of a study of celebrity culture reveals something more: the spectacles Barnum stages do not just appeal to popular opinion on race and culture or participate in ongoing discourses about whiteness, civility, and savagery; they contribute to a culture in which such spectacles are central to a commercial market for amusement. Barnum helps make it possible for individual Americans to understand such spectacles as harmless and pleasurable—and, moreover, as valuable commodities. Barnum's patrons do not simply objectify the people he exhibits. They pay for the privilege, and doing so—being in the position to do so—is a constitutive feature of their social and cultural dominance.

Barnum's amusements literally make fun of these excluded persons—they convert their experiences and selves into the objects of audiences' amusement. To do so required more than a stage or a museum niche, and explaining his life's work in his autobiographies, Barnum reveals how he constructed the apparatus for his audiences' pleasure. Barnum worked hard to justify his work as uplifting his middle- and working-class patrons, and indeed he depicts himself as good-hearted and fun-loving, and his enterprises as sources of welcome respite from a workaday world. He also strives to differentiate himself from his audience: "I myself relished a higher grade of amusement, and I was a frequent attendant at the opera, first-class concerts, lectures and the like; but I worked for the million, and I knew the only way to make a million from my patrons was to give them abundant and wholesome attractions for a small sum of money" (*ST* 115). Attempting to differentiate himself from both his reputation and the audience that supported him, Barnum acknowledges a self that is inaccessible to the public. That private self redeems Barnum, or so he assumes, by tempering his disreputable business practices and distinguishing the humbug from the man. Barnum reserves for himself privileges he denies to the people he exhibits. That duplicity registers an important trait of the public figure, who recognizes himself as apart from, above, the public fray even when he is in its very midst. Such a judgment is erroneous, however: as a public figure, he is always subject to the same kind of objectification and judgment as the other human beings he places before the public gaze—otherwise, he would not need to work so hard to maintain his privacy. But this is not to say that Barnum was oppressed by the public gaze as his human exhibits were. From the outset of his career as a showman, Barnum capitalized on certain privileges his whiteness granted him—assumptions of his kinship with his white audience, a fluency in the discourses of whiteness and racial distinction, and an ability to shape, though not entirely control, the terms on which he would be seen and judged.

In the chapters that follow, we will see other celebrity authors make similar efforts to establish and maintain their privacy in the midst of a demanding, even invasive public. Like Barnum, these figures reveal what is at stake in the struggle to balance publicity and privacy: the selfhood that is the basis of their political legitimacy and cultural authority. To varying degrees, these figures must all come to terms with the fact that their cultural authority is inevitably limited, challenged by the competing authoritative visions of a pluralistic public.

CHAPTER 2

WALT WHITMAN
Mediation, Affect, and Authority in Celebrity Culture

If BARNUM ESTABLISHED THE PRACTICES OF PUBLICITY THAT DOMINATE nineteenth-century celebrity culture, Walt Whitman repurposed those practices for personal advancement, rhetorical power, and aesthetic effect. Whitman is rightly regarded as the most enthusiastic promoter of his own authorial vision, celebrating and singing himself to all who would listen. Late in his life, however, he doubted whether his songs of himself had been heard. In the 1888 essay "A Backward Glances o'er Travel'd Roads," he wrote, "That I have not gain'd the acceptance of my own time, but have fallen back on fond dreams of the future . . . that from a worldly and business point of view 'Leaves of Grass' has been worse than a failure—that public criticism on the book and myself as author of it yet shows mark'd anger and contempt more than anything else . . . is all probably no more than I ought to have expected."[1] In assessing his reception, Whitman characteristically relates his book to his self, and he associates both with the commercial marketplace. His disappointment registers the book's purchase as an expression of approbation and even desire for the author himself. This view is consistent with celebrity, a condition of public life in which "the body becomes a commodity . . . an object of consumption, designed and packaged to generate desire in others and achieve impact in public."[2] For Whitman, this consumption is an intimate act that would return the "affection" the poet has lovingly bestowed on his audience through his close observation of public life and inscription of it into his poems.[3] Were this exchange of affections to take place as Whitman imagines, it would of course be uneven: granting even the largeness of the poet's affections, he imagines a mass audience. Such large-scale reception resembles the dynamics of celebrity, in which mass audiences bestow on a particular public figure an amount of interest disproportionate to any attention that that individual could ever repay.

The period in which Whitman came of age is the same period in which mass culture and celebrity emerged and transformed the critical public sphere. In the first half of this chapter, I examine Whitman's journalism from the period 1840 to 1842, the primary expression of his developing vision of a public life that is equally committed both to the model of critical discourse associated with the public sphere and to the close attention to public individuals that characterizes celebrity. Journalism provided Whitman's training as a writer and instilled in him a keen sense of publicity. Although his poetry is generally written in a much different tenor than his bombastic journalism, the two forms share an understanding of the public sphere as a site of both critical discourse and personal feeling—as a site where the union of critical discourse and personal feeling is politically productive. At the same time, Whitman's *Aurora* journalism reveals that the personal public sphere challenged the ambitious journalist who sought public acceptance as a voice of authority. The challenges of public reception and authorial control are on display in Whitman's "Calamus" poems as well, to which I turn in the second half of this chapter. Considered Whitman's most personal poetry, the "Calamus" poems reveal Whitman as he wishes to be read: "Lovers, continual lovers, only repay me," he writes.[4] Using Lacanian gaze theory, I argue that in the "Calamus" poems Whitman objectifies himself and shapes an affective response to his own persona and to his work. Turning, finally, to Whitman's great Lincoln elegy, "When Lilacs Last in the Dooryard Bloom'd," I take up the question of what happens to public affect when its object is no longer present in the public sphere.

As a journalist Whitman understood the newspaper to be a tool for individual self-culture and social improvement. His friend and biographer John Burroughs notes, "He loved the common, democratic character of the newspaper; it was the average man's library."[5] Though devoted to individualism, he sought to channel the self-authorizing confidence of individual readers into avenues of public life that he considered conducive to the development of republican culture and democratic union. Whitman had a strong sense of the newspaper's potential to shape communities of readers gathered around the identifiable persona of a strong editor. During his brief tenure as editor of the *New York Aurora* in 1842, Whitman adopted the aggressively argumentative editorial style typical of the penny papers. In particular, Whitman's attacks on Bishop John Hughes incited readers' accusations of anti-Catholic bigotry and Know-Nothingism. Such attacks "reveal Whitman as a master of invective, in which any editor worth his salt at the time had to excel."[6] At the same time, in his observational pieces he began to cultivate his flâneur persona, through which he projected an authoritative vision of the life exhibited in New York's public spaces. In these two strains of his *Aurora* experience, the editor and the flâneur, Whitman demonstrates the dynamic tension between commercialized institutional or cultural authority and individual judgment that motivates and complicates antebellum public life.

This paradoxical embrace of both individual and didactic authority is the particular offshoot of a public sphere tested by the social transformation brought by industrialization and urbanization; it is the practical expression of the artisan republican political philosophy through which Whitman and other journalists revived the egalitarian ideals they associated with the American Revolution.[7] Amid the increasing economic stratifications of social and political life, the newspaper fosters a public sphere of discursive exchange among readers of differing social classes. By adapting to print a vernacular style rooted in orality, the penny press sought to shrink distances among readers and generate a sense of immediacy in public discourse, even as the expansion of the press makes the newspaper available to a mass audience. The newspaper potentially reconciles the anonymity of modern urban life with the desire for community and connection among individuals that is the basis for Whitman's vision of political union. In the process, it also facilitates the spread of celebrity culture that invests personal feeling in the representations of public figures.

Antebellum celebrity culture regards public figures' successes as manifestations of their personal traits on a large scale. That is, celebrity does not magnify the character of the public individual, so much as it suggests that an enlarged or capacious character engenders celebrity. This is the model of self that Whitman ultimately celebrates in 1855. But Whitman the journalist does not offer faith in celebrity figures per se; rather, he encourages his readers to regard the strangers they encounter as projecting magnified representations of their selves on the public stage, and to regard themselves as the interpreters of this play of selfhood. This model of publicity offers a few advantages. First, it builds on the personalized relations and exchanges within the public sphere, encouraging further personalized relations and in the process fostering sympathetic union. Second, it both supports and conveys republican virtues, which Whitman understands as virtues of character. Finally, it encourages readers to balance the passions and sympathies that accompany personal experience with critical judgment. Such, at least, is the ideal of publicity that Whitman models with more or less success in his editorial writings. In general, he seeks a mode of publicity through which reasoned exchange and critical judgment can be infused with, informed by, personal feeling. But the controversies that accompanied Whitman's nativist editorials indicate as well the danger to republican union posed by the personalization of public life. Just as celebrities' meanings are always open to interpretation, the personal public sphere makes every citizen a critic with an idiosyncratic standard of judgment. The result is no mere relativism of critical judgment, but the destabilization of social and political community. Whitman's *Aurora* journalism is an example of how and why it is so difficult to reconcile individualism with political and social community in the era of mass culture.

Whitman's newspaper career started while he was quite young. In 1831, at the age of twelve, he began working as a printer's apprentice for the *Long Island Patriot*. He held a variety of jobs throughout his teen years, but by the time he reached his twenties, he seemed poised for a career in journalism. In 1840 and 1841 Whitman published "Sun-Down Papers from the Desk of a Schoolmaster" in several Long Island newspapers. In this series of related essays, Whitman experiments with a first-person, familiar style that draws heavily on sentimental conventions for their didactic power. For instance, "Sun-Down Papers" No. 1 uses the generic figure of the melancholy bachelor, sitting "in mine elbow-chair," reflecting on his lost youth and pending mortality.[8] The appeal of the piece rests not only in its conventionally melancholy pose but also in popular interest in the plight of the young bachelor, one of a type of educated and socially aware young man who was understood to make up the readership for newspapers.[9] Implicitly, the piece encourages such young men to fight the loneliness and isolation that come with the anonymity of city life and instead allow their sympathies to guide them into emotional connections with others. Other numbers of "Sun-Down Papers" similarly combine stylistic conventions to address familiar situations. A possible exception to this rule, No. 7 is typically read as an expression of Whitman's budding artistic ambitions: "Yes: I *would* write a book! And who shall say that it might not be a very pretty book? Who knows but that I might do something very respectable?" (WJ 22). While the association with a young Whitman makes sense, the piece also reflects the sense of possibility and self-confidence that characterizes the class of young professional men of which Whitman was a part. This persona reflects the optimistic spirit of democratic equality, in which every young schoolmaster is also a would-be writer, his potential checked only by his own confidence, drive, and willingness to risk the conciliatory comfort of loneliness by following his passion.

In the "Sun-Down Papers," Whitman exhibits stylistic tendencies that illustrate his absorption of the conventions of contemporary journalism. The "newspaper revolution" of the 1830s and 1840s gave rise to not only a dramatically expanded print culture but also an intensely personal style of journalistic writing that drew on conventions of oral culture.[10] First-person journalism, such as Whitman uses in "Sun-Down Papers," reaches out to readers as if individually; it presumes the possibility of conversational exchange among strangers and promotes an idea of the newspaper as a forum for public discourse across social classes. The daily papers cultivated a vernacular style that combined fact-based reporting with first-person editorial content,[11] through which they established their public identities as extensions of their editors' personal characters and political values. This "middling style" brings to printed texts the directness and sense of immediacy prized in oratory while eschewing the elitism that restricted classical eloquence to the genteel classes.[12] In addition, the newspapers drew on their historic origins as public correspondence, raising the possibility and even expectation that readers would respond to what they read. Indeed, frequent publication of readers' letters originated in newspapers of the previous century, which promoted the newspapers' "forum function" as part of their larger civic mission.[13] In both the eighteenth and nineteenth centuries, the publication of readers' letters built on the notion of letters as "written conversation" that pervaded eighteenth-century correspondence manuals.[14] In doing so they aimed to recreate in print the conversational exchanges associated with coffeehouse culture and the dialogic public sphere of the eighteenth century; likewise, they brought about the "convergence of oral and print cultures" in the effort to promote critical exchange about matters of public import.[15]

Projecting an eighteenth-century model of discourse through modern means of production, the penny press extended and democratized the public sphere. Such a claim, however, contradicts the view that the commercialization of print culture in the early nineteenth century brought about the decline of the rational public sphere theorized by Jürgen Habermas. The public sphere is, as he puts it, "the corollary of a depersonalized state authority." In other words, the civic life that develops in the eighteenth century counters the state's claims to depersonalized authority with the personalized expressions of a dialogic public space. Newspapers facilitate the public sphere's debates by providing information about matters of the state and trade. Habermas argues that the commercialization of news in the early nineteenth century degrades and weakens the public sphere's functioning as a political counterweight to state authority. While commercialization expanded the penny papers' readership, "it paid for the maximization of its sales with the depoliticization of its content—by eliminating political news and political editorials on such moral topics as intemperance and gambling"—developments, he suggests, that diluted the public sphere's effectiveness.[16] As a portrait of the American penny press, however, Habermas's descriptions are limited; he conflates the penny press with the many new forms that emerged in the press's expansionist period, such as story papers and illustrated weeklies. The penny press itself never abandoned its interest in politics, and indeed it provided the model for publicity associated with moral reform movements such as abolition and temperance.[17]

Subsequent investigations suggest, moreover, that the public sphere that Habermas identifies was not effaced by industrial capitalism but complicated and, in some ways, enriched by it. Habermas's larger concern is that the commercialization of mass media blurs the interests of the private and public spheres. Feminist scholarship, however, has pointed out that "public" and "private" are never wholly discrete categories but conventional designations that historically have been used to uphold conventional expectations of gender and class roles.[18]

The penny press itself challenged this expectation of public versus private life. Its "London system" of daily production and on-the-street sales gradually replaced the weekly subscription model of newspaper distribution; this shift made newspapers widely available to all but the most destitute of readers, and it brought the discussion of civic affairs out of the coffeehouses and into the streets—or the railway cars, or the taverns, or the private home, anywhere, in short, that a newspaper might be read.[19] The very portability and availability of the newspaper extended the means of public participation to those who are notoriously excluded from the Habermasian public sphere—namely women, unpropertied men, and nonwhites.

Yet the commercial press's extension of public access should not be considered a wholly productive cultural development. Trish Loughran associates the unprecedented growth of print culture with "the ongoing integration of the local into the national" that accompanied the emergence of industrial capitalism more generally, and she argues that the threat to the local community led to the eventual breach of the Union in the sectional crisis and Civil War.[20] Her critique is useful in reading Whitman's journalism, which is shaped by the social transformations Loughran describes. His work encourages further examination of the relationship between the idealized public sphere of enlightenment debate and the equally idealized "imagined community" of the nation. To the extent that the newspaper revolution is part of a larger industrial revolution, the penny press both contributes to and attempts to atone for the social transformations that accompany industrialization. The displacement of artisans in an increasingly capitalist economy, the fragmentation of communities that occurs as young people, especially young men, move from the countryside to the city—the penny press attempts to counter these social changes by giving voice to the artisan republican ideology of the working class and generating a community of sympathetic readers centered around the recognizable figure of the editor. The penny press aims, that is, to adapt an older model of publicity and community to the circumstances of modern life.

Indeed, mass production and commercialization do challenge the newspaper's ability to generate dialogic exchange, and in their personal, vernacular style and modern commercial methods, the antebellum newspapers faced an apparent contradiction. As David Henkin explains, "Newspapers . . . struggled with the problem of creating personal credibility within a system whose power lay precisely in the establishment of impersonal authority. While particular papers were famously and often notoriously identified with their idiosyncratic editors, the public power of the metropolitan press lay in the idea that newspaper space as such belonged to no one in particular, that its columns were available for open purchase, and that its words were being read by an impersonal public."[21] At stake in this struggle between impersonal and personal modes of authority are ideas of truth rooted in either market success or humanistic relations, the latter of which is associated with an older, pre-capitalist ideal of discursive exchange. In the effort to assert personal authority, the penny papers rely on the "legitimating charisma" of the editorial voice.[22] This emphasis on the oral qualities of newspaper discourse contradicts Michael Warner's influential claim that print culture is an arena of impersonal expression abstracted from the writer. At the same time, print's "unrestricted dissemination" remains a powerful source of the newspapers' authority,[23] as their wider commercial practices enable them to reach ever larger and more spread-out readerships. The penny press claims its authority from both the immediacy of orality and the widespread availability of print, without questioning whether these two modes of authority are compatible or mutually supportive. Whitman's *Aurora* journalism registers just this conflict, as he relies on the paper's middling style to generate communities of sympathy while at the same time insisting on the social authority associated with print.

Whitman therefore participates in a periodical press working on these issues of personal and impersonal authority at the same time as they are competing with one another commercially. Whitman understood that in this context the struggle for authority was a struggle for both truth and dollars. As editor of the *Aurora*, Whitman oversaw increased circulation.[24] This commercial success may reflect readers' appreciation of what Douglas A. Noverr calls the "writerly qualities" he brought to the paper—the "sense of fluent spontaneity and natural public talk" that characterizes Whitman's best editorial writing.[25] But Whitman was fired when his aggressive, nativist-leaning editorials put him at odds with publishers Anson Herrick and John F. Ropes.[26] His dismissal suggests the tenuousness of Whitman's claims to authority as an editor in the employ of others. Unlike prominent editors such as Horace Greeley and James Gordon Bennett, Whitman held no stake in the ownership of the papers he edited, and therefore he was less free to express his political views.[27] On the one hand, Whitman's firing suggests that social and political authority are aligned with neither oral nor print expression, but with the interests of capital. On the other hand, Whitman's editorships raise the question of whether the convergence of his writerly style and his newspapers' commercial successes ratifies the authority of his editorial claims. The editorial experience encourages Whitman to accept popular success as the signal of an ascendant social or political authority.

Whitman pursued that popular authority in the role of the bombastic and politically judgmental editor during the two months he oversaw the *Aurora*. In contrast with the melancholy bachelor of his "Sun-Down" phase, at the *Aurora* Whitman used his position as editor and the conventional personal style of the antebellum press in the service of vitriolic editorials filled with personal attacks.

The editorials represent Whitman's efforts to articulate the "Americanism" that ultimately figures in some of his mature poetry, but their aggressive editorial style contributes to a persona that is not merely brash but in some instances bigoted. Specifically, Whitman responded to the "schools question," an issue of whether the city would help fund Catholic parochial schools. The measure was promoted by the Ireland-born bishop of New York, John Hughes, as an alternative to a public-school curriculum that promoted a Protestant understanding of history and encouraged scriptural and other readings that contradicted Catholic belief and practice. Opposition to the measure was fueled in part by nativist anxiety that Catholics—largely Irish immigrants—were undermining American sovereignty by acting on the authority of the foreign pope. Whitman's editorials on the schools question staunchly defended the Public Schools Society and its Protestant curriculum, arguing that Hughes's efforts represented special interests taking advantage of public welfare and a pernicious anti-Americanism. But even as he claims the newspaper's inclusiveness and lack of prejudice, in an editorial of March 7, 1842, Whitman makes direct, personal attacks against the character of Bishop Hughes, who seemed to Whitman to manipulate the Catholic faithful to gain political advantage: "The Aurora is no puritan. We open our arms very wide—taking into our good wishes, professors of every creed and doctrine, and tenet. We are prejudiced against no sect, as such—and love all men equally well, whatever be their religion. But this Hughes—this cunning, flexible, serpent tongued priest, who has had the insolence to appear in the political forum, and pour vials of discord amid us and the discussions we engage in on questions appertaining to the laity alone—we feel called upon to condemn in the strongest terms" (WJ 43). Speaking on behalf of the *Aurora* to its readers, Whitman projects the newspaper as a pluralistic entity unified by affect, tolerance, and consensus. In the paradoxical exclusion of Hughes, however, Whitman's editorial shifts the debate over the schools question to a debate over personalities. Against the singular "serpent tongued priest," Whitman offers the "we" of the *Aurora* as an inclusive agent of public good. The two dominant personalities in this debate, Hughes and Whitman (as the *Aurora*), are understood not merely as representatives of political positions but indeed as the animators of the public itself. Whitman's third-person editorial argues that, beyond their effects on curriculum, Hughes's methods of persuasion would change the mechanisms of public participation, disrupting the unity of (perceived) consensus but also introducing the private matters of religion into civic debate. Instead of the rhetorically powerful appeals of Hughes's charismatic personal authority, itself bolstered by his proximity to the pope, Whitman projects public participation motivated by *feeling*. The problem is, Whitman's "we" is actually an "I"—he offers a fiction of consensus that is constantly belied by the very debates the editorial engages.

In his outrage over foreign and religious influences in civic matters, Whitman evokes his hero Thomas Paine. Like Paine, he uses vernacular polemical rhetoric to muster republican fervor among his readers and generate a nationalistic community through the power of his words. This backward glance, so to speak, suggests the revolutionary urgency of the moment: as he urges vigilance against external threats to America's emerging political and cultural identity, Whitman implicitly denies that the work of founding is certain or complete. His efforts to establish a personal authority in shaping the public debates—including determining who may participate in those debates, and how—draw on the newspaper's ability to combine oral and print forms of expression. That is, his confrontational vernacular style claims the charisma of spoken utterance, while the medium of print amplifies and disseminates his utterances.[28] Against the apparently inescapable presence of Hughes and his supporters, Whitman projects an omnipresent editorial self whose authority is bolstered by its access to and control of printed newspaper texts, the very avenue of publicity.

Newspaper editorials were only one arena in which this particular political battle was fought, and Whitman made his arguments in the midst of continuing political wrangling that often spilled over into social demonstrations and even violence. Whitman responded to such events with outrage, seeing them as proof of his arguments against Hughes, and he continued to assert the social and political authority of a public debate mediated not only in print but by particular public individuals. He used his editorial position to arbitrate events that occur in the city's public spaces. For instance, in an editorial of March 17, Whitman claims that a demonstration of support for the Public Schools Society held on the previous day had been disrupted by harassment and violence from pro-Catholic "foreigners": "We saw Irish priests there—sly, false, deceitful villains—looking on and evidently encouraging the gang who created the tumult" (WJ 57). Feeding anti-Irish, anti-Catholic anger, these depictions carry the violence and outrage of the street demonstrations into the newspaper. Provoked readers on the other side of the issue wrote letters in response. On March 18 Whitman published "The Aurora and the School Question":

> A communication was received yesterday at this office, strongly reprehending the course we have taken upon the public school question. The writer says:
> "A personal and political friend of Bishop Hughes, as I am, I cannot but be amazed at the strictures you have given utterances to in relation to that gentleman. Are you not afraid that so abusive, malevolent, and groundless an attack will bring a tempest around your ears that it will be hard to allay?"
> The Aurora, we imagine, among people who know it, needs no certificate of its character for courage. We do *not* fear, either the attacks of those whom,

by exposing their wickedness, we have made enemies of—nor any "tempest" that our conduct may bring down upon our head. We have nerve enough to face the fire of battle, and stand by our colors, and peal out the rallying cry to the last, in support of any cause which we sincerely believe to be holy and patriotic. (WJ 59)

This editorial reveals the complicated claims to authority that compete with one another both within and without the newspaper's pages. Which carries more weight, the first-person claims of Hughes's "political and personal friends" or the editor's observations from the critical distance of his position? By keeping the letter writer anonymous, Whitman neutralizes the letter's claim to personal authority. Instead, the letter is subsumed within his own editorial statement, which characterizes those who disagree with the *Aurora* as its "enemies." Whitman thus uses the epistolary structure of dialogic exchange to rhetorically shut down the dialogue. Whitman justifies the paper's position with patriotic, martial, and religious language that communicates shared values and sets up a dichotomy between insiders and outsiders on the issue. As a result, it echoes and even encourages the violence that is occurring in the streets.

These epistolary exchanges challenge not just Whitman's editorial views but increasingly his authority and judgment in sociopolitical matters. Of course, Whitman the editor did not have to incorporate readers' letters or use epistolary exchange to structure his editorial comments. That he did so suggests his general commitment to dialogue as a means of promoting the didactic work of the newspaper and achieving social and political consensus. Letters from critical readers inevitably put Whitman on the defensive, but they also pressed him to refine and clarify his politics.[29] Again using the device of responding to a reader letter, on March 30 Whitman published "Defending Our Position," an editorial in which he attempts to distance himself temperamentally and philosophically from the nativist element: "We have no antipathy or bigoted ill will to *foreigners*. God forbid!" he states. The editorial claims that "anti-American" forces in the society threaten to undermine the national project of "evolving the Great Problem—the problem of how far Man, the masterpiece of cunningest Omni-conscience, can have his nature perfected by himself, and can be trusted to govern himself" (WJ 85). Such perfection, Whitman argues, will occur when foreign influences are eradicated from the culture and Americans enjoy freedom from external influence. Thus linking values of Jacksonian individualism, small government, and religious faith, Whitman rhetorically elevates his position above crass bigotry, and from these heights of republican idealism he excuses the paper's invective against Hughes: "The farthest stretch of condemnation cannot go too far against any proceedings which put in jeopardy the soundness and purity of the elective franchise" (WJ 86). The personal attack on Hughes acknowledges the potential of a personal public sphere to become antidemocratic. The schools question and Hughes's role in it illustrate the problem at the heart of a personalized public sphere: the potential for a single or singular public figure to wield excessive influence over others.

At the same time, as editor, Whitman attempts to exert a similar persuasive authority over his readers. When, for instance, the state legislature adopted a compromise school bill,[30] Whitman opposed it as a capitulation to pro-Irish interests, and he urged readers to abstain from voting in the upcoming Common Council elections so that neither party should benefit from the compromise (WJ 107). Whitman's suggestion was apparently widely ignored; nevertheless, it is astonishing that Whitman, the eventual bard of democracy, would encourage a politically energized population to withhold its votes as a protest. It demonstrates the intensity of the political moment for Whitman, the ardency and hubris with which he held to his role as editor of a daily newspaper.[31] More to the point, it also demonstrates the multidimensionality of the newspaper public sphere, as Whitman's *Aurora* balances claims for social authority and judgment against the competing authority and judgment of its readers. This editorial shows just how difficult this balance can be, particularly when the editorials include personal attacks on an individual figure: under rhetorical pressure, a personalized public sphere can split apart, and assumptions of a unified public can turn contentious and even violent.[32]

Whitman's two months at the *Aurora* demonstrate, in a particularly accelerated context, the play of competing claims of personal authority that ensues when the public sphere's functioning hinges on the actions and words of strong personalities. But these challenges and exchanges are characteristic of an emerging celebrity culture, in which the significance of a singular public figure is subject to interrogation and negotiation among members of a mass audience. It is possible to see how Whitman might have become invested in celebrity as a model of both artistic success and republican social authority. Drawing massive public attention to singular individuals, celebrity claims market success as a form of authority that parallels if not rivals that of more traditional figures of authority, such as elected officials. P. David Marshall explains that the celebrity's claims to authority are the outcroppings of the public life that emerges from a modern political and economic state: "Our modern focus on the new public realm or even the expanded public realm beyond the confines of the church and somewhat refined by the growth of the state is another feature of seeing new forms of public representations outside of the classic metaphors and symbols of power and influence."[33] Understood in this way, celebrity accompanies a widening public sphere that is also increasingly personalized. In a democratic society such as the United

States, those public representations are not simply alternatives to the authority of the church or elected officials; they are parallel to them, and to some degree they are parodies of them. The allure of this kind of "election" is particularly strong where democratic representation is explicitly associated with character. Considering the efforts of commercial promotion that generate celebrity's mass appeal, David H. Blake claims, "Celebrity, with all its surrounding commotion and hype, was democracy's ironic cousin, a system of value that did not measure virtue or talent as much as an individual's cultural profile."[34] Celebrity might be regarded as democratic because the celebrity is understood to represent ideals and values relevant to the public; it is ironic because the public figure's "election" takes the form of commercial success that in turn feeds popular interest in the celebrity's person rather than his work or ideas. Whereas election reflects a definitive, collective judgment about a public figure's character, celebrity involves an ongoing interpretation of character, a negotiation over the meaning of the celebrity persona that the celebrity figure may participate in but cannot completely control. Controversy over the public figure's meaning and value is therefore inherent to celebrity and a feature that distinguishes it from the near-uniform approbation of fame.[35] In this sense, celebrity reveals election itself to be at best a tentative judgment of character, and its appeal lies in the competing claims to authority among not only the celebrity figure and his audience as a mass, but also among individual members of that mass audience. The ironies of celebrity therefore make any claims to authority that it carries deeply complicated and always contingent, as the personal public sphere of Whitman's *Aurora* demonstrates.

However aggressively Whitman attacked Hughes and pro-Irish political interests, toward his readers he expressed gratitude and humility. But in thanking readers for their continued support of the *Aurora*, Whitman tacitly acknowledges the link between commercial success and individual cultural authority: "The consciousness that several thousand people will look for their Aurora as regularly as for their breakfasts, and that they expect to find in it an intellectual repast—something *piquant*, and something solid, and something sentimental, and something humorous—and all dished up in 'our own peculiar way'—this consciousness, we say, implies no small responsibility upon a man. Yet it is delightful. Heavy as it weighs, we have no indisposition to 'take the responsibility'" (WJ 105). In its evocation of the breakfast scene, Whitman's comment highlights the newspaper's ability to cross thresholds and bring the public world into the private or domestic sphere. Moreover, Whitman's repetitions underscore the notion of consciousness as the point at which public and private intersect—where awareness extends beyond the self and applies perception to the tests of sensibility and judgment—guided by Whitman himself, whose consciousness drives the *Aurora*'s work. Even in his less aggressively political editorial writings, Whitman manages to celebrate himself.

The scene of reading that Whitman offers is important in its effort to incorporate the *Aurora* into experience presumed to be universal. Like the fleeting images of a blacksmith or a president in the catalogues of "Song of Myself," Whitman here particularizes a type of activity and conveys the feeling of the individual in a paradoxically generalized image. In fact, this is a gesture with a history in "Sun-Down Papers," one that Whitman honed in his cultural reporting of the *Aurora* period and after. In his city sketches and cultural pieces, Whitman projects a much more amiable though no less authoritative persona than in his Americanist *Aurora* editorials. At the *Aurora*, Whitman generated his city sketches from the walks he took each workday, while the compositors prepared proofs of his morning's work. He casts himself as a recognizable urban type, the flâneur, whose intellectual detachment from the crowd and singular analytical ability allows him to "read" the crowd as if it were a text.[36] Characteristically, the flâneur is a European figure. Whitman Americanizes the flâneur, however, not only by adapting his behaviors to an American cityscape but more importantly by using the flâneur as a critic of particularly republican tastes.

An early piece from the *Aurora* is practically a template for Whitman's flâneur style. As in the note to the readers, Whitman's flâneur promotes his personal vision as deriving its authority from its comprehensive, universalizing power: "On an afternoon of one of those pleasant days, we sauntered out of the west gate of the Park, feeling in an observative mood, we recollected an old custom of ours, long since disused—we went up the stairs of the American Museum, entered the first room, took a chair, placed it in a roomy niche made by the settling in one of the front windows—and in that chair ensconced we ourself. Out before us was the busiest spectacle this busy city can present. One mighty rush of men, business, carts, carriages, and clang" (WJ 66). That act of settling into the chair echoes the melancholy bachelor of the "Sun-Down Papers," who sits in his "elbow-chair" to reflect on the passage of time. Typically a bachelor, the flâneur manifests not the melancholy of alienation but the bemusement of detachment as he reflects on the scene he has just left. Whitman represents himself here as entirely solitary, "ensconced" in his private niche, but his language challenges his ostensible isolation: the imperious pronoun "we" marks him as at once a self-authorized individual and part of the mass he seems to escape. As in his political editorials, Whitman frequently uses the first-person plural in scenes where it is obviously representing only himself. In this play with the ideas of the individual and the larger social whole, Whitman's editorial "we" is the antecedent to the comprehensive "I" of *Leaves of Grass*.

Remarkably, Whitman rejects the curiosities of Barnum's American Museum, preferring the human curiosities of Broadway at midday to Barnum's exhibits of grotesque or freakish nature. From his vantage point above Broadway, Whitman is able to observe and represent the street as a sweeping panorama of New York social types.[37] Assuming the interpretive authority of the flâneur, he attempts to classify each "specimen" that he encounters, using a diction heavy with racial and gendered distinctions. He comments on the omnibuses and their drivers, "a unique race," as well as the ladies of fashion. Whitman critiques the gentleman of fashion, the dandy whose clothes and attitudes undercut the republican ethos that Whitman prizes in the urban experience and that he associates most strongly with robust masculinity. At first he considers this "Broadway aristocrat" amusing, but "it is no joke, after all. These gentry discover their consummate folly in this sort of aping of the customs of Europe. We have no aristocracy in this country; but these poor, deluded people think that by wrapping themselves in the cloak of the true aristocrat they will be able to pass for genuine. They should remember the ass in the lion's skin" (WJ 67). In singling the individual "aristocrat" out of the crowd of passers-by, Whitman's social vision objectifies the Broadway aristocrat as an outsider who does not share the national identity. The ersatz gentleman is no threat in himself, but as a representative of a class that values European style and attitudes, he threatens the republican values of democracy and individualism. He is neither a man nor a woman; aping European fashion, he is certainly not entirely American. He is, in short, a grotesque social type who transgresses categories of social distinction. In this sense, he is very much like the fraudulent and transgressive displays in the halls of Barnum's museum, except that the "Broadway aristocrat" does not wink at his transgressiveness.

A few years later, writing in the *Brooklyn Daily Eagle*, Whitman notes Barnum's ability to express concisely the difference between the European and American characters. He quotes Barnum on his European travels: "'There, every thing is foreign—kings and *things*—formal, but absolutely *frozen*: here is *life*. Here it is freedom, and here are *men*.' An entire book might be written upon that little speech of Barnum's."[38] The comparison captures Whitman's distaste for fashion as imitative, cold, and lifeless. Whitman's city observations tend to return to these themes of honest self-representation and "natural" social markers in an urban society that is crowded and visually complex, and he consistently associates the natural and genuine with an American egalitarianism. Each description challenges the observer to discern the genuine from the ungenuine: is the fashionable lady a woman or a painted woman? Is the gentleman of fashion elegant or a buffoon? Whitman assumes that the external visual cues of the individual's dress and mien in turn indicate qualities of character—an assumption that emerges as much from the discourses of sentimentality as from phrenology, theater, and the theatrical street culture of parades and public festivals.[39] The connection Whitman invites between individuals' behaviors and nationalistic spectacles suggests the individuals' capacity to express values and ideas from a vantage point outside of the elaborate ideological rituals of nationhood.[40] In observing these anonymous public figures, Whitman separates himself from the crowd he describes, obtaining both visual, panoramic perspective and critical distance.

Having come to observe street scenes as exhibits or forms of theater, it takes little adjustment for the flâneur to perceive scenes of art and amusement as socially expressive. As a critic of New York's social and cultural scene, Whitman resembles fellow journalist and man-about-town Nathaniel Parker Willis.[41] However, Whitman was openly critical of the cultural consumption that Willis and other popular journalists encouraged, and he contrasted mere consumption with a more genuine appreciation—what he might later call "absorption"—of art. His position emerges in his slightly ironic *Aurora* review of Emerson's 1842 lecture on "The Poet":

> The transcendentalist had a very full house on Saturday evening. There were a few beautiful maids—but more ugly women, mostly blue stockings; several interesting young men with Byron collars; lawyers, doctors, and parsons; Grahamites and abolitionists; sage editors, a few of whom were taking notes; and all the other species of literati. Greeley was in extacies whenever any thing particularly good was said, which seemed to be once in about five minutes—he would flounce about like a fish out of water, or like a tickled girl—look round, to see those behind him and at his side; all of which very plainly told to those, both far and near, that he knew a thing or two more about these matters than other men. (WJ 44)[42]

Distancing himself from the "literati," Whitman implicitly identifies with the majority of individuals who possessed the capacity to comprehend Emerson's lecture and its significance, but who were not part of any literary, intellectual, or economic elites. The lecture itself receives scant attention from Whitman: "But it would do the lecturer great injustice to attempt any thing like a sketch of his ideas," he writes. "Suffice it to say, the lecture was one of the richest and most beautiful compositions, both for its matter and style, we have ever heard anywhere, at any time" (WJ 44). Whitman's interpretation shifts the emphasis from Emerson and his lecture to the social drama of the event as a whole, and it registers the tendencies of a personal public sphere to give exaggerated credence to received opinion, represented in a parody of *New-York Tribune* editor and Emerson booster Horace Greeley. Greeley's enthusiasm for Emerson's lectures was evident in the *Tribune*, where he published substantial summaries of all six lecures in Emerson's series "The Times." Reflecting on the entire course of lectures, the *Tribune* commented, "As far-seeing and profound commentaries upon passing events giving to every thoughtful mind high and rare instruction and a new, living reality to what before seemed dead, they will be prized by all reflecting minds; while the strength and purity of the language, the harmony and beauty of the style and the eloquent sentiment mingled with the most genial humor by which they were uniformly marked will commend them to the approval of every man of cultivated and scholarlike taste."[43] Certainly these comments reflect journalism's didactic tendencies. By contrast, Whitman's review of "The Poet" is rather tepid, especially considering Whitman's later claim that "Emerson brought me to a boil." But as a specimen of Greeley's preference for "cultivated and scholarlike" company, this puff puts Whitman's parody of Greeley into perspective. Whitman's review of "The Poet" reflects a distrust of received opinion based on social designations and a preference, instead, for individual sensibilities.

In both the Broadway scene and the Emerson review, Whitman offers descriptions that cohere in their movement from crowd to individual and back again. The "Broadway aristocrat" emerges from the crowd as if by a subtle shift of focus, and Greeley's "extacies" push him into the foreground of an extemely crowded frame. "Out of many, one"—but Whitman senses that the process can be just as easily reversed, as one nation or community is broken down into individuals of distinct backgrounds and characters, or else reassembled into a unified vision of one mass of people. Betsy Erkkila articulates the problem of pluralism as fundamental to Whitman's poetic art: "Whitman attempted to seal the Union imaginatively by placing the paradox of the many and the one at the thematic and structural center of *Leaves of Grass*," she explains. "The problem of reconciling private or factional interests within the single identity of the Union was at the root of the political crisis of the 1850s as it was at the foundation of the American republic."[44] Her comments are equally relevant to his journalism as to his poetry, although in the 1840s, as we have seen, the Union was threatened more by immigration and the related nativist controversies than by the sectionalist disputes incited by the Compromise of 1850. These issues share a concern with union but more specifically with the authority to determine who would be a part of the Union. To a large degree, that authority rested on matters of interpretation— not only of the goals and values of the founders, but also of the meaning of those members of the social body whose presence seemed to challenge or threaten larger philosophical values. In the *Aurora*, Whitman's flâneur promotes republican values of natural and genuine character and at the same time provides a critical model for making such interpretive judgments.

MANY OF THE FEATURES THAT CHARACTERIZE WHITMAN'S POETRY are present in his 1840s editorial writing. In particular, the editorials aggressively promote Americanist political and cultural values and highlight the relevance of everyday life to shared experience and collective identity. Although his former employers claimed he was lazy, as an editor Whitman conducted himself professionally. In keeping with the conventions of his profession, he adopted the first-person, vernacular style that dominated the contemporary press, he developed an outsized editorial persona, and he embraced the bare-knuckles strategies of an intensely personal public sphere. But his affinities with his profession were more than posturing: stylistically evoking the polemical writings of the revolutionary era, Whitman signaled his commitment to the ongoing work of social renovation and nation making; he likewise embraced the artisan-republican ideology that the penny press as a whole tended to promote as it widened newspapers' audience and scope. In his two journalistic modes, as an editor and a flâneur, he is both a participant in and observer of the life of his community and nation, and that double status gives him a valuable critical vantage point and interpretive power. Moreover, he communicates the idea that newspaper readers occupy a similar status—they also participate in the life of their communities, and they observe that life through the newspaper itself. Adhering to the conventions of a personalized newspaper public sphere and extending that personalization of public figures (such as newspaper editors) to strangers in the streets, Whitman extends the features of celebrity culture to the public at large. But Whitman's editorial experience also suggested the fragility of the sympathetic community formed by these means. In the personal public sphere, the critical vantage points multiply with circulation numbers, and as readers took up the newspaper's invitation to comment on public events, Whitman sometimes struggled to find a viable model of social authority.

In his poetry Whitman projects public relationships, such as those between the poet and his readers, as intensely intimate. This version of public relationships among strangers extends and aestheticizes the public sphere that Whitman experiences in his journalism career. As the self-proclaimed bard of democracy, the figure who gives voice to the voiceless, the poet Whitman attempts to use the mechanisms of celebrity in a very specific way: putting the accent on celebrity's representative status, he establishes a poetic persona that ironically parallels the politics of representative democracy by calling attention to those on the social and political margins. But Whitman's project is complicated by the competing claims of authority that emerge in readers' interpretations of his public and poetic efforts. As Kerry C. Larson has argued, Whitman wrestled with these issues of authorial and interpretive authority in his poetry.[45] The paradox of individualism and authority that runs throughout Whitman's poetry is evident also in his journalism, where readers in a personal public sphere are explicitly encouraged to develop their critical skills so long as they share the author's critical values.

The competing claims to interpretive authority challenge social and political unity. In some cases, such as New York's 1842 nativist controversy over school funding, competing interpretations of public individuals can lead to dissent and even violence. As one *Aurora* reader puts it, Whitman maintains a disposition to "ultraism" even as he participates in a newspaper life that in its form and conventions encourages just such personal responses from his readers. The "newspaper revolution" that created mass culture and celebrity is also blamed for the demise of the rational public sphere. Whitman's work in the *Aurora* demonstrates how these phenomena—mass culture, celebrity, and critical discourse—can in fact coexist. But it also highlights the complexities of their coexistence, the ways in which mass culture multiplies the vantage points for criticism and extends interpretive authority among an increasingly diverse public.

THE TASK OF MAKING JUDGMENTS SEEMS LESS PRESSING TO WHITMAN the poet than to Whitman the journalist. In the preface to the 1855 *Leaves of Grass*, he claims that the poet "is judgment. He judges not as the judge judges but as the sun falling around a helpless thing. He sees the farthest and has the most faith."[46] Such judgment is enlightening, magnanimous, even prophetic in its ability to illuminate a path forward. In the poetry, this form of judgment comes through as a self-conscious effort to represent both the beauty and corruption of human experience without flinching or accusing:

> The little one sleeps in its cradle,
> I lift the gauze and look a long time, and silently brush away flies with my hand.
>
> The youngster and the redfaced girl turn aside up the bushy hill.
> I peeringly view them from the top.
>
> The suicide sprawls on the bloody floor of the bedroom,
> It is so . . . . I witnessed the corpse . . . . there the pistol had fallen.
>
> (1855 *LG* 31, ellipses in original)

The suicide's despair is rendered vivid in its juxtaposition with the promise of the innocent baby and the urgency of the young couple's hilltop tryst. Any suggestion of meaning seems to arise from the details of the images. Even as the speaker claims a wide-ranging vision, he is no flâneur; for one thing, he is not limited to public scenes, and, for another, he seems to hold in check the kind of judgmental claims that characterize both the flâneur and Whitman's editorial persona as a whole.

The poetry carries that struggle into new arenas. Whitman persists in challenging cultural and institutional figures of authority with his capacious, all-encompassing self. The poet's apparently infinite capacity to receive all he sees makes the flâneur's judgment seem petty, even bigoted: unlike the journalist who attacked Bishop Hughes, the poet Whitman asserts, "I do not despise you priests; / My faith is the greatest of faiths and the least of faiths, / Enclosing all worship ancient and modern, and all between ancient or modern" (1855 *LG* 75). His is a faith in the act or process of recognizing and absorbing variety, and in feeling the power of greatest and least both individually and in composite. The "I" that sees this—that all faiths, even those yet untried, "cannot fail" (1855 *LG* 76)—assumes an authority in its ability to comprehend all. Thus showing "folks" "the path between reality and their souls" (1855 *LG* 10), the poet helps establish the conditions of a new world in which Hughes and his ilk are obsolete: "There will soon be no more priests," he prophesies in the 1855 preface. "Their work is done. . . . A superior breed shall take their place . . . the gangs of kosmos and prophets en masse shall take their place. A new order shall arise and they shall be the priests of man, and every man shall be his own priest" (1855 *LG* 22). Whitman revises the skepticism of his hero Tom Paine ("my own mind is my own church"), shedding Paine's bellicose criticisms of theology and revelation. Indeed, in his prophetic mode, Whitman claims the authority of revelatory vision, and he maintains that the poet's role is the apocryphal unveiling of realities, including "the exquisite beauty and reality of the soul" (1855 *LG* 22), which are fundamental to the social and political union he seeks.

The priests that pass out of use include the poets themselves. In his closing to the 1855 preface, Whitman posits a scenario where the poet is invisible: "The proof of a poet is that his country absorbs him as affectionately as he has absorbed it" (1855 *LG* 24). Paradoxically, the poet's invisibility—his complete incorporation into the country—marks his presence: his absorption is "proof" or evidence of his effectiveness. Moreover, the sentence insists that this absorption occurs with, perhaps through, affection. Whitman mandates an affective response to the poet that reciprocates his embrace of his country. What all this amounts to is that Whitman promotes an ideal form of reading in which author and reader, text and its comprehension, are completely, seamlessly integrated. It is a reading without types or texts, exchange without presence, unmediated revelation and reception.

To say Whitman cherishes an affectionate response from his country is to say he seeks popular acclaim. At least popularity, or celebrity, is the nearest practical exhibition of the metaphysical condition he envisions. But, as we will see, the "absorption" that comes with celebrity does not eliminate but in fact enunciates the problems of mediation that Whitman seeks to avoid. As David H. Blake has shown, Whitman avidly participated in the celebrity culture of his day, because he understood that the popular poet was one who "could truly be said to represent [the people] in a democratic society." Celebrity would therefore fulfill Whitman's desire for attaining cultural authority, as it would acknowledge his role as representative of all America, giver of "the sign of democracy" (1855 *LG* 48). Blake's important study of Whitman's engagement with celebrity culture builds on the poet's own claim that the poetry and the poet are one. The mass readership that would affectionately "absorb" him would do so through his poetry, the verbal expression of a personality created by and for public performance. Tracing the complexities of Whitman's responses to celebrity culture, Blake argues that Whitman generates "a poetics of hype, a poetry that consistently sells its value to a public it already claims to represent."[47] This poetics, Blake notes, is heavily influenced by advertising, a rhetorical form innovated by P. T. Barnum and disseminated through the newspapers. In these career-long "campaigns," Whitman sold not only poetry but also himself.

What exactly is the distinction between Whitman's personality and his self? The answer may be found in the "Calamus" poems that Whitman added in the 1860 edition of *Leaves of Grass*, a sequence frequently regarded as Whitman's most personal poetry. The poems assume a confessional mode—"No longer abashed," the speaker of the opening poem promises "To tell the secret of my nights and days, / To celebrate the need of comrades" (1860 *LG* 341, 342). The "Calamus" sequence holds a privileged place in the Whitman canon, to "celebrate the need of comrades"—a need the "Calamus" speaker claims as his own. On publication, the "Calamus" sequence was deemed unremarkable, at least in comparison with the "Children of Adam" sequence that accompanied it. For their frank depictions of heterosexuality, "Children of Adam" earned the 1860 *Leaves* the sobriquets "Whitman's Dirty Book" and "smut."[48] Unlike the contemporary reviews, modern criticism has turned to "Calamus" with interest. Encouraged by the poems' confessional style, biographers approach the sequence as a record of Whitman's internal experience; others regard his depictions of "manly attachment" as integral to a radical, even utopian vision of a queer public sphere.[49] For Blake, the "Calamus" poems are intentionally misleading: Whitman is "coy," working in the confessional mode without really disclosing anything of significance about himself. These efforts support his quest for a celebrity that thrives on self-exposure. Whitman "invokes the artifice of privacy to counter the artifice of publicity, but both, in effect, are inverse expressions of the same promotional energy," Blake writes.[50] Always, the kelson of creation is hype.

Blake's portrait of Whitman as the Barnum of poetry does not acknowledge the subtlety of Whitman's critical response to the culture of celebrity, which comes through so strongly in the "Calamus" cluster. These poems are indeed remarkable in their apparently personal content, but to me, they are even more remarkable for representing scenes of desire and intimacy in public settings. As Helen Vendler notes, lyric poetry such as Whitman's generates intimacy between the speaker and unseen listeners through modulations of tone; in turn, such intimacy articulates "a more admirable ethics of relation, one more desirable than can be found at present on the earth." In Whitman's case, this "utopian" project would generate more tolerant, sympathetic relations.[51] Acknowledging the radical possibilities of Whitman's vision of a public sphere where men may express their desires for one another freely, I note that Whitman does not challenge the masculine character of the public sphere. But the intimacy he represents makes a strong contrast with the vitriolic and aggressive discourse that characterize Whitman's early journalism. Whitman proposes an alternative to the hypercompetitive, agonistic relations between men in the public sphere. The public sphere he imagines in these poems favors acceptance, intimacy, and satisfied desire among men even as it questions the reliability of such claims of knowing others in a highly mediated mass culture.

Whitman's poetics of intimacy may reflect his own erotic and emotional struggles in a society that does not accept same-sex love. Vendler claims that "the creation of this sort of [lyric] intimacy springs from a fundamental loneliness," and biographical critics emphasize the personal origins of Whitman's poetry of homoerotic longing.[52] The ideal for public life that follows from this intimate vision is indeed utopic: Whitman's "homosexual utopia," as Tom Yingling calls it, is one in which "male bonding . . . is not based on a displacement of desire but on its enactment freely and openly between two men whose sexuality requires no mediating other." Yingling references the notion that desire itself is always mediated—"neither internally nor externally is the object of desire pure or purely itself"—and sees Whitman's "Calamus" poetry as articulating an alternative to or route around the mediating forces that regulate desire.[53] In contrast with Yingling's claims, Larson argues that the "Calamus" poems dramatize Whitman's struggle with "a mounting despair over the efficacy of written documents, poetry foremost among them, to bind, mediate, or reconcile."[54] Does the visionary poet project a utopia of unmediated social relations, or does he see poetry serving a mediating function to generate social union? This question cannot be answered without attending to the dynamics of the celebrity culture in which Whitman positioned himself, in which he sought both personal and professional satisfaction—and in which mediation is an inherent, unavoidable force.

The "Calamus" poems represent the speaker turning away from the very field of publicity in which Whitman himself worked as a journalist and critic and into which he consistently inserts himself as an author seeking public acceptance. He rejects and, in some cases, attempts to correct the public version of himself as "one who would destroy institutions," and he instructs his readers and would-be lovers—"élèves," he calls them elsewhere—in the best methods of responding to him: kisses, touches, embraces. Considering that these physical responses to the public person are not possible for the vast majority of Whitman's readers, it is fair to say that Whitman imagines a response to the public person that is far different from the illusion of intimacy and judgmental authority available to most observers in the public sphere. In other words—and to take this back to Blake's claims about Whitman's own desire for celebrity—I see the "Calamus" poems as addressing and representing desire as it motivates relations among men, mostly strangers, in celebrity culture. The "Calamus" speaker is both desiring of others and the object of others' desires. The speaker desires to be seen for who he really is, or who he thinks he is, to have that self acknowledged and affirmed through intimate gestures such as touches, kisses, and reciprocated glances. At the same time, the speaker's discontent with his public reception and his fear of unrequited desire indicate the inevitable misrecognition that occurs in celebrity culture, where selves never encounter one another directly but are mediated through images.

If nothing else, "Calamus" reminds us that intimacy and privacy are not synonymous, and that they are not necessarily even related. The intimate exchanges in these poems frequently occur in public spaces, though they may go unseen or unrecognized by others. The speaker portrays such scenes as if he observes them, and his own role in them, from the outside, as in the poem Whitman later titled "A Glimpse":

> One flitting glimpse, caught through an interstice,
> Of a crowd of workmen and drivers in a bar-room, around the stove,
>   late of a winter night—And I unremarked, seated in a corner;
> Of a youth who loves me, and whom I love, silently approaching, and
>   seating himself near, that he may hold me by the hand;
> A long while, amid the noises of coming and going—of drinking and
>   oath and smutty jest,
> There we two, content, happy in being together, speaking little,
>   perhaps not a word.
>
> (1860 *LG* 371)

The tableau of hand-holding lovers is itself an interstice of quiet intimacy amid the noisy sociability of the barroom. This public setting acts as a metonym for the public sphere in general, which is characterized by voluble, often combative speech. Whitman's "Glimpse" focuses, however fleetingly, on the intimacy that occurs in a public sphere that cannot recognize it, distracted as it is by its own boisterous exchanges of "oath and smutty jest." In contrast with that profane imitation of pleasure, the lovers here experience the real pleasures of physical and affective companionship. Their intimacy is world-making, in that "it creates spaces and usurps places meant for other kinds of relation."[55] Throughout "Calamus," such loving exchanges are understated to the point of invisibility to most observers, who are unable to recognize the "secret and divine signs" with which lovers "discover" one another (1860 *LG* 376).

In keeping with Yingling's observations of intimacy between men in Whitman's poetry, the intimacy in "A Glimpse" appears to be unmediated: the lovers have no need for speech or other means of recognizing one another, and Whitman figures the immediacy of their reciprocal affection in the physical contact of clasped hands. Locating a moment of intimate pleasure in the crowded bar, Whitman speaks to the mass culture that attempts to mediate individual affect. The affective dimension of the personal public sphere is a characteristic of mass culture generally, including celebrity. As Jonathan Elmer puts it, "mass culture founds itself on the terrain of pleasure—or more broadly, an affect—that it simultaneously provokes and regulates."[56] In Elmer's rendering of mass culture, pleasure must be mediated to control for or shunt away excess affect; the regulation or limiting of affect is the means by which a personal response to the cultural object transforms into or joins with a collective response. Regulation therefore mediates social relationships so that the individual and the collective come to identify with one another. In the case of celebrity culture, a subset of mass culture, the affect in question is not pleasure but desire. Celebrity mobilizes "abstract desire" among audiences, that is, a desire "not confined to the technical accomplishments or aesthetic public face of the celebrity, but [that] extends to emotional, sexual, spiritual, and existential identification with the celebrity."[57] In other words, celebrity culture fuels and is fueled by desire not for what the celebrity figure does but who the celebrity is, or seems to be. Such desire is satisfied, at least momentarily, by consumption of the celebrity image, which is a complex array of signifiers at large in the culture, including texts the celebrity figure produces, reviews or descriptions of those texts, and renderings of the person of the celebrity figure in photographs, drawings, or written descriptions that circulate through popular media. The desire at the heart of celebrity culture is therefore always mediated, as spectators lack direct access to the celebrity object of their desire.[58]

The notion that the celebrity image reflects observers' desires clearly parallels the Lacanian theory of desire. For Lacan, the object *a* is itself meaningless—contentless—but gains significance in relation to the subject, whose lack or desire it appears to fulfill. In this way, the object *a* mediates the subject's own identity. The power of the gaze to construct both desire and the subject means that the subject can know himself only by representation: as Lacan puts it, "*I see myself seeing myself.*"[59] This is the glimpse through the interstice, the image of the self not as subject but as object. Thus in contrast with Yingling's claim that Whitman represents same-sex intimacy as unmediated and therefore utopic, I would argue that in fact Whitman creates a poem in which the apparently unmediated intimacy in turn represents or mediates the speaker's desire for intimacy itself. As in others of Whitman's "Calamus" poems, this "glimpse" is in actuality a vision, a dream, or a fantasy. Interpreting Lacan, Slavoj Žižek writes, "It is precisely the role of fantasy to give the coordinates of the subject's desire, to specify its object, to locate the position the subject assumes in it."[60] As Whitman represents intimacy that occurs in a crowded public space, he fantasizes a public sphere in which such intimacy can go forward.

The desire constructed by Whitman's gaze is, then, intimacy unencumbered by the gazes of others in the public sphere—intimacy unaffected by the collective gaze. That this fantasy responds directly to the mediating power of the mass public gaze is evident in other "Calamus" poems, where the poet-speaker dissents from his popular reception. "When I heard at the close of day how my name had been received with plaudits in the capitol, still it was not a happy night for me that followed," he confesses (1860 *LG* 357). Instead, the speaker finds happiness in the knowledge that "my dear friend, my lover, was on his way coming" and in the experience of sleeping with him "under the same cover in the cool night" (1860 *LG* 357, 358). Whitman substitutes the highest cultural approbation with the reciprocated intimacy of lovers. Yet despite Vendler's claim that "Calamus" privileges the physical intimacy of lovers in the present tense, he does extend his vision to include "readers-in-futurity" as well as he attempts to secure his legacy:

> You bards ages hence! when you refer to me, mind not so much my poems,
> Nor speak of me that I prophesied of The States, and led them the way of their glories;
> But come, I will take you down underneath this impassive exterior—
>   I will tell you what to say of me:
> Publish my name and hang up my picture as that of the tenderest lover,
> The friend, the lover's portrait, of whom his friend, his lover was fondest,
> . . .
> Who oft as he sauntered the streets, curved with his arm the shoulder of his friend—while the arm of his friend rested upon him also.
>
> (1860 *LG* 356–57)

Whitman's skepticism of critical readings reaches back to the 1855 edition, where he teases readers who "felt so proud to get at the meaning of poems" (1855 *LG* 26), and even to his 1842 review of Emerson's lecture, where he makes light of Greeley and the rest of the New York "literati." Here, he extends that skepticism to include a critical legacy for the poetry's political aims. Among Whitman's poetry, this is perhaps the clearest statement of a legacy that he leaves, and as such it glosses his statement in the 1855 preface that the success of a poet can be measured by the degree to which he has been "absorbed" by his country. Seen in the light of this poem, that "absorption" is a figure for an affective exchange, an intimate embrace.

Throughout "Calamus," Whitman struggles to control the terms on which he is seen by others, and in the process he unveils his vision for how he would like to be seen. "Calamus" is about Whitman's desire to be desired, and not merely as an image but as a self. He tries again and again to sweep aside the various barriers to an immediate engagement with the multitude of strangers who regard him and whom he regards. For instance, "Calamus" 19, the poem eventually titled "Behold This Swarthy Face," includes a poetic self-portrait that echoes the frontispiece engraving of Whitman in the 1860 *Leaves of Grass*, as well as the image of the poet published in the 1855 edition. As Ed Folsom details, these representations were central to Whitman's public identity, created and deployed in a self-conscious effort to shape a public image. As the images reinforced Whitman's equivalence of the book and its author, they fostered the reciprocal exchange of glances that promote intimacy: "he wants the reader, via the poem and portrait, to look deeply into his face . . . and he in turn looks deeply into all faces, including his own."[61] "Behold This Swarthy Face" attempts just such an exchange of glances, even as it shows readers how to understand what they see:

> Behold this swarthy and unrefined face—these gray eyes,
> This beard—the white wool, unclipt upon my neck,
> My brown hands, and the silent manner of me, with-out charm;
> Yet comes one, a Manhattanese, and ever at parting, kisses me lightly
>   on the lips with robust love,
> And I, in the public room, or on the crossing of the street, or on the
>   ship's deck, kiss him in return;
> We observe that salute of American comrades, land and sea,
> We are those two natural and nonchalant persons.
>
> (1860 *LG* 364)

Like the barroom of "A Glimpse," the pun on "public rooms"—literally pubs or taverns—brings the poem and the "Calamus" project in general into the center of male social life, in rooms that are public insofar as they are open to anyone and intimate in the type of relations they facilitate. In both the pictures and the poetic description, Whitman offers his image as a visual object for the reader to engage. In this respect, he reverses the dynamic of the writer's relationship with his audience. The audience observes him, just as he—writer, social critic, flâneur—observes them. Whitman thereby brings to the poetry the reciprocity that is a central element of the personal public sphere; he acknowledges and builds into his art the idea of a public sphere in which everyone is seen, everyone is an observer. But Whitman is not content to allow readers to engage with his image however they choose. As he describes the "Manhattanese" who "kisses me lightly on the lips with robust love," Whitman idealizes his preferred response to his image. Whitman's directive, "Behold this swarthy and unrefined face," like the frontispiece itself, demands to be seen. Whitman recognizes his public status as an image, and, in the Lacanian sense, he attempts to "trap" his reader's gaze. Lacan's gaze theory makes clear that by capturing the gaze, the image registers as the object of the subject's desire. Whitman self-consciously positions his own image in the line of his reader's gaze, making himself the object *a*.

"Calamus" rejects poetry as the gauge of the poet's reception and instead instructs readers in how to respond to the poet himself. That shift of emphasis is not an ironic commentary on the failure of criticism so much as it is an embrace of a personal public sphere that equates the public person with his work. Whitman frequently associates his poetry with his person, as when he addresses the reader "holding me now in hand"—the personal pronoun elides the poet and his book—or, more intimately, when he urges

> Or, if you will, thrusting me beneath your clothing,
> Where I may feel the throbs of your heart, or rest upon your hip,
> Carry me when you go forth over land or sea;
> For thus, merely touching you, is enough—is best,
> And thus, touching you, would I silently sleep and be carried eternally.
>
> (1860 *LG* 346)

Whitman imagines a kind of physical reciprocity as the poet feels the throbbing heart as if through the book's pages. The reader carrying the book so close to his body, like the lover sharing the bedclothes, is a figure for the loving intimacy unmediated by institutional or culturally sanctioned reception. But, again, the intimacy here is a fantasy in which the poet imagines or even scripts a loving, intimate response from an ideal reader. He recognizes the fragility of the exchange he posits here, as in the very next lines he foils the reader's assurance:

> But these leaves conning, you con at peril,
> For these leaves, and me, you will not understand,

> They will elude you at first, and still more afterward—I will certainly
> elude you,
> Even while you should think you had unquestionably caught me,
> behold!
> Already you see I have escaped from you.
>
> (1860 *LG* 346)

Whitman's evasiveness supports Blake's reading of "Calamus" as an exercise in hype. Whitman opens the sequence with a promise of self-revelation and intimacy that he never intends to fulfill; he teases readers attuned to a celebrity culture that publicizes the innermost self. But in doing so, he draws attention to the inevitable failures and false promises of celebrity culture. Intimacy fails because the exchange is inevitably mediated: in the end, you're embracing a book, not the body of your lover. Whitman's apparent elusiveness in fact indicts the personal public sphere for its own failure to fulfill its promise of intimacy—a promise that attracts the poet as well—because in the public sphere, everyone is an image and therefore elusive. In an updated version of his flâneur persona, for instance, Whitman conjectures about a "passing stranger": "You give me the pleasure of your eyes, face, flesh as we pass—you take of my beard, breast, hands in return" (1860 *LG* 366). The glance between strangers in the street unfolds a past and future of intimate pleasure; Whitman collapses the scope of human relationships into a fleeting instant—but it is indeed fleeting, a moment that exists only to be remembered: "All is recalled as we flit by each other, fluid, affectionate, chaste, matured," he writes, and concludes by reminding himself to keep the image of the intimate stranger ever present in memory:

> I am not to speak to you—I am to think of you when I sit alone, or
> wake at night alone,
> I am to wait—I do not doubt I am to meet you again,
> I am to see to it that I do not lose you.
>
> (1860 *LG* 366–67)

Such reciprocity as the speaker enjoys with the passing stranger occurs only in the initial encounter; after that, all the effort to maintain this imagined intimacy comes from the spectator alone. I cannot imagine a clearer portrayal of the audience's response to the celebrity figure than this: the spectator keeps the image of the celebrity ever present in memory or imagination, nurturing it like faith.

WHITMAN'S "CALAMUS" POETRY RESPONDS IN PART TO THE IDEA that celebrity culture encourages individuals to develop personal and intimate relationships with people they know only as images and with whom they have little or no actual physical contact. This model of sociability fits well with Whitman's ideal of democratic union, in which desire and intimacy counteract social differences and even hatred. Putting the body in the center of his poetic and social vision, Whitman takes on the "task," Martha Nussbaum argues, "of getting [his audience] to accept longing," as distinguished from "a cleaned up and superficial sex," as a fundamental, shared human experience.[62] To a certain extent, this is the task of celebrity culture as well, which seems to focus on the superficial even as it claims to look through it to the self that lies within. But, as the "Calamus" poems also demonstrate, the affective ties in Whitman's imagined democratic community wrap around an inevitably absent object: the desired person is an image, an absence, a void in which the subject projects himself and his own lack. This is the problem of celebrity culture as well. The "Calamus" sequence never resolves this problem, but it illustrates how the poet, like everyone else, simply lives with it and in it, sometimes accepting the image as object, other times drawing attention to desire as constitutive of the subject, elsewhere railing against the foolishness of spectators who fail to recognize their own complicity in this illusion of intimacy among strangers. Nonetheless, these intimacies are imperative to the Union Whitman prophesies: "I believe the main purport of These States is to found a superb friendship, exalté, previously unknown, / Because I perceive it waits, and has been always waiting, latent in all men" (1860 LG 374). Whitman's "friendship" is an elastic term incorporating intimacy that may be erotic, fraternal, or sympathetic.

Of course, the quality of the nation's sympathy was sorely tested by the Civil War. In his writings on his time as a nurse to the wounded, however, Whitman testifies to the power of the kind of fleeting, intense intimacies he depicts in "Calamus." In addition, his writings on Lincoln reveal his own tendency to personalize public figures. In Lincoln, Whitman finds the ideal American and object of his desire: his Lincoln mirrors Whitman's own values for unaffected manners, good sense, humor, and vernacular style. That "the only truly individual object of love in Whitman's poetry" is a public figure whom Whitman never met personally is striking.[63] Whitman writes of Lincoln with the conviction of personal insight. Lincoln is the "passing stranger" identified, that person with whom the poet would seem to have shared his youth, a companion he must never lose and who returns to him with every returning spring. Ironically, the relationship's endurance owes to its illusory nature: like most Americans, Whitman never knows Lincoln except as an image, and as an image, Lincoln becomes omnipresent in the individual and popular imagination.

As an image, Lincoln contains multitudes. Gary L. Bunker points out that the Lincoln image was created by "media smithies"—illustrators, cartoonists, engravers, and lithographers—who "wrought not just one but many versions of Lincoln" depending on their political leanings.⁶⁴ Starting with the Republican National Convention in 1860, printmakers produced Lincoln imagery in many media, including sheet-music covers, "separate-sheet portraits for home display, illustrated broadsides for posting on fences, walls, and tree trunks, and engraved and lithographed cartoons" for inclusion in the partisan newspapers.⁶⁵ Such illustrations competed with photographic *cartes de visite* of Lincoln, which individuals purchased for their personal scrapbooks. Tracing the rise of Lincoln imagery to his presidential nomination in 1860, Harold Holzer, Gabor S. Boritt, and Mark E. Neely Jr. note that "In Lincoln, [printmakers] were given artistically and commercially stimulating raw material: an all-but-unknown face, which the nation would soon be clamoring to see. The opportunities for complementing such presentations with allegorical and biographical accompaniment would arise as well."⁶⁶ In other words, popular artists worked to create not just a likeness of Lincoln but an image of him. The flood of imagery made Lincoln, in Bunker's words, "the most visually conspicuous political figure in the history of the republic [to that point]. With an unprecedented surge of synergy, popular art commenced to create and recreate Lincoln's public persona."⁶⁷

The prominence of Lincoln imagery, Bunker claims, owes as much to the radical transformation of the print industry as to Lincoln's own appeal as a visual subject. Similarly, Holzer emphasizes the commercial dimension of Lincoln imagery in a mass market for printed images: printmakers' "goal was to find timely, potentially appealing subjects whose illustration would sell widely and enduringly." As a result, he claims, prints and other images created for the mass market "truly reflected public sentiment about Abraham Lincoln"—sentiment that took many forms over the course of his presidency.⁶⁸ In contrast with the public appetite for Lincoln imagery, Lincoln himself appeared indifferent to his visual representations. He was a difficult subject for portrait painters, rarely sitting still for them, and he consistently played down his own ability to judge the portraits of himself.⁶⁹ Nonetheless, his readiness to allow portrait painters access to himself suggests his awareness of the political expediency of such personal imagery in the public sphere.

Whitman's prose writings on Lincoln reflect the influence of the many visual representations of the president in the popular press and participate in the process of interpreting and constructing Lincoln imagery. In sketches published first in the *New York Times* and later collected in *Specimen Days*, Whitman recalls the occasions on which he observed Lincoln in Washington, D.C.: "I see the president almost every day, as I happen to live where he passes to or from his lodgings out of town" (*PW* 59). Proximity and familiarity give Whitman the claims of authority and insight despite his lack of access: "I see very plainly ABRAHAM LINCOLN's dark brown face, with the deep-cut lines, the eyes, always to me with a deep latent sadness in the expression," he writes (*PW* 60). Whitman turns the public setting and his role as spectator to his advantage here, drawing on the observational techniques and interpretive authority of the flâneur that he learned as a young journalist. Developing his reading of Lincoln's melancholy, Whitman relates an occasion when the president acknowledged him personally: "He bow'd and smiled, but far beneath his smile I noticed well the expression I have alluded to. None of the artists or pictures has caught the deep, though subtle and indirect expression of this man's face. There is something else there. One of the great portrait painters of two or three centuries ago is needed" (*PW* 61). Popular images make Lincoln's visage recognizable, but Whitman questions whether those images reveal Lincoln's inner self. He seeks an imagery that more fully participates in and supports the affective union he seeks. Since Whitman was hardly an art critic, his callout to "the great portrait painters" of another age rings empty; he is less interested in portraiture than interpretation, and that work, he indicates, is best done by artists such as himself. Expressing his disappointment with contemporary portraits of the president, Whitman obliquely criticizes the politically partisan culture of image making, which disregards the inner character or self of the political subject.

This is not to say that Whitman's portrait of Lincoln is politically neutral. Emphasizing Lincoln's plainness, Whitman adds to the mythology of Lincoln as a self-made man of the people: Lincoln's plain appearance and unpretentious guard suggest his strength; a true man of the people, Lincoln "looks about as ordinary in attire, &c., as the commonest man" (*PW* 60). Never overtly conjuring the image of Lincoln splitting rails, Whitman nonetheless emphasizes his appeal as the plainspoken, self-taught westerner: "Lincoln, underneath his practicality, was far less European, was quite thoroughly Western, original, essentially non-conventional, and had a certain sort of outdoor prairie stamp," Whitman recalled years later (*PW* 603). For Whitman, Lincoln embodies the republican masculinity he celebrates in his poetry. As David Reynolds puts it, Lincoln was for Whitman "virtually the living embodiment of the 'I' of *Leaves of Grass*. He was 'one of the roughs' but also, for Whitman, 'a kosmos,' with the whole range of qualities that term implied"[70]—such as the ability to embody the Union in all its contradictions and conflicts as well as the immense sympathy that Whitman's ideal of affective political union requires. Whitman's Lincoln reveals not just the roughness of the outdoorsman or the heavy responsibilities of the president; he is the carrier of and conduit for all the pain of the war and the struggle of national reconciliation.

Whitman claims the president "bow'd and smiled," returning his gaze. We cannot know if this passing glance occurred as Whitman represents it or, indeed, how familiar Whitman was to Lincoln. According to Jerome Loving, it is possible Lincoln recognized the poet, who passed the White House daily, but the story that Lincoln said of Whitman, "Well *he* looks like a *man*," is "possibly apocryphal." Nevertheless, Lincoln "undoubtedly read" Whitman's sketches of him in the *New York Times*.[71] This tantalizing historical detail puts Lincoln in the position of Whitman's reader—of the rest of us—and upholds the poet's self-appointed public function as the agent of democratic union. At the same time, it evokes the hall of mirrors in which the celebrity lives: reading Whitman's *Times* sketches, Lincoln encounters not himself but Whitman, as refracted through Lincoln's own image.

In Whitman's prose representations of Lincoln, the personal affinity Whitman came to feel for Lincoln may have verged on the erotic. Loving connects Whitman's prose descriptions of Lincoln to the "Calamus" poems. "I love the President personally," Whitman wrote in an 1863 notebook.[72] In light of such comments, Vivian Pollak builds a case for Whitman as "a Lincoln lover . . . [who] admits no erotic rivals. Living beyond time, under no temporal circumstances can he be displaced by his beloved's beloved."[73] Lincoln appeals to Whitman as a lover-in-perpetuity, to paraphrase Vendler. Setting aside the psycho-erotic dimensions of Whitman's life and poetry, I would like to point out that this arrangement is made possible by celebrity culture. As it mediates the subject through complex verbal and visual images, celebrity culture lifts the public figure out of his immediate, material contexts—out of his own lived experience. Objectified as an image, the public figure lives as he circulates discursively, sustained by the attention of an audience of spectators. As Barthes notes, the process of objectification is "a micro-version of death."[74] Folsom claims that "Whitman was well aware of the death-objectification built into any act of representation," and he points to the poet's self-representations in *Leaves of Grass* as part of his effort "to keep alive and make perpetually elastic that transitional moment of subject becoming object."[75] In "When Lilacs Last in the Dooryard Bloom'd," he does the same for Lincoln. The poem shows how the affective relationship—the romance—between a spectator and a public figure may proceed even in the public figure's death. Typically, celebrity is distinguished from fame by its temporality: celebrity is a perishable state of public existence that reflects shifting values and interests of a diverse, fluctuating marketplace for personality. But Whitman shows the appeal of celebrity as a model of publicity that transcends death precisely because it resembles it so closely. Existing in the public consciousness as an image, the celebrity is already absent—already, in a sense, dead. The Lincoln elegy grapples with the implications of a loss so irrational: knowing the man himself to be dead, the speaker nevertheless persists in loving the image of him, which returns in many as-yet-unimagined guises.

"Lilacs" is deeply concerned about images and their uses. From the start, it establishes a strong set of symbols—the Western star, the hermit thrush, and the lilac itself—that connect art to nature and cycles of transition. These symbols correspond to the poem's central ideas of the figure of the beloved, the "thought of him I love," and the speaker's effort to address or honor his lover. The poem dramatizes the struggle to express love in the lover's absence: "O how shall I warble myself for the dead one there I loved?" (*SDT* 6). The speaker turns this into a question about images:

> O what shall I hang on the chamber walls?
> And what shall the pictures be that I hang on the walls,
> To adorn the burial-house of him I love?
>
> (*SDT* 7)

In one sense, these lines draw attention to the poem itself as the speaker questions the best way of honoring the fallen lover in art. This reading is supported by the poem's inclusion of the hermit thrush, whose death carol is the prototype for a poetic language of grief. The images he chooses for the chamber walls represent panoramas of the American landscape, as well as the president's funeral cortege that moves through it and becomes the focal point of a national spectacle of mourning. Further, Whitman's images emphasize his own understanding of Lincoln as the figure of national union:

> Sea-winds, blown from east and west,
> Blown from the eastern sea, and blown from the western sea, till there
>   on the prairies meeting:
> These, and with these, and the breath of my chant,
> I perfume the grave of him I love.
>
> (*SDT* 6)

Whitman's "chant" reorients the national compass, replacing the north-south axis of discord with an east-west axis of union and reconciliation. But this national union is not matched by personal union between the lovers. Their intimacy, represented as a moment of conversation, is imperfect and one-sided:

> O western orb, sailing the heaven!
> Now I know what you must have meant, as a month since we walk'd,
> As we walk'd up and down in the dark blue so mystic,
> As we walk'd in silence the transparent shadowy night,
> As I saw you had something to tell, as you bent to me night after night,
> As you droop'd from the sky low down, as if to my side, (while the
>   other stars all look'd on;)

> As we wander'd together the solemn night, (for something I know not what, kept me from sleep;)
> As the night advanced, and I saw on the rim of the west, ere you went, how full you were of woe,
> As I stood on the rising ground in the breeze, in the cool transparent night,
> As I watch'd where you pass'd and was lost in the netherward black of the night,
> As my soul, in its trouble, dissatisfied, sank, as where you, sad orb,
> Concluded, dropt in the night, and was gone.
>
> (*SDT* 5–6)

Despite the apparent intimacy of the speaker and his lover, the passage emphasizes the lover's absence—their meeting is remembered, not relived. In their remembered encounter, the lovers fail to generate a satisfying, communicative union. Now, the speaker must accrue meaning and recreate intimacy in his lover's absence. He attains insight too late into the "latent sadness" both Lincoln and the Western star conveyed in their looks. The speaker remembers his lover as having been "full of woe" he could not express. Only in the presence of both the thought of death and the knowledge of death does the speaker understand that his lover's sadness signifies foreknowledge of his own death and, with it, the insufficiency of his efforts to generate either personal or national union. Claiming to understand his lover's meaning in retrospect, the speaker admits he was "dissatisfied"—a significant negation of Whitman's characteristic term of union and pleasure.

In contrast to the failed communication between the lovers, the speaker hears the hermit thrush clearly. "I hear—I come presently—I understand you," he insists (*SDT* 6). So clearly does the speaker hear the thrush that the speaker's most satisfying intimacy in the poem is with the bird, not his lover. Moreover, the thrush's song, or death carol, suggests intimacy with death herself, the "Dark Mother, always gliding near, with soft feet," against whose oceanic embrace he imagines "the body gratefully nestling close" (*SDT* 9, 10). This idea of death-as-mother gives way to visions of actual mothers whose suffering in grief and longing for the dead contrast with the "rest" of the dead who "suffer'd not" (*SDT* 11). The dead are not so much comforted as inert, negated, not suffering. The speaker's vision aligns him with the grieving widows, while it aligns the fallen president with the armies of war dead.

As it takes up the experiences of living and dead, "Lilacs" revisits the subject on which Lincoln himself meditates in his famed speech at Gettysburg. Just as

Whitman's poem worries over the best ways to honor the dead with language, Lincoln notes the inadequacy of speech that "the world will little note, nor long remember." Called on to dedicate the battlefield as a cemetery, Lincoln reminds his audience that dedication is shown through actions, not words: "it is for us the living, rather, to be dedicated here to the unfinished work which they who fought here thus far so nobly advanced." His vision of active citizenship includes engagement in the work of remaking the nation—the work of the war. Lincoln imagines a citizenry that redeems and is redeemed by the work of death, of the dead: he asks the living to recommit themselves to the work of not only the dead soldiers but also "our fathers" who "brought forth" this nation, as well as the principles in which the nation was "conceived."[76] Lincoln seeks to revivify, re-embody, a dead and abstract nation. Whitman's "Lilacs" likewise seeks continuity between the living and the dead, but the only renewal it envisions is that of the ever-returning spring of grief. Through death, the president's body disappears, finally, from public view, and he exists only as the abstraction of the fallen star. Russ Castronovo relates the "privatization and disengagement that stamps citizenship in the nineteenth century" to death.[77] Lincoln's death might be said to give him the most impermeable privacy. He is therefore the ultimate citizen, with a unique capacity to unite living and dead into an imagined community of grief. As such, he reveals that the satisfactions of citizenship can be fulfilled only in the privacy of the grave.

In "Lilacs," grief is not relieved but persists as the painful afterlife of desire for the dead. This is as true for the survivors of the war as it is for the speaker, whose grief for his lover returns "with every returning spring." The poem's power, in fact, comes from its representation of desire as unsatisfied, unsatisfiable, except by death. Only death, the negation of self, can absorb the lack that constitutes the subject's desire. In "Calamus," Whitman frequently returns to the pain and self-doubt that accompany desire:

> Of the terrible question of appearances,
> Of the doubts, the uncertainties after all,
> That may-be reliance and hope are but speculations after all,
> That may-be identity beyond the grave is a beautiful fable only.
>
> (1860 *LG* 352)

These uncertainties are quelled "when he whom I love travels with me, or sits a long while holding me by the hand." In such moments of reciprocal contact and loving exchange, "I am satisfied" if not assured: I live in the uncertainty, accepting that "I cannot answer the question of appearances, or that of identity beyond the grave" (1860 *LG* 353). "Lilacs" takes this problem further, addressing what happens when the lover does not return to grasp the proffered hand.

In keeping with celebrity culture, "Lilacs" represents the speaker's love for the public figure as a personal love, and his grief as a desire for him that cannot be satisfied. The poem's concern with finding pictures to honor the dead reflects a broader cultural effort to depict Lincoln after his assassination. Shocked by grief and buoyed by nationalism, many Americans sought to adorn their own chamber walls to honor Lincoln; they reinvigorated a market for Lincoln images, particularly "pictures that illustrated, occasionally imagined, Lincoln's transfiguration into national sainthood."[78] "Lilacs" participates in the national effort to depict the fallen president, and in this sense it is remarkable in its effort to illustrate a personal love from the public figure even as it reflects his national stature and significance—and even as it seems to omit the president himself from the verse. In addition, it equates the speaker's grief and desire with the suffering of every American grieving for someone lost in the war. Lincoln thus stands as representative of all the war dead, and grief for him encompasses a national mourning for him, for the thousands killed in war, and for a nation rent apart. This nationalistic reading is consistent with contemporary representations of Lincoln as a martyr for the national cause. But more than this, "Lilacs" asserts the continuity of personal and public affect. The "adhesiveness" or homoerotic desire that he celebrates in "Calamus" as the basis of national identity is love for both the anonymous passing stranger and for the illustrious public figure. They are alike unknowable except as objects on whom one's own desires—for intimacy, mutual recognition, and the momentary relief from self-doubt—are projected. While Whitman looks to both love and death to satisfy desire—"what indeed is finally beautiful except Death and Love?" he asks (1860 *LG* 343)—ultimately he acknowledges death's inevitable tendency to "dissipate this entire show of appearance" and thereby answer desire with "the real reality" (1860 *LG* 344).

Revisiting "Calamus" and "Lilacs," it is difficult to imagine they were written by the same man who issued verbal assaults against Bishop Hughes twenty or so years prior. Whitman's early journalism, his "Calamus" poems, and "Lilacs" are disparate moments in a rich body of writing, and I do not propose that such fragments as I assemble here can be glued together into a solid literary vessel. But in revisiting these milestones of Whitman's career, I hope to have demonstrated Whitman's investment in and critical response to celebrity culture and the personalization of public life. Most importantly, Whitman's work responds to the power of affect in a highly mediated popular culture. The questions of affect and intimacy that Whitman addresses in his "Calamus" sequence and "Lilacs" deal with, in their way, the questions of authority that he confronts in his newspaper writing: when the object of the popular gaze is an image, neither individual interpretive authority nor affective response can be entirely satisfactory or true, except as reflections of the subject's own self. Seeking the reciprocal exchange of glances and touches as the basis of political and social union, Whitman puts himself, his own image, before the public gaze. But the intimacies Whitman imagines fulfill his own long-held desires. His is a willful vision, an expression of authority that he claims is his right as the poet par excellence. The authority Whitman seeks as a journalist parallels the intimacy he seeks as a poet: each is a form of desire that shows how affect is the currency of popular culture.

Moreover, Whitman's "Calamus" poems and "Lilacs" alike take up the relations among men in public, exploring them explicitly in their affective dimensions and in awareness of the mediated nature of their encounters. In the meetings of lovers in "Calamus," the speaker encounters his ideal self—his satisfied self—through the mediated form of his lover. In "Lilacs" he struggles both to understand the lover as he is and was and also to find the form through which to express his own feelings. The poem draws on the romantic idea that truth must be mediated by and through nature—here, the thrush—to evoke the incongruity of personal feeling and public life in a mediated society. But if the desires for intimacy prompted by mediated others are themselves unsatisfied, Whitman remains committed to the promise of union they hold forth. The alternative, after all, is the erasure of the image by death, and the certain suffering it brings to those who remain.

CHAPTER 3

RALPH WALDO EMERSON
The Impersonal in the Personal Public Sphere

WRITING IN HIS JOURNAL, RALPH WALDO EMERSON INCLUDES P. T. Barnum's name on a list of individuals he considers among the worst of the age: "My countryman is surely not James Buchanan, nor Caleb Cushing, nor Barnum, . . . But Thoreau & Alcott & Sumner & whoever lives in the same love and worship as I; every just person, every man or woman who knows what truth means."¹ Emerson's rancor here registers his concerns about the Democrats, Know-Nothings, and other threats to the ideal society he envisions. He distinguishes himself and his "countrymen" from others who, as it turns out, are in fact his countrymen, and in doing so he reveals the very personal terms with which he understands political differences in a fractious time. The passage articulates a tribalism that turns up from time to time in Emerson's writing, as when, in "Self-Reliance," he remarks, "There is a class of persons to whom by all spiritual affinity I am bought and sold; for them I will go to prison, if need be."² This line comes in the context of his discussion of popular philanthropy, and while I recognize his effort to withstand the pressures of conformity, I think such statements reveal Emerson at his most snobbish. Nonetheless, the ideas he conveys in these instances are significant to his engagement with his times. Rejecting Barnum as one who does not know "what truth means," Emerson does more than echo contemporary criticisms of the showman as a fraud; he addresses his own quest for authenticity and meaning, and he personalizes the tendencies within the culture that make that quest both difficult and necessary.

In his own career, Emerson tried to reconcile the demands of commercial society with those of scholarly devotion, and he did so in part through a celebrity akin, but by no means identical, to Barnum's. As much as has been written about Emerson, his popular appeal—his celebrity—remains a fact more acknowledged than understood. Emerson lectured to packed halls until late in his life, and he retained the reputation for genius that drew ardent readers and listeners, mostly young men, not just to his public appearances but even to his doorstep. Part of his success owes to his skills as a lecturer. Emerson studied oratory from his youth, and in his journals he astutely critiqued oratorical performances, including his own. In an age that prized oratory, Emerson ranked among Edward

Everett, Frederick Douglass, and Henry Ward Beecher as one of the best and most influential speakers of the era. But a cultural value for oratory does not quite account for Emerson's celebrity, because celebrity indicates a kind of relationship between a singular public figure and his audience. In the first place, oratory, and the reputation for eloquence, concentrates on each performance independently. The oratory establishes a unique connection with the audience, a sympathetic union, that unites the entire group as if by an electric current. This understanding of eloquence highlights its temporality: it exists only in the time and place of the utterance, and it depends on the physical presence, voice, delivery, and language of a charismatic speaker. Emerson apparently achieved this kind of success and built a reputation on it, but his celebrity presumes to extend that charismatic power beyond the lecture hall and into the culture at large. As Barnum's example shows, celebrity supposes the public figure's ubiquity, a presence beyond the body. The celebrity, in this respect, is less like the public speaker, who appears intermittently before specific audiences and then retreats, than he is like the printed text or image, which extends the figure's presence into spaces he does not physically occupy. The significance of the body notwithstanding, celebrity is a metaphysical, even transcendental, condition.

But let's not get carried away. My language might indicate that Emerson's celebrity is of a piece with his philosophies: it presumes that the leading spokesman for the ideas commonly called transcendentalism sought or at least tolerated celebrity as a manifestation of a spiritual reality in the shared material world of mass culture. I do not go so far as that in this chapter, because Emerson was highly skeptical of celebrity and its tendency to equate the physical person with his private self. As we have seen, celebrity culture operates in a personal public sphere characterized by the presumption of familiarity and even intimacy among strangers. This sense of intimacy arises from the seeming availability of the celebrity image, his or her physical presence, before a mass audience that presumes the image conveys the celebrity's self. This understanding of self runs counter to the idea of abstract selfhood that Emerson champions: he takes as his central subject "the infinitude of the private man" (*JMN* 7:342), by which he means the metaphysical self that one nurtures in solitary study and reflection. Strengthened by such self-culture, the Emersonian individual enters the public sphere, the realm of "action," as he says in "The American Scholar." Identifying and nurturing this metaphysical self is Emerson's primary business, even though—perhaps because—it was increasingly challenged by contemporary realities, especially a celebrity culture that equated self and body. Emerson's transcendentalism consists to a large degree in his efforts to recalibrate the popular understanding of self that a burgeoning celebrity culture helps promulgate. In simplest terms, Emerson asserts the primacy of the abstract self, whereas the popular culture increasingly identifies self with the physical person. But Emerson's philosophy of self—his concept of self-reliance—is part of a critique of mass culture, including celebrity culture. Emerson calls for nonconformity as an act not just of self-assertion but also of resistance; he urges the self-reliant to live out their values even in opposition to the "vulgar prosperity that retrogrades ever to barbarism," to use a memorable phrase from "The American Scholar." Emerson recognizes and is wary of the connection between capitalist consumerism, mass culture, and Jacksonian individualism. His reassertion of abstract selfhood would reestablish a precapitalist public sphere even in the context of his acquisitive, capitalist society.

Such a claim risks characterizing Emerson as nostalgic for an idealized public sphere of a past age. Likewise, scholars of celebrity tend to see Emerson as backward-looking. Leo Braudy dismisses Emerson's studies of "great men" in *Representative Men* (1850) as "anachronistic" because they claim that "through great men . . . individuals could connect with their own cultures and histories."[3] Similarly, P. David Marshall associates Emerson with Thomas Carlyle and William Hazlitt, all of whom argued that "the danger of the new celebrity is that it has slipped the yoke of historical validation."[4] These analyses represent the difficulty modern readers have in trying to situate Emerson historically. Interested in history as a force bearing on the present, Emerson nevertheless cautions his audiences against an undue reverence for the past. Noting individuals' inevitably subjective interpretation of the past, he claims, "There is properly no History; only Biography"; but he also wonders, "Why should we grope among the dry bones of the past, or put the living generation into masquerade out of its faded wardrobe?" (*CW* 2:6, 1:7). If the men of past ages (and they are always men, for Emerson) compel his interest, he nonetheless refuses to be ensnared by the past's claims on the present. Emerson's critique of mass culture is similarly shaped by an awareness of a powerful social force, public opinion, and a recognition of the potential for individual "great men" to marshal that power. He at once admires these men for their personal ascendancy and is wary of their threat to his own.

Such complexities extend to his thinking about capitalism as well: Emerson's concerns about the consumerist society in which he lived did not lead him to try any alternative—he did not retreat to Walden Pond, nor did he join his friends at Brook Farm. He skillfully managed his own lecture tours and publishing agreements, as well as publishing agreements for friends such as Carlyle. And, more to the interests of this chapter, he courted popular success by crafting and cultivating a public image or persona even as he challenged the mainstream idea of celebrity and selfhood that fed into his popularity. In doing so, Emerson entered into the cultural discourse over self and individualism and rejected the ideas of an embodied self that characterized much of the celebrity culture that supported him. Put another way, Emerson's contrarian speech challenges the popular authority of the mass audience and assumes the traditional authorial role of cultural authority. This role may seem contradictory to the ideas that made him famous—particularly, the concept of self-reliance, which indicates that the individual has access to the universal or impersonal forces within himself. Encouraging nonconformity, Emerson licenses individual authority insofar as that individual heeds the universal law that governs his or her conscience. Emerson's own nonconformist philosophy resists and revises popular ideas of the self and the individual that shaped the very celebrity culture that brought him before the mass audience. He promotes impersonality in a culture that favors personality.

Contemporary audiences treated Emerson as a kind of spiritual spectacle, meaning they accepted his oratorical performances as a display of genius or spirit. What caused them to see Emerson in this way? The reverence with which audiences regard him seems at odds with his own philosophy of nonconformity, but at the same time it shows the influence of his impersonal methods. What I am saying is, if audiences did not regard Emerson impersonally—indeed, they were quite attentive to both his physical person and his public personality—they did not fail to understand him as the agent or representative of impersonal forces. Emerson rejected much of this popular culture out of hand. As his dismissive reference to Barnum shows, he distrusted spectacle as delusion, mere appearances designed to provide sensation without offering substance. He does not accept the premise that commercial performances such as these can participate in serious discourses about spirit, truth, or democracy. But rather than retreat from popular culture he found unrewarding, Emerson made a career and became a celebrity out of the effort to challenge or correct popular understanding of mass culture itself. That effort begins with a redefinition of the concept of self that responds to contemporary concerns about individualism in a democratic, capitalist society. "But now we are a mob," he admonishes in "Self-Reliance," distinguishing the thoughtful congress of abstract selves from the physical and intellectual chaos of a modern public sphere (*CW* 2:41).

Whether or not Emerson succeeded in these efforts is a question that does not allow simple answers. Assuming the role of cultural spokesman, Emerson sought a form of power, the power to influence popular thought. At the same time, in the personal public sphere, every individual observer may "read" and interpret public men such as Emerson in word and mien. To the extent that Emerson and his audiences worked at cross-purposes, understanding self as either abstract or embodied, an eminence or a spectacle, they cannot be reconciled. Yet audiences embraced Emerson as the embodiment of genius, a representative of the very wisdom he thought they craved and could find through an impersonal self-reliance. In the years following his death, Emerson's first biographers carried this personal response to Emerson even further as they sought to establish his permanent legacy. Their readings of Emerson used the same techniques made common by the personal public sphere: they read his physical eloquence as a lecturer to affirm his status as a genius. Rather than making Emerson and his ideas available to the masses he addressed, these biographers set him apart from them. Their work minimizes—erases—Emerson's attempts to engage with his times and risks transforming him from an active scholar to "a valetudinarian,—as unfit for any handiwork or public labor, as a penknife for an axe" (*CW* 1:59). At the same time, these early biographers minimized the popular audiences' abilities to judge, evaluate, and interpret his meaning—to exercise their own self-reliance.

REMINISCING IN THE 1890S, CHARLES JOHNSON WOODBURY DESCRIBES seeing Emerson lecture in 1865. After his lecture, Emerson "descended from the enforced dignity of the platform. . . . His bearing and con[duct] had the exquisite power of a moral nature which has never been impaired by a willful transgression. Nobility characterized his deportment." Reading, in retrospect, Emerson's body and movements, Woodbury claims to see Emerson's "nobility" expressed therein. His gestures convey the spiritual insight that presumably made up the substance of his lecture. From such heights of wisdom—"so lifted and extraordinary was the elevation from which he approached the subjects he discussed"—he does not step down but *descends*. Yet, Woodbury contests, "Elevating is a weak word with which to describe the influence of his gentle serenity upon men; for even quite above themselves were they lifted by his presence, and found their highest moments his common ones." The scene of Emerson's talk is characterized by a rugged spiritual topography, and Emerson himself tops every peak. The words of the orator whose "thoughts and life were abreast of the Holy Spirit" do not elevate or instruct, but they illustrate the differences between the speaker and his audience. Throughout his reminiscence, Woodbury emphasizes Emerson's greater nature. "After parting" from Emerson's company, Woodbury writes, "you remembered, more even than his vivid talk, his simple ways, the home-like feeling he diffused, and the forgetfulness that you were in the presence of our foremost American."[5] To be in Emerson's presence, this suggests, is to experience a double amnesia, forgetting first the very words Emerson uttered, and then the reputation that was surely rooted in his language. For Woodbury, Emerson's words are incidental to his greatness: Emerson communicates not ideas but spirit; he cannot be read or heard, but must be experienced.

Woodbury's portrait is not atypical. As I will discuss later in this chapter, Emerson's first biographers praise him as a saintlike figure whose every syllable and glance revealed a providential wisdom beyond the ken of mortal understanding. Contemporary reviews of Emerson's lectures and the firsthand accounts of those who knew him attest to his celebrity by demonstrating the audience's intense interest in his physical person, often at the expense of the lectures or his ideas. At least two sources of note discuss this persistent interest: first, in their introduction to *Emerson in His Own Time*, Joel Myerson and Ronald A. Bosco point out that Emerson's contemporary observers frequently "betray an almost uniform preoccupation with his physical appearance both at the lectern and away from it."[6] This kind of attention to the physical appearance of public figures is not unique to Emerson, but in fact it is a condition of celebrity. As we will see, both Frederick Douglass and Fanny Fern experienced similar scrutiny, though it was inflected by mainstream ideologies of racial and gender identity. Thomas Augst attributes contemporaries' attention to the bodies of Emerson and other lecturers to popular interest in physiognomy.[7] Physiognomy is just one example of popular interest in the body and its meaning: nineteenth-century audiences were increasingly attentive to a variety of popular amusements—theater and dance performance, circuses, freak shows, novelty acts—that emphasized the spectacular display of the human body, and many of those amusements shared the same stage as the popular lecturer. Attention to Emerson's and other celebrities' physical presence on the lecture platform reflects his culture's increasing visual emphasis, which grew out of widespread hunger for spectacle fed by a carnivalesque print marketplace.[8]

Emerson's celebrity bridges the distance between his audience's sense of his significance and his own ambitions for the secular ministry of his lecture career. Seeking a role of cultural influence on par with that of the minister, Emerson was nevertheless drawn to the lecture hall partly by worldly concerns. The commercial dimensions of his lecturing career connect his lecturing to both his idealized public office and the popular amusements of the period. Emerson's account books and personal correspondence demonstrate his attention to the economic aspects of lecturing, which supported him and his family and enabled him to devote his summers to writing and publishing essays. Audiences accepted his participation in a market-driven profession—after all, they paid the required admission fee. And this shared understanding of lecturing as a paid, even entrepreneurial venture surely affected how audiences responded to it. Audiences were able to associate the public lecture with the many other entertainments they saw advertised in the same newspapers and handbills and that frequently appeared at the same venues as an Emerson lecture.[9] In such an environment, the presence of the speaker is especially important. Gustavus Stadler explains, "the value of [lyceum] attendance hinges on the very fact of coincident, physical presence with [the speaker] as much as on the content of the address." Stadler links this claim about lyceums to Emerson's particular case, noting the "excitement and anxiety in Emerson's experience of his own body's new significance in the national cultural field."[10] In the lecture context, the distinct pressures of Emerson's ideals for oratory and his audience's attentiveness to his physical presence each generate expectations and responses that may not agree with one another but are, in themselves, essentially correct. Observers may "read" his body's cues and find meaning in them that is separate from his words and potentially out of his control. In short, the lecture's emphasis on visual encounter and physical eloquence gave the audiences greater interpretive authority than they might experience as readers or listeners only.

In claiming to have forgotten Emerson's conversation in the aura of his semi-divine presence, Woodbury puts a positive spin on the old complaint that Emerson was incomprehensible. This trait of Emerson's has two sides: it reflects the difficulty of his ideas and unruly compositional style, as well as the idea that Emerson's intellect was too subtle for the masses to follow. Critics generally accept that Emerson's audiences consistently misinterpreted or failed to fully understand his lectures. Mary Kupiec Cayton's influential work on Emerson and the nineteenth-century culture industry explores the distinctions between Emerson's lectures on "Wealth" and his midwestern audiences' misinterpretations of it.[11] Cayton highlights the ways that the marketplace shapes audiences' expectations of an Emerson lecture. She argues that audiences encountered a particular Emerson, a cultural icon whose reputation for greatness preceded him to the platform. In attending one of his lectures, audiences therefore could assure themselves of having seen something historic, culturally important, or personally improving—even when they misheard his message. Cayton's study opens up the cultural and economic contexts of Emerson's lectures, but it is limited by its commitment to the Frankfurt School analysis of popular culture, with its thesis that mass culture is "mass deception." If we consider the significance of Emerson's physical presence in the lecture hall, we can say that there is no deception, no misinterpretation, only interpretations of lectures that do not cohere with interpretations of complementary texts. Moreover, interpretation of the lecture, understood as a visual as well as verbal performance, helps audiences gain access to a figure whose reputation for greatness actually was enhanced by the difficulty of his prose.

Evidence shows that the tendency for readers and listeners to misconstrue Emerson's ideas began much earlier than the 1840s, when his celebrity was in its ascendancy. Sarah Wider has shown, for instance, that at least one of Emerson's parishioners at the Second Church "heard" Emerson preaching conventional messages of faith in God and the church when in fact the sermon texts led to more ambivalent sentiments and suggested Emerson's more theistic self-reliance.[12] Such misunderstandings helped define Emerson's reputation—indeed, to a certain extent, Emerson himself contributed to this part of his reputation. Claiming to "speak the rude truth in all ways" (*CW* 2:30), Emerson acknowledged the cultural power of controversy and even scandal as a means of challenging conventional beliefs. One of the earliest and starkest examples is the 1838 Divinity School "Address" and the controversy that followed.[13] To his mentor Henry Ware Jr., he wrote, "It strikes me very oddly & even a little ludicrously that the good & great men of Cambridge should think of raising me into an object of criticism. I have always been from my very incapacity of methodical writing a chartered libertine free to worship & free to rail lucky when I was understood but never esteemed near enough to the institutions & mind of society to deserve the notice of the masters of literature & religion."[14] The lines are self-deprecating and also a little disingenuous. Known at this point principally for his self-published tract *Nature*, Emerson presents himself as beneath the notice of "the good & great men of Cambridge." He presumes his inconspicuousness—his limited publicity—gives him freedom from literary conventions as well as from conventional thought. Emerson attempts to retain his intellectual autonomy by preserving his right to be misunderstood without sanction. The letter may be an antecedent to the aphorism "To be great is to be misunderstood" (*CW* 2:34). Read as such, it explains that great, or at least genuine, ideas are difficult to understand because, unconstrained by particular schools of thought, they are unfamiliar to "the institutions and mind of society."

Like the reviews of the Divinity School "Address," reviews of *Nature* emphasized the difficulty of his prose and the unorthodoxy of his ideas, and they show that in the mid- to late 1830s Emerson was gaining a reputation for pantheism, mysticism, and occultism that was supported as much by the idealism of *Nature* as by Emerson's innovative and difficult prose style. "Mystic" may serve as code for "obscure." Typical reviews wondered that they could hardly understand Emerson. For instance, at the outset of his favorable treatment of *Nature*, Orestes Brownson epitomizes a strain of comment on Emerson's style and philosophy: "We cannot analyze it; whoever would form an idea of it must read it" (*ETCR* 3). Elizabeth Palmer Peabody perhaps gets closest to explaining the difficulty when she labels *Nature* a "poem . . . written in prose" to suggest that the work appeals to an imaginative capacity in order to convey its metaphysics (*ETCR* 18–23). Similar comments accompanied reviews of his lectures and other books. Considering the development of Emerson's essays out of lectures he delivered in Boston in 1840, reviewer C. C. Felton sums up the challenges of Emerson's style: "It was not very easy to make out from the varying reports of hearers, what these discourses really were; it was not much easier to say what they were, when you had heard them yourself; and the difficulty is not greatly diminished now they have taken the form of printed essays" (*ETCR* 80). Such comments indicate that an encounter with Emerson's language, either read or heard, is an experience that demands something other than the ability to correctly interpret texts; it is an "extraliterary" experience, to borrow Jonathan Bishop's description of reading Emerson's essays.[15] This growing reputation for difficulty might cause some readers to expect to struggle with Emerson's meaning, to regard his complexity as a sign of his "genius," and to forgive their own failed comprehension.

Audiences around the country need not have been familiar with any particular accounting of Emerson's difficulty or mysticism, but they are likely to have been aware of a version of his reputation culled from reviews of his publications and mediated through a newspaper editor. Emerson's lectures and print publications were related not only in his own compositional practices but also in his audiences' imaginations. However, to attribute such awareness to a mechanistic "culture industry" is to overlook the agency of individual readers or auditors in attributing significance to any particular author or literary activity. Thomas Augst's work on nineteenth-century literary practices provides a way of understanding how individual readers' participation in the personal public sphere influenced their expectations and values. He argues that nineteenth-century literary practice occurs "within a social framework of received opinion," which I take to be more of a communal practice than an imposition from a larger cultural force. The misapprehension associated with Emerson's lectures reflects changing literacy practices in the period. As Augst writes, "Like writing in a diary, or borrowing a book from a library, attending a popular lecture was a means of spiritual exercise or a technology of the self—a practical means by which ordinary people sought to define and exercise moral agency."[16] That is to say that attending the lecture— and attending to it, by writing about it in a diary or letter, discussing it with friends, or reading a review of it—was understood as a morally improving way of participating in ongoing social conversations about literary and moral values. These ideas were supported by the lyceum itself, which, as an institution, sought to provide lectures that were personally edifying and morally sound. "As a site where public selves and public cultures were constituted," the lyceum promoted individual self-culture as a communitarian and even nationalistic enterprise even as it strove to remain politically neutral.[17] Over time, the lyceum transformed from a system for "mutual education" to a commercial enterprise that capitalized on appearances by recognizable stock types of speakers, even as it held onto its original ethos as an educational institution.[18]

Lyceums competed for attention with a host of other entertainments available in the marketplace of cultural commodity, including theater, dime museums, musical and dance performances, and exhibitions of all kinds.[19] The lyceum's political neutrality may have given it the luster of intellectual purity, but it arose from the same cultural forces that made P. T. Barnum's American Museum, Moses

Kimball's theater at the Boston Museum, and an array of dime museums and musical halls that sprang up in urban centers. The emergence of an urban working class created a market for amusement; the lyceum and the self-culture movement more generally offered morally wholesome and edifying entertainments, and in doing so sought to preserve an ideal of self seemingly endangered by mass culture. In this effort, for instance, William Ellery Channing's 1838 lecture "Self-Culture" is a useful touchstone. One of the leading figures in Unitarianism and a major influence on transcendentalism, Channing preached the integration of a divine influence with the human mind. Echoing Francis Hutcheson's philosophy of the passions, Channing encourages his audiences to avoid the temptations of modern, urban life and embark on a disciplined program of self-improvement. Recognizing that industrial capitalism intensifies class differences, exacerbates poverty, and lumps individuals together into a mass, Channing remains optimistic: "The grand distinction of modern times is, the emerging of the people from brutal degradation, the gradual recognition of their rights, the gradual diffusion among them of the means of improvement and happiness, the creation of a new power in the state, the power of the people." This republican power will be felt through the instruments of mass communication, which in turn facilitate individual self-culture. He heralds the transformation of the press as a tool for self-education via newspapers—"the literature of the multitudes"—inexpensive books, and circulating libraries, as well as public schools.[20] Channing's individualism seeks continuity with the past in that it maintains social class structures. As David Robinson points out, Channing's writings on labor "appealed to the workers to keep their place in the social order in a proper moral perspective."[21] If, therefore, singling out the man from the multitude, Channing is not as dour as Emerson, who notes, "But now we are a mob," neither does he seek a "revolution in all the offices and relations of men" (*CW* 2:41, 44).

In contrast with Channing, at least, Emerson is a radical. He regards self-culture as a means not just of self-reform but also of social reform, or "revolution-by-consciousness" that looks a lot like religious conversion.[22] The lyceum was one stage for bringing about such revolution. As they offer alternatives to the various amusements and spectacles that threaten the self's development, lyceums and other institutions of self-culture relocate the work of self-making from the private to the public sphere. Emerson himself was a fixture in lyceums from 1837 onward, a period that included the lyceum's heyday as a cultural force. Like the lyceum itself, he began his lecturing career in Massachusetts and gradually expanded through New England and the Northeast, and then westward.

Part of the appeal of an Emerson lecture was the opportunity it provided for interpreting the moral character of one of the nation's leading moral critics. Audiences consistently looked to Emerson's physical presence in the lecture hall for evidence of his character. Descriptive reviews of his performances attempted to recreate his appearance and the atmosphere of the lecture. They seem to regard his physical person not as the vehicle that delivers the lecture text but as a text in itself. In interpreting that text, audience members and review readers can claim an intimacy with the man himself. Interpreting Emerson's person is therefore an authoritative act available to as many people as have access to his presence, either in the lecture hall or in print. While reviewers presume intellectual engagement with Emerson, their analysis tends to overlook the lecture content, concentrating instead on Emerson's physical bearing and dulcet voice. This may owe, in part, to Emerson's efforts to keep his lecture content out of the newspapers in an age when newspapers tended to fill columns with verbatim transcripts of lectures. Respectful reviewers therefore omitted the details of his speech, focusing instead on the details of his performance. For instance, a reviewer for the *Cincinnati Gazette* describes Emerson's appearance at an 1857 lecture: "Mr. Emerson is a tall man, full six feet high, but slender and bony, and in his plain suit of ill fitting black, looked not unlike a New England country schoolmaster. His face is thin and strongly marked, his nose large, and his eye-brows highly arched and meeting. He rarely looks his hearers full in the face, but at emphatic expressions has a habit of turning his eyes backward as though he desired to look in at himself. His voice is like his sentences—not smooth or even, yet occasionally giving a tone of considerable sweetness, and he has an [oracular] way of delivering himself that is calculated to impress the audience."[23]

The *Gazette* review attempts to link Emerson's wisdom and insight to physical traits such as the look in his eye or his posture. Other reviews are likewise attentive to his facial features, especially his eyes and his voice. A review from the same Ohio lecture tour remarks that Emerson's eye "has a mysterious and undefinable blight in its depth," while "his voice is full, strong and rich, but he speaks with a sort of hesitation . . . as if he were struggling with a thought too great for immediate utterance."[24] Rather than conveying the ideas Emerson shares, the review describes Emerson's experience of impersonal truth as a performance. Emerson's physical ungainliness and halting delivery manifest his genius and add to his oratorical power. Newspaper reviews such as these build Emerson's celebrity by extending his image beyond the site of his actual appearance and rendering his body as a text for interpretation. The *Gazette* review strikes key notes that resound in descriptions of Emerson: the "sweetness" of his voice, his introspective tendencies, the physical traits and behaviors that set him apart from the masses. Hence Emerson's philosophy of impersonality gets converted into personality, the physical manifestation of his unique self. In pointing out Emerson's attempts "to impress the audience," the reviewer distinguishes him- or herself as a practiced spectator. Any power Emerson's oratory may have sought is countered by the judgment of the reviewer and, by extension, Emerson's entire audience. However appreciative of Emerson's sweet tone and skillful delivery, this audience is unlikely to be swept away by Emerson's intellectual power. Even as the reviewer claims a privileged position as observer of the speaker, the review provides a portrait of Emerson that readers might use to make their own independent judgments of his character and relevance.

Physical descriptions of Emerson suggest that newspaper readers can achieve some measure of closeness to the lecturer through the medium of print. They provide enough of a portrait of the speaker to allow readers to assume familiarity with him, even if they are not acquainted with his writings or speeches. By attending an actual lecture, however, audience members could enjoy even greater proximity to Emerson. In accounts of their father, written years after his death, the Emerson children suggest that value of his physical presence to lecture audiences and avid readers. His daughters described the crowds of well-wishers who gathered around their father after a lecture and the groups of young Harvard students who sought him out at home. In 1902 Ellen Tucker Emerson wrote, "People who knew him were pretty sure to go up afterwards to see him, and Edith and I meanwhile, when we were at the lectures, had often little talks with his friends or ours that were no small part of our happiness."[25] Edith Emerson Forbes recalled, "About 1853 or 4 Harvard students began to ask leave to come to see Father. I think it was a great pleasure to him. From three to twelve would come" at a time and be welcomed into the house.[26] These memories attest to Emerson's availability, practically unheard of among modern celebrities. They also suggest that intellectual affinity for Emerson's ideas was complemented or even intensified by contact with the man himself. They indicate the unique combination of affect and intellect, sympathy and judgment, that characterizes Emerson's celebrity—and indeed celebrity in general. To be close to Emerson is to approximate genius itself. A nineteenth-century audience would have understood "genius" not as singularity of achievement only but singularity in spirit, a conjunction of the soul and the effort. Thus "genius," like the celebrity that accompanies it, distinguishes the individual from the mass at the same time as it endears that difference to the mass. Gustavus Stadler argues that the assumption "of possession by *alterity*" that is central to concepts of genius in the period is alienating to the audience, and that "genius and genius figures invite affective and psychic attachments that overflow their 'representative' significance."[27] Emerson—"genius," celebrity—is in this sense representative of abstract qualities that his audience appreciates, perhaps desires, and may perceive as unattainable to themselves except via the intimate act of interpretation. To use Emersonian terms, the effort of interpretation impersonalizes the public figure. Far from being anti-intellectual, audiences sought correspondence between Emerson's physical and intellectual expression. Interpretations of Emerson's genius depend on the attentiveness of the observer, his or her sensitivity to the meaning of the body as well as his participation in the communal practices of literacy itself. Interpretation of Emerson's person therefore is both highly subjective and widely available. This democratic availability is especially important because, as nearly all of Emerson's early biographers point out, he lectured to audiences of diverse intellectual backgrounds, from the East Coast elite to the merchants and farmers of rural communities. Emerson's physical characteristics of voice and carriage provided the link to his genius shared by all audiences.

The crowds of eager auditors manifest the availability of Emerson's genius in mass culture. However patiently Emerson himself forbore his eager spectators, others sought ways to isolate him from an apparently indiscriminate public. Of particular interest, Nathaniel Parker Willis wrote two reviews of Emerson's 1850 lectures on "The Signs of the Times" in New York City. A celebrity author himself, Willis captures the Emerson lecture in its full social context and accounts for the ways Emerson's reputation may influence his reception. Willis therefore intervenes into ongoing critical discussions of Emerson and his significance. He remarks on the size of the crowd, the setting, and the quality of the lighting in the lecture room, and he provides a vivid description of the speaker himself. Importantly, Willis also accounts for the personal context of the lecture—his own preconceptions of Emerson, whom he knew slightly as a child in Boston. He recalls Emerson as "one of those pale little moral-sublimes with their shirt collars turned over, who are recognized by Boston schoolboys as having 'fathers that are Unitarians.'" Such a beginning, he suggests, did not presage Emerson's development into "the deity of an intellectual altar, upon which, at that moment, burned a fire in our bosom."[28]

Distinguishing between Emerson's appearance and his influence, Willis forms the central theme of his essay. His review of the lecture performance emphasizes the same distinction:

> Emerson's voice is up to its reputation. It has a curious contradiction, which we tried in vain to analyze satisfactorily—an outwardly repellant and inwardly reverential mingling of qualities, which a musical composer would despair of blending into one. It bespeaks a life that is half-contempt, half adoring recognition and very little between. But it is noble, altogether. And what seems strange is to hear such a voice proceeding from such a body. It is a voice with shoulders in it, which he has not—with lungs in it far larger than his—with a walk in it which the public never see—with a fist in it, which his own hand never gave him the model for—and with a gentleman in it, which his parochial and "bare-necessaries-of-life" sort of exterior, gives no other

betrayal of. We can imagine nothing in nature—(which seems, too, to have a type for everything)—like the want of correspondence between the Emerson that goes in at the eye, and the Emerson that goes in at the ear.[29]

Describing Emerson's physical appearance and voice, Willis contrasts his unexceptional physique with his intellectual strength. The result is to negate the body, emphasizing instead the disembodied or abstract qualities of Emerson's intellectual achievement. Referring to "the Emerson that goes in at the eye," Willis of course alludes to Emerson's physical appearance, but the line also resonates with Willis's subsequent comments on reading Emerson's lectures as written texts. When encountered on the page, Willis claims, Emerson's words do not communicate the "surprises" he uses to oratorical effect: "in delivery, his cadences tell you that the meaning is given, and the interest of the sentence is all over, when—flash!—comes a single word or phrase, like lightning after listened-out thunder, and illuminates, with astonishing vividness, the cloud you have striven to see into."[30] Here again, Willis emphasizes a distinction between the expectation and the experience as the signature of Emerson's power. That "flash!" is the speaker's impersonal power illuminating the audience's own capacity for understanding.

Willis's positive review of the lecture is not typical. Bosco and Myerson point out that "The Spirit of the Times" was often poorly received. Some audiences laughed derisively, having found the gravity of Emerson's delivery inappropriate, as the lecture's content was so familiar.[31] In short, Emerson's presumption of intellectual authority was insulting. In this context, Willis's comments redeem Emerson as a gifted orator who, to be sure, "speaks . . . from his superatmospheric elevation," but who also "handles things without gloves, as everyone knows."[32] But Willis also clarifies that Emerson is not for everyone. He notes the intellectual and cultural eminences who attend the lecture—Horace Greeley among them, just as he was in the audience for the 1842 lecture Whitman reviewed. In contrast with Whitman, Willis claims that these elite figures constitute the ideal audience for Emerson, and he effectively dismisses a mass audience that reduces the celebrity orator to a spectacle. Those who see Emerson as "a national joke, the type of the incomprehensible, the byword of the poor paragrapher" are not equipped to hear or judge him aright.[33] These judgments, Willis tacitly acknowledges, rest on the assessment of his masculine power. Interpreting Emerson is difficult for lecture audiences because he relocates masculine power that conventionally resides in the body; he derives his power not from the shoulders and fists but from the intellect, figured as the voice that expresses it. The "want of correspondence" between Emerson's physical and intellectual expression challenges commonplace assumptions of what is "natural" and powerful. Willis ironically acknowledges Emerson's philosophy of correspondence between nature and spirit while also pointing out the gulf in perception between Emerson and his audience, which interprets "nature" as "body."

Although Willis is ultimately "vexed" that Emerson addresses a "miscellaneous audience,"[34] his reading responds to and incorporates habits of spectatorship that are common to celebrity culture. In imagining a restricted audience for Emerson, moreover, Willis attempts to cordon off access to the representative American genius, thus preserving and enhancing his cultural value. Willis's Emerson essays anticipate an entire body of biography that emerged after Emerson died. Indeed, the first generation of Emerson biographers devotes considerable energy to questions about audience reception. While they can be aggressive, even hagiographic, in their praise of Emerson, their language illustrates the connections between his physical characteristics as a lecturer and contemporary ideas of his genius. For Lowell, whose essay on "Emerson the Lecturer" has been influential, Emerson's ability to transcend the intellectual differences among his audience is the proof of his genius. Audiences were attracted to Emerson's appreciation for and expressions of beauty. Contra Willis, Lowell argues that Emerson's aesthetic sensitivity powers his "masculine faculty of fecundating other minds."[35] Thus Lowell rescues Emerson as a thinker and as a man from the ridicule of an uncomprehending public. The combination of beauty and manliness occurs in Oliver Wendell Holmes's accounts of Emerson's genius as well. He recalls that "wherever he appeared in the lecture-room, he fascinated his listeners by his voice and manner; the music of his speech pleased those who found his thought too subtle for their dull wits to follow." The comment brings together an intense appreciation for Emerson's genius with condescension toward his less intellectually sophisticated audience. But Holmes himself is not unresponsive to the physical power of Emerson's oratory. He goes on to acknowledge an emotional rather than intellectual effect of Emerson's speech, claiming that there was "a sweet seriousness in Emerson's voice that was infinitely soothing. So might 'Peace, be still,' have sounded from the lips that silenced the storm."[36] This is Emerson as both nurturer and godhead, whose rhetorical force inspires profound affection.

Whereas Lowell and Holmes identify intellectual differences among Emerson's audience, George Santayana argues that Emerson's appeal was in his character, not his intellectual power: "[Audiences] flocked to him and listened to his word, not so much for the sake of its absolute meaning as for the atmosphere of candour, purity, and serenity that hung about it, as about a sort of sacred music. They felt themselves in the presence of a rare and beautiful spirit, who was in communion with a higher world."[37] The fact that Santayana, a philosopher, emphasizes the alluring presence of the speaker rather than the quality of his ideas is significant. Writers such as Santayana, Holmes, and others of their generation anticipate twentieth-century critics, many of whom either hesitate to take Emerson seriously as a philosopher or dismiss contemporary audiences as unable to fathom Emerson's intellectual achievements. The language of spirit that Santayana uses reaffirms the idea that Emerson's genius distinguishes him from his audience even as it denies Emerson the masculine intellectual power that Willis and Lowell saw in his oratorical performance.

A few important points arise from considerations of these remembrances of Emerson. First, there is a considerable effort to solidify and preserve Emerson's legacy in the years following his death. And while the bulk of these efforts are complimentary—exceedingly so—they tend to foreclose the possibility for individual interpretation evident in the contemporary reviews of Emerson performances. Second, the consciousness of Emerson's celebrity is a matter of some concern for these later critics. They share an impulse to account for the effect that Emerson had on mass audiences, on the nature of the "genius" that compelled their affection. Third, Emerson's physical characteristics provide the most ready explanation for his power and appeal. Reviewers and biographers alike struggle to assimilate Emerson's appeal to higher truth with the very earthly power of his performances; physical traits such as voice and facial expressions provide the link between these two realms of experience. But, and this is the final point, later critics do not seek to make Emerson available to later audiences. They do not provide portraits available for readers' interpretation, as the earlier reviews do, but instead attempt to create an authoritative interpretation that will secure Emerson's legacy. These reviews therefore wrest authority from the masses in order to glorify Emerson's genius, tamp down a specific interpretation of his significance, and rescue the "real" Emerson from the fate of mere celebrity. But as they canonize Emerson, these early biographies rob audiences of the interpretive power that is intrinsic to his celebrity, and that is the first stage of self-reliance.

THE BIOGRAPHERS' ANXIETY ABOUT EMERSON'S CONTEMPORARY audiences and his legacy represents a conservative response to his celebrity. These biographers distrust the claims of intimacy and authority that accompany celebrity and seek to establish their own claims on the man they knew. In doing so, they in fact perpetuate Emerson's celebrity: through their firsthand accounts, these men revise and extend Emerson's image in the public sphere, making him available to new readers. Hence, insisting that the best way of knowing Emerson is to spend time in his presence, whether in the lecture hall or the parlor, their written accounts extend his presence even as they mediate it. And in attempting to pin down Emerson's meaning, these writers betray their distrust of popular opinion as a reliable gauge of cultural value.

To an extent, Emerson shared this distrust. He respected and valued public opinion as a tremendous social force, but he also took seriously the potential for strong individuals to resist public opinion and even reshape it. His interest in public opinion dates to at least 1828, when he wrote to his brother Charles about the subject: "What makes the value of any one man as precise & as well known as the stamp of a coin? Public opinion. What is a throne? What is a legislature? What is a Congress? What is a Constitution? Mere pipes, mere mouth-pieces for the expression of public opinion" (*Letters* 1:245). Emerson identifies public opinion as the foundation for all great powers. Against this great force, however, he pits the individual encouraged by "*private opinion*": "Why, then, what a clean Damascus blade of an inference can you not draw about the value of a brave lad in the world, that knoweth how to keep his hands clean & heart pure & then write a tract or speak a speech?" (*Letters* 1:246, 247). Already, Emerson frames individual self-reliance as oppositional to the forces of popular or collective values. He heralds the "brave lad"—the nascent great man—who can both remain independent of public opinion and transform it with his insights. Ten years later, in a journal passage that anticipates "Self-Reliance," Emerson identifies public opinion as one of the "hobgoblins" that smother individual thought: "It seems as if the present age of words should naturally be followed by an age of silence when men shall speak only through facts & so regain their health. We die of words. We are hanged, drawn, & quartered by dictionaries. We walk in the vale of shadows. It is an age of hobgoblins. Public Opinion is a hobgoblin, Christianity a hobgoblin, the God of popular worship a hobgoblin. When shall we attain to be real & be born into the new heaven & earth of nature & truth?" (*JMN* 7:240). Emerson diagnoses as cant the endless chatter that forms the basis of popular beliefs. Tocqueville worried that popular opinion would create a political force impeding democracy by strengthening the majority and stifling opposition. Emerson's concerns are less overtly political. He sees that public opinion and other "hobgoblins" impede the advance of truth among the people. As they distort reality, Emerson's hobgoblins are the counterparts to Barnum's humbugs, without either the playfulness or the promise of providing something else of value. Why can Emerson respect public opinion as a culture-making power in 1828 and then dismiss it as a "hobgoblin" ten years later? Emerson's change reflects, in part, his maturity and experience: by 1838 he had emerged on the public stage to much criticism and controversy. In addition, his early view regards public opinion as a register of universal currents, the moral law that governs human progress. In the 1838 view, however, he sees public opinion as a substance molded by circumstance and personality, and in his hope of "attain[ing] the real," he calls on the messianic presence of universal or impersonal truth among human society.

Among the factors that shape the "hobgoblin" of public opinion, spectacles and popular amusements especially rankle Emerson. Indeed, Emerson sees little fun in the kind of spectacular manipulations of nature that form the basis for many popular amusements. He regards popular amusements skeptically, as temptations to the greatest transgression imaginable: passive acceptance of surface appearances. Emerson tends to regard audiences as willingly stupefied by sensationalistic stunts and oddities rather than seeking the intellectual stimulation of genuine curiosities. Increasingly popular throughout the nineteenth century, the circus epitomized Emerson's distrust of spectacle for its own sake. In an illustrative journal entry, Emerson describes a circus he attended with his oldest son, Waldo: "I went to the circus & saw a man ride standing on the back of two galloping horses, a third horse being interposed between the two. As he rode, the sinews of his limbs played like those of his beasts. One horse brought a basket in his teeth, picked up a cap, & selected a card out of four. All wonder comes of showing an effect at two or three removes from the cause. Show us the two or three steps by which the horse was brought to fetch the basket, and the wonder would cease. But I & Waldo were of one mind when he said, 'It makes me want to go home'" (*JMN* 7:358). Emerson affirms the child's power of discernment, suggesting that maturation and socialization weaken individuals' ability to gauge the genuine. The discipline involved in self-reliance is in fact the careful calibration of the innate moral intuition that governs one's earliest responses to the world. As he writes in *Nature*, "few *adult* persons can see nature. . . . The sun illuminates only the eye of man, but shines into the eye and the heart of the child" (*CW* 1:9, emphasis added). Young Waldo's dissatisfaction with the circus riders therefore justifies his fathers'—but just what in the performance dissatisfies the two of them? The typical circus stunts Emerson describes, tricks of horsemanship and displays of equine intelligence, entertain the crowds by symbolically inverting understood hierarchies that elevate human beings above brute animals.[38] The performance satirizes the values that shape social hierarchy, including the display of the physical body, the body's service to physically demanding activities, and claims to higher forms of reason. But Emerson is unresponsive to such satirical critique: he is less interested in effects than their causes, preferably their First Cause. Later, in "Fate," Emerson returns to the image of the circus rider as a metaphor of double consciousness: "A man must ride alternately on the horses of his private and his public nature, as the equestrians in the circus throw themselves nimbly from horse to horse, or plant one foot on the back of one, and the other foot on the back of the other" (*CW* 6:25). The quotation speaks to the central dilemma of publicity as experienced by Emerson and others in the period. The public self is of a different "nature" than the private self, and transitioning between the two spheres of being requires certain psychological and rhetorical dexterity. Physical expression matters for Emerson as a metaphor of subjectivity wherein contingencies of persons give way to abstractions of higher truth.

Emerson is not immune to the pleasures of public amusement; he enjoys performances that metaphorically express the truths he constantly seeks. But the tensions between public expression and private character, or between spectacle and genuineness, are always present. For instance, in 1841 he saw a performance by the celebrated ballerina Fanny Elssler. He appreciated her dancing as physical eloquence, the work of a poet of the body, so to speak. In his reflections on the performance, however, Emerson more directly addresses the anxiety about erotic physical display and its effects on observers that is muted in his consideration of the trick riders at the circus:

> But over & above her genius for dancing are the incidental vices of this individual, her own false taste or her meretricious arts to please the groundlings & which must displease the judicious. The immorality the immoral will see, the very immoral will see that only, the pure will not heed it, for it is not obtrusive, perhaps will not see it at all. . . . I can easily suppose that it is not the safest resort for college boys who have left Metaphysics, Conic Sections, or Tacitus to see these tripping satin slippers and they may not forget this graceful silvery swimmer when they have retreated again to their baccalaureate cells. (*JMN* 8:110–11)

Just what, exactly, the "immoral" and the college boys will see in Elssler's dancing, Emerson does not care to enumerate, but it is likely that he worries about the very consciousness of the body that the dance evokes and that might arouse the young men to sexual transgression in their "baccalaureate cells." In this concern, he touches lightly on the associations between men's self-mastery and republican citizenship that motivates contemporary anti-onanist discourse.[39] The problem is compounded for Emerson by the ways the dancer seems to encourage such responses in the audience. He suggests her performance is more than a spectacle or display, but a form of communication between dancer and audience. Like all forms of eloquence, this physical discourse ought to be handled carefully. Failing to "uplift" her audience, Elssler engages an exhibitionism more dangerous than the circus performer's, because it courts approval by arousing desire. Consciously or not, the presence and display of the female form threatens to bring the young men who observe her into a fuller physicality, thereby undermining their quest for impersonal truth and virtue.[40]

Emerson believed that a too-great attention to persons could potentially take the form of public eroticism. Only idealized as expression of divine truth can Elssler's dancing be understood as eloquent. Emerson is concerned with the uses audience members make of public men and women: do they attempt to discern how the card trick is affected, or the genius of Elssler's movements? More importantly, will they be able to leave these performers behind—return to their

Metaphysics and Conic Sections, as it were? While Emerson recognizes genius in Elssler's dancing, he could not ultimately acknowledge it as great, because it does not help the spectator out of himself—it does not liberate him from the "hobgoblin" of mass culture or popular opinion. The erotic response to her may be individual in that it occurs to each man singularly, but when enacted on the mass scale it becomes grotesque. In "The Uses of Great Men," he describes the human aggregate in vivid imagery: "Enormous populations, if they be beggars, are disgusting, like moving cheese, like hills of ants, or of fleas,—the more, the worse" (*CW* 4:4). The young men watching the dancer, reduced to instinct and appetite, are equally disgusting. If mass culture is the site where pleasure is regulated,[41] Emerson would prefer stricter controls. He would have audiences disassociate the body from the material world of sensory stimuli and regard it as symbolic.

As the reference to "The Uses of Great Men" suggests, Emerson's concerns about public persons' influence are not limited to popular amusements but extend into their social, political, aesthetic, and spiritual lives as well. Indeed, Emerson's concerns about the circus and dance indicate that he resists dismissing such events as mere amusements. In this respect, he takes mass culture as seriously as anyone. Conversely, his most sophisticated lectures and essays resist the influence of social reformers whose zeal paradoxically trivializes their purposes. It is as though Emerson resists spectacle precisely because he recognizes its significance in unifying an audience in a shared pleasure. These shared experiences can give undue attention to the trivial or trivialize matters of political import, and in each case, spectacle creates a moral obstacle to self-reliance. In the introductory lecture on "The Times" and "Self-Reliance," Emerson justifies his turning away from abolitionism, temperance, and other philanthropic causes because, in their failure to abstract the ideas behind their efforts from the persons involved in their movements, they encourage intellectual and social conformity. Reformers, he argues, rely "on men, on multitudes, on circumstances, on money, on party; that is, on fear, on wrath, and pride" rather than the moral sentiments. They fail to recognize "that then are we strongest, when most private and alone" (*CW* 1:176). We are strongest when alone presumably because solitude allows us to see truth unclouded by personalities, money, and other circumstances. "Self-Reliance" is based on the allied premise that "nothing is at last sacred but the integrity of your own mind" (*CW* 2:30)—not the antislavery or equal rights movements, or even Christian ministry. "I am ashamed to think how easily we capitulate to badges and names, to large societies and dead institutions," he claims with a tone of defiance and confession mixed, continuing: "Every decent and well-spoken individual affects and sways me more than is right. I ought to go upright and vital, and speak the rude truth in all ways. . . . If an angry bigot assumes this bountiful cause of Abolition, and comes to me with his last news from Barbadoes, why should I not say to him, 'Go love thy infant; love thy wood-chopper: be good-natured and modest: have that grace; and never varnish your hard, uncharitable ambition with this incredible tenderness for black folk a thousand miles off. Thy love afar is spite at home'" (*CW* 2:30). The apparent hard-heartedness of the passage's idealized self-reliant individual represents the most unsavory aspect of Emerson's impersonal philosophy, its potential disregard for human suffering. But the passage's speaker confesses his very susceptibility to sympathetic appeal. He braces himself against these appeals because they threaten to flood his sensibilities and overwhelm his impersonal judgment. Emerson is concerned about an activist zeal that is blind to immediate relations; in overpersonalizing "black folk a thousand miles off," the abolitionist ignores the "rude truth" of human relations closer to home. This is not to defend Emerson's ambivalence about race but to point out the depth of his regard for individual moral authority and his confidence in the meliorative influence of the impersonal on the individual.[42] By undertaking the impersonal reckoning Emerson advocates here, the activist can in fact improve personal ties, renewing what elsewhere he calls the "moral sentiments" that are, in fact, forms of love. Emerson's judgments are clear if harsh: cooperation with social movements that are intrinsically flawed is a kind of conformity. Like the thrill of a circus stunt, it relies on miscalculation of the significance of persons at the expense of intellectual clarity.

In "The Uses of Great Men," Emerson claims that the great man is "greater, when he can abolish himself, and all heroes, by letting in this element of reason, irrespective of persons" (*CW* 4:14). Reason abnegates the self, all selves, in the attainments of the impersonal truth. This argument is especially salient in the context of a mass culture that prizes spectacle and persons, in the sense of both bodies and personalities. While Emerson wrote and lectured about "the infinitude of the private man," he did so in the face of a culture that mistook the public personality for the materialized self. One way he addresses this phenomenon is by referring to public men as "persons," whose allure he acknowledges but whose meaning he questions. In the controversial Divinity School "Address," for instance, he argues that, instead of reflecting on the truths Jesus teaches, "historical Christianity . . . has dwelt, it dwells, with noxious exaggeration about the *person* of Jesus" (*CW* 1:82). Emerson alludes to theological questions about Christ as expressing both human and divine characteristics, and he criticizes a Christianity that emphasizes such questions to the exclusion of cultivating the truths Jesus represents. Emerson continues, "The soul knows no persons. It invites every man to expand to the full circle of the universe, and will have no preferences but those of spontaneous love." Emerson's critique of "historical Christianity" is concerned with the formalism and ritualization of Christian practice, which elevates Jesus as a "demigod, as the Orientals or the Greeks would describe Osiris or Apollo." Instead of guiding worshippers to venerate icons, Emerson urges his clerical audience to encourage religious self-reliance: "That which shows God in me, fortifies me" (*CW* 1:82). For Emerson, the emphasis on God's humanity in the "*person* of Jesus" does not make God more recognizable or approachable. Instead, it creates a distance between the faithful and the deity that can be spanned only by an intermediary. Worshippers fail to recognize the God within because they focus instead on God as accessed through the person of Jesus.

In the Divinity School "Address," Emerson advocates Unitarianism's evolving into the religious expression of self-reliance, rejecting imitative, conformist worship. "Dare to love God without mediator or veil": Emerson presses the continued "reformation of the Reformation" (*JMN* 3:70). As in his other treatments of self-reliance, he acknowledges the difficulties. To go alone is to trade "the commendation of society" for "the influx of the all-knowing Spirit"—or a secular pleasure for a sacred one (*CW* 1:90, 91). Although the Divinity School "Address" concerns questions of theology and pastoral practice, his analysis of Unitarian orthodoxy reveals an overlap between religion and celebrity culture. In a secular society, celebrity is often regarded as a substitute for religion. Chris Rojek accounts for the connection: whereas traditional religion "addresses the fundamental questions of being in the world," celebrity "is now one of the mainstays of organizing recognition and belonging in secular society."[43] In this analysis, religion explains the appeal of celebrity. In the Divinity School "Address," however, we can see how celebrity explains religion—how the veneration of persons in the secular sense can resemble the veneration of persons in the theological sense. Emerson indicates that the result is ritual, performance, and mediation, all of which cut off individuals from the God they seek and give them instead a person they desire.

Emerson's introductory lecture on "The Times" similarly explores a culture-wide interest in persons, one that more directly responds to celebrity culture. Here, he draws on another notion of "persons": "What is the reason to be given for this extreme attraction which *persons* have for us, but that they are the Age? they are the results of the Past; they are the heralds of the Future. They indicate,—these witty, suffering, blushing, intimidating figures of the only race in which there are individuals or changes, how far on the Fate has gone, and what it drives at. . . . How I follow them with aching heart, with pining desire! I count myself nothing before them" (*CW* 1:168–69). The passage captures the complex, affective relationship between the individual and a public figure. The erotic power and charisma of the public person carries through an eloquence of word and gesture; to the observer, body and mind seem united and, as a result, the public figure is doubly attractive. But the passage also hints at Emerson's eventual rebellion from this affective trap, in which the subject is diminished, even annihilated, by the object of his desire. Emerson cautions against the stupefying pleasures of observing such persons: "But we are not permitted to stand as spectators at the pageant which the times exhibit: we are parties also, and have a responsibility which is not to be declined. A little while this interval of wonder and comparison is to be permitted us, but to the end that we shall play a manly part" (*CW* 1:171). Emerson's language reflects his dissatisfaction with a public life that is merely spectacular and that encourages individuals to become passive observers rather than critical participants. The "manly part" he advocates is the critical effort of seeing through the spectacle of persons to the reality of the self, to "unmask the king as he passes" (*CW* 1:171). Thus in a span of a few pages, Emerson rejects the celebrity culture in which personality and affect "deceive" people with erotic promise.

In their different ways, both the Divinity School "Address" and the lecture on "The Times" speak to the seemingly religious appeal of the charismatic person and the ways his irrational, erotic appeal circumvents the self. Emerson is not opposed to irrational power—his theory of self-reliance privileges spontaneous insight—but his concern is with *persons*, the attention and even devotion to a public figure as the embodiment of ideas. More specifically, he is concerned about mediation: he would rather "read God directly" than through a medium, even if that medium be Jesus Christ himself. Similarly, the devotion to charismatic persons inhibits observers' firsthand engagement with the ideas and experiences the persons represent. Emerson anticipates postmodernists who argue that mass media and other forms of spectacle tend to intervene in human experience, substituting real experience for a simulation.[44] Emerson's concerns about mediation are reflected in his own oratorical style and practice. While he sought a role of public influence, he attempted also to craft an oratory that deemphasized his person and focused the audience's attention on his language and ideas. In doing so, he deliberately countered the prevailing culture, which, emphasizing personality, implicitly understood the medium and the message to be one.

Emerson takes measure of the public scene he is himself entering, attempting to set the terms for his own reception. His decision first to leave the pulpit and then to become a public lecturer reflects his drive for popular success and influence. Bosco and Myerson point out that, as an "entrepreneurial individual," Emerson enjoyed financial success as a lecturer, but lecturing was "more than a financially driven alternative career." As a lecturer, they claim, Emerson "tried out 'Ralph Waldo Emerson,' the public persona he both adopted and was forced into by his audiences."[45] This passage conveys the push and pull of public identity in celebrity. Emerson's efforts to craft a public version of himself inevitably conflict with versions of himself circulating in the public sphere. As we have seen, Emerson's image was transmitted through press coverage he received—reviews of his lectures and books—and, eventually, biographies. Paradoxically, Emerson built his public identity on the principle of genuineness, the idea that his public utterances expressed his inner self without mediation. In this respect, Emerson was, ironically, a walking advertisement for his lectures and books, the living embodiment of the principles of self-reliant individualism and impersonal thinking that he advocated. Observers thus encountered the Emerson image, a mediated representation of Emerson, even as they sought—and often claimed to perceive in the image—the man himself.

Emerson's theory of eloquence highlights the paradox of his position as a speaker who performs genuineness—for whom authenticity is an art. Emerson had high appreciation and high ambitions for oratory as a public office and an important form of mass communication. He respected the orator as a person of tremendous influence over his audiences, and he understood the art of oratory to originate in the orator's ability to express truth with conviction and genuineness. "Genuine" expression was Emerson's primary goal, a concept he explained with references to heroes such as the Quaker George Fox. He quotes Fox more than once: "What I am in words, I am the same in life" (*JMN* 4:33, 37). On the lecture podium, that genuineness is both artful and spontaneous, and it follows from the speaker's ability to impart truth even as he receives it: "[A lecture] is an organ of sublime power, a panharmonicon for variety of note. But only then is the orator successful when he is himself agitated & is as much a hearer as any of the assembly. In that office you may & shall (please God!) yet see the electricity part from the cloud & shine from one part of heaven to another" (*JMN* 7:224–25). Identifying the orator as an auditor, Emerson evokes a unity between the speaker and his audience. But the crowd is not held rapt by his speech; all are in the thrall of the universal force as it is channeled through the speaker. Emerson uses a metaphor of electricity to convey this power.[46] As the conductor of this power, the orator must be receptive to the very truths that he is communicating to his audience, as if experiencing them for the first time. In "Intellect," he claims that the activities of the intellect can be either "receptive" or "constructive." The "intellect receptive" registers the material world; it is the primary mode of the self-reliant individual, who trusts his perceptions or feelings as registers of moral truth. The receptive intellect practices what George Kateb calls "mental or philosophical self-reliance," through which the individual maintains "the readiness to treat with sympathetic understanding ideas and values that have no sympathy for one another." This receptive thinking, Kateb explains, is democratic in that it recognizes that "each idea or value, practice or movement, has an equal right to exist, even if it does not have a right to an equal influence."[47] Emerson's oratorical practice attempts to enact or perform this model of mental activity. In the moment of oratorical utterance, it is as if the Emersonian speaker is allowing the impressions he has attained unconsciously to rise to the surface, so that he can put words to them for himself and his audience. Moreover, the facts that he then utters are not valuable as mere images or "impressions on the retentive organ" (*CW* 2:198); the language of the orator conveys the emotive force of those images or impressions. Witnessing the passion of the speaker, the audience is in turn impassioned—and persuaded of the speaker's genuineness.

As we have seen, descriptions of Emerson's lecturing attempt to convey this by emphasizing his body, especially his eyes and voice. That emphasis on his person actually recreates the very problem Emerson's impersonal method seeks to avoid, the problem of mediation. But how could it be otherwise? Sharon Cameron helps reconcile the seeming paradox of the embodied impersonal while also noting the potential for confusion. Explicating "The Over-soul," she notes the "incarnations" of the Over-soul in physical traits, "not separate from and also not equal to any particular trait, but also manifesting itself only through recognizable peculiarities." These physical manifestations of impersonal power can, she notes, lead to confusion: "In fact, it could be argued that it is the Over-soul's visibility *in* action, function, property, and person that permits us to mistake action, function, property, person for the manifestational power which animates them."[48] From an Emersonian standpoint, this error helps explain the "attraction to persons" that shapes celebrity culture. The physical manifestations of the impersonal may best be illustrated by Emerson's portrait of Napoleon, whose accomplishments owe as much to his physical vigor as to his receptive powers: "He had a directness of action never before combined with so much comprehension" (*CW* 4:133–34). In his own career as a lecturer, Emerson similarly serves as a kind of a vessel for the universal, impersonal authority—a representative of genuineness. But he is less a mediator of the universal authority than a transmitter of it, because he does not presume to alter its content by his delivery of it.

To what extent does Emerson succeed at enacting his philosophy? Certainly his eloquence of genuineness involves a fiction—a fiction of immediacy. It presumes that the speaker is himself transparent, a hearer rather than a speaker. It denies that the speaker exists for his audience as a personality—that is, as an image or assembly of signs that incorporates his words. In accounting for Emerson's eloquence, however, it becomes clear that the personality is ever present, and that even in his performance of selflessness, Emerson exerts a charismatic appeal over his audiences. Moreover, his efforts from the platform can seem quite manipulative. Transformation, not manipulation, is the goal of an oratory rooted in Unitarianism and the self-culture movement, and that goal presupposes the authority of the speaker to inspire change, if not bring it about through his art.[49] Along these lines, John H. Sloan has emphasized the "miraculous uplifting" that characterizes Emerson's relationship to his audience: "Rejecting the notion that the speaker should adapt by 'lowering his thought' to the level of the audience, Emerson proposed that the auditors should adapt by identifying themselves with the idealized concepts of the speaker."[50] The observation takes for granted that the speaker and audience are separated by a disparity of intellectual ability and personal achievement, and it assumes the constant risk of communication's failure. Sympathy might overcome that disparity, and Emerson had various techniques for achieving it. Shuffling his manuscript pages and pausing between words and sentences exhibited his "genius in creating a sense of spontaneity on the platform."[51] In fact, Emerson mastered these gestures with practice. In reminiscences of their father, both Ellen Emerson and Edith Emerson Forbes detail his habits of reciting poetry during walks and rehearsing the children's school recitations with them.[52] In addition to honing his performance techniques, Emerson might appropriate popular forms of discourse to suit his purposes or use the first personal plural form of address to "take sides" with his audiences. These are techniques Emerson developed as a preacher, and in his lecturing they amount to a "dialectical eloquence" that synthesizes Emerson's ideas with those of his audiences.[53] Audience members begin to recognize higher truths through their sympathetic identification with the speaker. When the sympathetic connection is strong, however, it can have a power of its own not clearly associated with the larger concerns of the lecture. Emerson's theory of eloquence does not acknowledge the risk of listeners' overidentifying with the orator at the expense of receiving higher truths. This risk is especially striking in Eric Cheyfitz's account of Emersonian eloquence, which argues that the Emerson lecture is less a dialectic of reason and sympathy than a seduction, and that as lecturer Emerson plays the ultramasculine role of coercing listeners to take his side.[54] The lecture-as-seduction coaxes and teases the audience, unifying all present in erotically charged sympathy—not exactly the grounds for intellectual receptivity.

It is difficult to imagine that a seduction like this could be analogous to an intellectual "uplifting" or that the erotic charge could somehow be made impersonal. Considering Emerson's concerns about the erotic effects of performances such as Elssler's, it is difficult to believe he sought a similar effect as an orator. Moreover, the idea of Emerson's seductive oratorical power contrasts with the emotional impotence and discomfort with his body that he frequently associates with his personal character. In the journals he commonly characterizes any feeling of emotional inadequacy or discomfort as a physical sensation rooted in his body. His ambivalence about his physical self permeates an 1839 journal entry that both confirms the correlations between rhetorical and physical power and laments that his power as an orator does not carry into his daily life:

> S[arah] M[argaret] F[uller] writes me that she waits for the Lectures seeing well after much intercourse that the best of me is there. She says very truly; & I thought it a good remark which somebody repeated here from S[amuel] S[taples] that I "always seemed to be on stilts". It is even so. Most of the persons whom I see in my own house I see across a gulf. I cannot go to them nor they come to me. . . . And yet in one who sets his mark so high, who presumes so vast an elevation as the birthright of man, is it not a little sad to be a mere mill or pump yielding one wholesome product at the mouth in one particular mode but as impertinent & worthless in any other place or purpose as a pump or a coffee mill would be in a parlor or a chapel? (*JMN* 7:301–2)

In a telling gloss on Fuller's comment, Emerson understands that the "best" self who appears on the lecture platform is his best physical self—comfortable in his own body, not awkward or "on stilts"—and he acknowledges a "gulf" between himself and others in his own home but not in the lecture hall. He fuses the intellectual performance with the physical appearance, revealing his consciousness of lecturing as a physical action. By contrast, the social conversation was uncomfortable perhaps because it was trivial and ornamental as feminized domestic life in general; it lacked the "heroism" that characterized manly public speech.[55] In this domesticated oral context, he represents himself as scatological and debilitated, unable to control his verbal product—but this physical failure also reassures him of his budding genius in his lecturing career.[56] The observation of Emerson's power as a lecturer coming from Margaret Fuller is especially interesting considering the erotic charge of their highly intellectual friendship—like lecturing, another instance of physical and intellectual conflation.[57] However, the fact that their charge was neutralized by Emerson's "inhospitality of soul" (*JMN* 7:509) suggests that Emerson remained "on stilts" with Fuller as with others. The "gulf" between him and others that is an advantage in the lecture hall is an impediment in the parlor; only on the lecture platform, before a mass audience, can he trust his powers and express himself as physically vigorous and controlled.

Distinguishing the lecture hall from the parlor, or the public sphere from the private, Emerson associates the public sphere with a mastery of his own body and language as well as of their effects on others. In "The American Scholar" Emerson urges the scholar to balance the solitude of reading and reflection with the action in the social world. His intellectual geography allows for no in-betweens: it is privacy or publicity, solitude or action, binaries he represents as natural as the inhalation—or inspiration—and exhalation of breath. But the imposition of social and personal obligations is a tragic distraction and detour from these binaries. In the feminized "middle social sphere," the semipublic, semiprivate setting of the parlor,[58] Emerson confesses confusion; he cannot ride the two horses at the same time, and so he struggles to balance the natural expression a domestic scene invites with the performative expression of the lecture hall. The obligations of the parlor are, for Emerson, feminized, embodied, and deceitful, forever embarrassing him with their unpracticed candor.

All this is to say that Emerson rejects the idea that body and self are the same, even as he acknowledges that the body is the link to nature, the scene of his most productive solitude and the locus of impersonal power. Emerson's worries about his body's expressiveness in social settings do not affect his confidence in its receptivity to the material world of nature. It is important to notice that sense perceptions, themselves rooted in the body, govern Emerson's discovery of truth and hence self-reliance. In the transparent eyeball passage of *Nature*, for instance, Emerson provides a richly sensuous response to the material world: "I feel that nothing can befal me in life,—no disgrace, no calamity, (leaving me my eyes,) which nature cannot repair. Standing on the bare ground,—my head bathed by the blithe air, and uplifted into infinite space,—all mean egotism vanishes. I become a transparent eye-ball, I am nothing, I see all. The currents of the Universal Being circulate through me; I am part or particle of God" (*CW* 1:10). In the moment of transcendence, the subject of the passage surely forgets his physical self and attains an impersonal knowledge of truth. The language of the passage reveals that that forgetfulness is made possible by the body itself and its receptivity to the stimulation of the physical world—the blithe air that bathes his head, the very acuity of his vision.[59] Such a moment leaves Emerson with no anxiety about his body as a vehicle for spiritual transformation, because his is the only human form he has to contend with. The problem for Emerson is apparently one of context and expectations; it is a problem not of bodies themselves but of bodies in relation to one another, in the lecture hall and in the parlor, contexts in which there are almost always elements of display and observation, expression and desire. He announces this anxiety early in his journals as a concern, for instance, for his blushing, which he relates to failed self-discipline. Comparing his own "silliness" to his brother Edward's seriousness, Emerson writes in 1828, "Edward had always great power of face. I have none" (*JMN* 3:137). Like his worries that in company he cannot regulate his speech, this confession reflects a concern with others' perceptions of him, which he is helpless to influence as his physical body broadcasts his feelings of disinterest or discomfort without his consent.[60] In his maturity, the imperative to master his physical expression leads him to distrust appeals to sentiment as overly sensational and intellectually weak.

Annie Adams Fields recalls Emerson's hilarity at a reading of Dickens: "he had laughed as if he might crumble to pieces, his face wearing an expression of absolute pain." After recovering himself, Emerson critiques Dickens's failure to balance his talent with "genius": "he is too consummate an artist to have a thread of nature left."[61] It is a telling remark. Emerson rejects Dickens for the very reason so many loved him: his skill in generating affect. His fictions exert a charismatic appeal that emanates from the artist himself, not an impersonal source, and as a result they dominate the reader emotionally. Emerson is embarrassed by his own mirth as it subjugates him, body and mind, to the "locomotive" of Dickens's talent.[62] In Emerson's oratory of genuineness, by contrast, he would circumvent the body, impersonalize himself, and segregate the spiritual from the material even while responding to concerns raised by the material world of nature.

Emerson's distrust of his own body's rebellious fragility endears genuine expression to him as the most promising means of successful communication. The lyceum was the most likely forum for enacting it. The end point of Emersonian self-culture is to become one "who in the midst of the crowd keeps with perfect sweetness the independence of solitude" (*CW* 2:31). In achieving such a masterful, self-mastering state, one need not dizzy himself with the oscillations between society and solitude—he need not withdraw at all. To maintain the sweetness of solitude in the midst of the crowd would be to enter a transparent state in which not just egotism but also personality vanishes: the face, the body, the gestures cease to exist as signifiers and dissolve into the universal or "Over-soul" they bespeak. Just as Emerson's scholar is one "who raises himself from private considerations," his great man is one who, like Napoleon, "almost ceases to have a private speech and opinion" (*CW* 1:62, 4:131). Yet rather than indicating a lack of depth, this loss of the private indicates the union of the great man with the impersonal, universal forces that constitute a public greater than the masses he addresses.

EMERSON RETAINS HIS REPUTATION AS A SAGACIOUS ADVOCATE FOR NON-conformity and a spokesman for the divine-in-self in an increasingly secular culture. But his critique of contemporary mass culture remains muted. His appraisal of Jacksonian laissez-faire capitalism and the materialism it promoted was, at best, deeply complicated by his commitment to an ameliorative "long-term teleology of change."[63] At worst, the structure of Emerson's "individualism defines freedom as submission to unmodifiable law," paradoxically limiting the very freedom it claims to secure.[64] Looked at another way, Emerson's impersonal philosophy is limited by its inability to fully account for persons: "If one tries to answer the question What is a person? no answer with any coherent substance can be produced with reference to Emerson's writing."[65] Perhaps for this reason contemporary audiences looked to Emerson's own person for coherence. But that fact leads to yet another failure: his contemporaries' intense focus on his person, and on his personality, leads to the misunderstanding of his message of self-reliance. Considering the vigor and consistency of Emerson's admonitions against slavish attention to persons, his celebrity is deeply ironic; it reflects his audience's capitulation to his own name and badge. But it is not only ironic. It is also revealing of the great difficulty in attaining self-reliance, of the challenges of Emerson's eloquence, and the transformative effects of public life for both the public person and the audience that observes him. Despite the clarity of Emerson's message of self-reliance and aversion to personal influence, audiences' continued and increasing reverence for him corroborates claims that he was popularly misunderstood. Why is this so? What did audiences think he was saying? Certainly it is true that Emerson did not speak explicitly on self-reliance every time he took to the podium, but it nevertheless makes no sense to conclude that audiences would celebrate a speaker whose very words they found incomprehensible.

Ultimately, I see two sets of responses to celebrity culture at work in Emerson's career. The first is the personal response that made Emerson a celebrity—the attention to not only his words but also his body and manner. Emerson's celebrity reflects the cultural tendency to regard public persons as physical manifestations of selfhood. Just what that self is—who Emerson is—is subject to debate. Misunderstanding Emerson results, in part, from his unorthodox ideas and complex writing style; Emerson challenges convention in the names of intellectual freedom and self-reliance, and he uses the ensuing scandals to bring light to the ideas he expresses. Misunderstanding results, also, from the diversity of audiences and texts in play: as participants in the personal public sphere, they respond to the image of the public figure that includes his body and representations of his character in tandem with his lectures and essays. Interestingly, Emerson's first biographers use the same methods of interpreting Emerson as the mass audiences do—they attend to his person as a text, reading in it the signs of the fundamental self. But they seek a definitive Emerson, eliminating the variety of responses that circulate through the personal public sphere. Their responses are therefore authoritarian, not democratic, in their rejection of a diverse and changeable popular opinion.

The second response to celebrity culture comes from Emerson himself. Like his biographers, he is skeptical of public opinion and a personal response to public figures, but for different reasons. Emerson does not want to close off debate; rather, he finds the debates in the personal public sphere to be methodologically insufficient, leading to inadequate understanding of the public figures in question. Perhaps because he practiced the performance of genuineness in his lecturing, Emerson recognized that personality is not transparent; it is a mediating agent that changes the substance—self, truth—that it presumes to convey. While not a direct response to the culture of personality, Emerson's impersonal method would avoid its pitfalls, and it would generate other results, too. Specifically, impersonal inquiry would reorganize our relationships to others in the public sphere, as it would require us to regard them not as persons (bodies manifesting inner qualities of self) or personalities (projected images of self). Instead, we could attempt to discern their relationship to impersonal universal truths. Emerson's impersonal would, moreover, reorganize our relationship to self. If the goal of self-reliance is to maintain in the midst of the crowd the assurances of solitude, responding to impersonal authority would, in a sense, erase one's person and transform oneself into an abstract self even when physically present to others. Oddly enough, in his reception as a "mystic," "sage," "genius," or even as a joke, Emerson attains the kind of transcendent abstract status he seeks—though these versions of his own transcendent selfhood derive from the responses—individual, popular, and indeed unpopular—to various combinations of his physical and verbal texts.

Emerson's discomfort with mass culture reflects his assumptions of and anxiety for his authority as a universal male subject. Audience authority imposes a limit on his own and requires him to acknowledge not simply the diversity of the public sphere but more pertinently the legitimacy of others' claims to social and cultural authority. Perhaps his dissatisfaction with popular amusements such as the circus is ultimately inconsequential. Of greater significance, he reportedly blocked Frederick Douglass's membership in the Town and Country Club, a fraternal association of Boston's intellectual elite.[66] If this story is true, it indicates the degree to which Emerson associated intellectual authority, masculine community, and social belonging with Anglo-Saxonism. Douglass is unlikely to have been aware of the snub, though he surely experienced others of which he was conscious. Though an astute reader of Emerson, Douglass had none of Emerson's assurances of citizenship; he could not, therefore, afford Emerson's skepticism of mass culture. In the next chapter, I turn to Douglass and his use of celebrity to help him claim the privileges of national manhood denied him by his race.

CHAPTER 4

FREDERICK DOUGLASS
Celebrity, Privacy, and the Embodied Self

On August 11, 1841, Frederick Douglass spoke before the convention of the Massachusetts Anti-Slavery Society at Nantucket, Massachusetts. The occasion was not Douglass's debut as a public speaker; his remarks at an antislavery meeting in New Bedford just two days before had earned him an invitation to Nantucket, and, indeed, Douglass had been honing his oratorical skills since his years in slavery.[1] Douglass's Nantucket appearance nevertheless takes on symbolic importance in his story as the moment at which he became a public figure. It was the first time that William Lloyd Garrison heard Douglass speak, as he reflects in his introduction to Douglass's *Narrative*: "I shall never forget his first speech at the convention—the extraordinary emotion it excited in my own mind—the powerful impression it created upon a crowded auditory, *completely taken by surprise*—the applause which followed from the beginning to the end of his felicitous remarks."[2] This notion of surprise is fundamental to Douglass's career as a public lecturer and antislavery activist: everything about his public performances was at variance with the social expectations and racial presumptions of his audiences. For his part, Douglass played on the rhetorical uses of his surprising publicity in various ways, presenting himself as an eloquent former slave, a mocking critic of slavery's logical inconsistencies, and a defiant outsider to the cultural privileges associated with white nationalism.

Douglass's Nantucket speech initiated his new career as a lecturer, first for the Massachusetts Anti-Slavery Society and then, from 1842, for the American Anti-Slavery Society (AASS). Throughout the 1840s, Douglass rose from obscurity to local notice, then, with the publication of his *Narrative* in 1845, he became a celebrity of the first order. Significantly, Douglass's emergence on the national stage coincides with Emerson's growing celebrity. I have argued that Emerson's message as a public speaker was complicated by audiences' responses to his physical presence on the lecture platform. For Douglass, the significance of his physical presence is shaped by his specific experience in ways that did not affect Emerson or, indeed, most popular lecturers of the moment. Emerson exemplifies a privileged form of public participation made possible in part by an intensely felt and carefully guarded privacy. The case is far different for Douglass, for whom attaining personhood is impossible. Karen Sanchez-Eppler has argued that "for both women and blacks" in the public spheres of abolition and women's rights, "their physical difference from the cultural norms of white masculinity obstructs their claim to personhood." For black public speakers, the physical self can never be forgotten or ignored: "the body of the slave attains the status of a text" by virtue of both the scars of slavery and, according to medical pseudoscience, through anatomical structures that supposedly suit the black body to socially inferior labor and status.[3] Audiences' responses to black public speakers inevitably conform to prejudgments based on their racialized expectations, which rule out the black speakers' authority to participate in the debates of the public sphere, let alone to possess the "genius" commonly ascribed to Emerson. In addition, we have seen that popular amusements such as Barnum's "What Is It?" promote forms of spectatorship that objectify and interrogate black bodies. The cultural associations of selfhood and citizenship with whiteness imply that Douglass is not merely an exceptional figure but indeed a curiosity. Facing the obstacles to personhood via the public sphere, Douglass charts an alternative path via the private sphere. He does so by making his private life, and the private lives of slaves in general, conspicuous in his writing even as he declines to describe them in detail.

Douglass acknowledges the prevailing skepticism about his authority to speak. He recalls, for instance, how the white leaders of the AASS presented him to audiences: "I was a 'graduate from the peculiar institution,' Mr. Collins used to say, when introducing me, '*with my diploma written on my back!*'" (*DA* 365; italics in original). The body is evidence of slavery's abuses and a rhetorical tool for condemning them. Metaphorically, Douglass reveals his scars by telling his story, but over time he resists even this rhetorical form of exposure, which limits his public identity and subject matter to his experience in bondage. He resists being made a Barnumesque side show, an exhibit that reinforces the authority of the white gaze. Throughout his career, audiences' inability to regard him as a person—their consistent focus on his embodied social and racial difference—reminds him of the distance that remains between freedom's promise and its realization. Writing therefore was extremely important to Douglass's self-fashioning. In his three autobiographies and voluminous journalistic writings, Douglass took advantage of print's ability to disseminate an abstract, disembodied authorial presence.[4] Moreover, both the slave narrative as a genre and his role within the Garrisonian movement constrained his ability to tell his story in his own terms and shake off racialized expectations of his story and his telling of it.[5] Douglass's career-long effort to control his personal story is therefore an effort to establish and maintain freedom beyond the nominal freedom from bondage that he effects with his escape; it is an effort to control his public image, which was forged under the specific conditions of mid-nineteenth-century celebrity culture.

As Douglass himself notes in the 1845 *Narrative*, his first steps into freedom were marked by his acquisition of literacy, and his exercise of rhetoric remains his most important method of asserting and practicing his freedom. Schooling himself and then his companions in bondage, Douglass commits crimes against the slave code and establishes a pattern he would follow throughout his career. Casting himself as a heroic figure in his early autobiographies, and as a self-made man in his late *Life and Times*, Douglass consistently represents a pattern of defiance and transgression as the means to self-development and freedom. Significantly, each of his acts of transgression brings Douglass farther into the public sphere—that is, the specific nature of his transgression is crossing the threshold between public and private spheres. He remains apparently unconcerned that he is regarded as a curiosity, recognizing instead that his public life brings him freedom that is renewed and expanded with each additional act.

The fact that Douglass identified freedom with celebrity is ironic. For contemporary figures, including Emerson, celebrity limited freedom by introducing competing interpretations of the public figure that threatened to undermine his goals. The celebrity's availability to a seemingly voracious marketplace led to the celebrity's "consumption" by the public comparable to the slave system's consumption of its human chattel.[6] But Douglass had not been consumed by slavery; he had survived it. His confrontational rhetoric encouraged competing interpretations of his meaning as a speaker and as a public figure. In these conflicts of interpretation, Douglass exposes and exploits a different parallel between slavery and celebrity, namely, the inscrutability of the objectified person. He generated meaning by exposing the discord of interpretations surrounding himself as a public figure and the black people, slave and free, whom he represented. The work of the critic John Ernest demonstrates the relationship between Douglass's uncertain identity as a black writer and his celebrity. He argues that the work of the slave narrative does not provide a comprehensive or definitive public identity: "writing one's way out of one racially inscribed identity does not mean that one has reached a free discursive space in which one can assert complete control over one's own story, and thereby over one's identity. But if one cannot escape, one can still teach one's readers to recognize how all-encompassing the prison is, and just how many are contained within its walls."[7] The slave narrator can draw attention to the ways that racially based notions of selfhood shape black identity, even if it cannot prevent the formation of such prejudicial interpretations. Indeed, as Ernest goes on to argue in *Liberation Historiography*, the complex framework of racial and ethnological ideologies that shape mainstream white culture generates a "multiply contingent selfhood" of the black author or speaker. In such a context, "each act, word, and gesture can be understood as a kind of performance (sometimes habitual, sometimes self-conscious) that is completed or fulfilled only when others, from a variety of cultural positions, respond appropriately. Viewed in this light, one's social identity is always delayed and in danger of being undermined as one's performance awaits verifying responses, reciprocal performances, in the field of social relations, responses that might well contradict one another."[8] Ernest's notion of performative identity suggests that every black figure is, to some degree, a public figure. Extending his analysis, I would point out that black public figures such as Douglass are always encountering the circumstances associated with celebrity, in which the meaning of the public figure is never absolute. Because the public is itself a pluralistic entity, its judgments are as well, and the celebrity's meaning is the subject of debates that parallel those over specific civic concerns. Ernest's discussion of the public's contradictory responses to the black public figure so nearly resembles the dynamics of celebrity that it is now possible to consider how celebrity can recreate even for white public figures the multiply contingent selfhood experienced by the nonwhite public figure.

One of Douglass's achievements is to recognize the potential rhetorical uses of controversy and multiple interpretations of his public self in generating productive exchanges that challenge and perhaps reform popular opinion. At the same time, he understands his own acts of physical and verbal defiance as essential expressions of self that were in themselves antithetical to slavery. Significantly, Douglass never considers freedom to be a purely political achievement. He distinguishes the slave from the man—an assertion of identity in the face of ideologies that denied the slave any sense of personhood. Douglass's defiance of social norms for public behavior and expression are part of a practice of selfhood that was crucial to Douglass's understanding of freedom, itself not an end point or constant status but an ongoing process that required regular renewal and exercise or else it would be lost.

Douglass's practice of freedom took the shape of public acts and expression. On one level, Douglass's publicity magnifies the processes of freedom that each individual must undergo. In this sense, Douglass's career dramatizes the individualism of the self-made man he eventually holds up as a hero. On another level, Douglass's aggressive publicity is a necessary antidote to the intense privacy that characterizes the slaves' condition. The designation of the slave as chattel restricts him or her to the private property and use of the slave master; the slave is associated with the accumulated property of the household and the complex familial dynamics of the plantation's emotional economy. As Douglass frequently points out, publicity undermined slavery's power: "Slavery is one of those monsters of darkness to whom the light of truth is death," he explains.[9] Through his public life and work, his celebrity, Douglass attempts to untangle the emotional, economic, and ideological ties that restrain him and confine him and other black Americans to a privacy so thorough as to render them invisible even as they are always embodied in the American public sphere.

Douglass's publicity also has the power to control or redirect the public discourse about himself. Rather than allow himself to be consumed by the audience's curiosity-driven desire for him, Douglass's confrontational methods refocus the public discourse on individuals and issues outside of himself. He makes slave masters public figures, subject to public scrutiny and interpretation; he pulls them out from the protection of the private sphere and in the process erects a bubble of privacy around himself. The achievement of privacy is always a goal Douglass pursues through his aggressive public career. His efforts suggest that the abstraction of the self in the public sphere of civic debate is not the apex of freedom; rather, it is the attainment of a protected sphere of privacy, in which he may cultivate his interests—play his violin, if you will—raise his family without interference, and associate freely with men and women of his own choosing without comment. Douglass seeks a privacy made valuable, paradoxically, by its visibility: as a refuge from the active public life, Douglass's privacy reflects freedom fully developed and on par with that of middle-class white society.

THERE IS NO QUESTION THAT DOUGLASS'S CAREER HINGED ON HIS deliberate rise from anonymity and slavery to a self-consciously public role. Late in his life, Douglass capitalized on his remarkable story by recasting it into the popular lecture "Self-Made Men," which brought an Emersonian idealization of self-reliance and representative men into a tradition of black achievement, relaying it in a popular-lecture forum associated with Barnumesque self-promotion. Although Douglass does not recount his autobiography in the speech, Waldo Martin links Douglass's "Self-Made Men" to the "heroic vision of himself" that he crafts in each of his three autobiographies. In Douglass's myth of heroism, Martin points out, race plays an important role; Douglass used "Self-Made Men" to publicize a black tradition of heroism typically excluded from or undermined by white historical narratives. Thus he compares heroes of the American Revolution to heroes of black liberation, such as Toussaint.[10] Comparisons such as this redouble the heroic associations with Douglass himself, whose autobiographies consistently associate his self-liberation from slavery with the revolution's quest for liberty.[11]

Douglass's efforts to extend an American heroic tradition to black leaders, including himself, are shaped by the structures of celebrity culture. This idea is captured by critic Wilson J. Moses, who compares him to Ralph Waldo Emerson,

Abraham Lincoln, and P. T. Barnum. Like these men, Moses argues, Douglass "manufactured" and capitalized on his public image; like them, he writes, "he interpreted his life as a moral precept, inviting his contemporaries to learn from his experiences and to weave them into the developing web of American values. His life symbolized the myth of American individualism, but it also symbolized the ideals of American communalism, altruism, and self-sacrifice. The successful man in America was expected to share the secret of his success and to enrich himself by doing so."[12] The interrelation of Douglass's commercial success and his public identity that Moses notes here is a fundamental trait of celebrity. Moses suggests that Douglass's success followed on his ability to market himself in terms that resonated with mainstream—that is, white—American cultural values. This is not to say that Douglass cynically presented himself in a manner designed to appeal to white audiences, but the work of self-presentation that Douglass began in the 1845 *Narrative*, and that informs his entire career, involves a complex appeal to values, such as self-reliance, that are not only promulgated by mainstream white leaders but moreover naturalized into pillars of the dominant ideologies. But Moses does not address the apparent source of this knowledge in Douglass. From his own accounts, we know how he gains his literacy, but how does he gain his publicity? That is, by what means is he educated in the methods of acting in a public context? The answer is slavery itself. As he describes it in his autobiographies, slavery involves an extremely complex structure of privacy and publicity, and as he becomes more fully conscious of the meanings of slavery and freedom, Douglass awakens to the related possibilities and limitations of publicity and privacy. As it regards slaves as property, the system of slavery consigns human beings such as Douglass to the master's private sphere. Southerners' aggressive efforts to maintain the slave system reflect their concern to keep their private affairs out of the public realm. At the same time, slaves learned to regulate their own behaviors under the watchful eyes of their white overseers and masters, a habit that reinforced a racial distinction between a white public sphere and a black private sphere all but invisible to the master class.

The concept of privacy has enjoyed a conspicuous public life. In the United States, the great jurists Samuel D. Warren and Louis D. Brandeis first acknowledged privacy as a civil right in "The Right to Privacy" (1890). Driven by concern about the growing invasiveness of the yellow press, Warren and Brandeis articulated privacy as the "right to be let alone."[13] The principle holds that individuals' personal information and activities may not be subjected to undesired publication or intrusion. Their argument relies on the notion that the individual maintains property in the self, and that he or she has the right to control access to the self and information related to it as he does to other properties he holds. Although this landmark article was published late in the nineteenth century, it is understood to articulate principles that long held sway in both common and tort law.[14]

The association of privacy with property is a vexing matter in the context of slavery. Hannah Arendt argues that the classical associations of slaves (and women) with the private or domestic sphere are essential to the creation of the private sphere as a haven or refuge from the pressures of public life.[15] In this view, the labor of slaves is necessary for maintaining the comfort secured by property ownership, which also sanctions the master's participation in the public life of the agora. The same sharp distinction between public and private spheres feeds into the domestic ideology of the antebellum South that is used to justify and continue the oppression of both blacks and white women. In the area of tort law, slaves' status as chattel led to exemptions from certain privacy protections. A 1981 article in the *Harvard Law Review* shows that throughout the nineteenth century, private property was protected from intrusion even when the intrusion was meant to reclaim the property of another—a protection clearly related to the constitutional protection against improper search and seizure. In a footnote, however, the *Harvard Law Review* reveals that in a case involving the physical trespass of "owners of goods seeking to retrieve them," the "statute permitted forcible entry to recover a slave adjudged to belong to the plaintiff."[16] In such a situation, the slave owner's right to property apparently trumps the rights to privacy of the harborer of fugitive slaves.

More to the point of Douglass's case, because slaves were considered property they were denied the rights associated with property ownership, including the right to privacy derived from property-in-self. In the sections of the *Narrative* where Douglass discusses hiring himself out for a wage, he associates the denial of his right to property—the wages he earned—with the denial of his freedom: "When I carried to [Hugh Auld] my weekly wages, he would, after counting the money, look me in the face with a robber-like fierceness, and ask, 'Is this all?' He was satisfied with nothing less than the last cent. He would, however, when I made him six dollars, sometimes give me six cents, to encourage me. It had the opposite effect. I regarded it as a sort of admission of my right to the whole. The fact that he gave me any part of my wages was proof, to my mind, that he believed me entitled to the whole of them" (*DA* 86). Douglass makes it clear that by denying him his wages, Auld was denying Douglass's selfhood. In escaping from slavery, Douglass takes possession of his self as property. The claim to property-in-self accompanies the escape effort because it is intrinsic to it.

Likewise, the claims of both property-in-self and freedom make it possible for Douglass to assert his right to privacy—what Warren and Brandeis identify as his "right to be let alone"—which he does most notably in the *Narrative* by omitting references to his relationship with Anna Murray, his future wife.

Douglass mentions Murray only briefly, when he relates his marriage to her in New York just a few weeks after his arrival there. Douglass's exclusion of Murray from his story to that point is noteworthy, considering her importance in his life in Baltimore and her contributions to his escape effort. Douglass's subsequent versions of his autobiography are also reticent about Douglass's relationship with Anna both before and during their forty-four-year marriage. The reasons for his omission are likely manifold: rhetorically, it suggests Douglass made his escape single-handedly and bolsters his claims of heroic masculinity. In addition, his silence regarding Anna across his three autobiographies reflects the gendered understanding of separate spheres associated with the contemporary domestic ideology: as Rafia Zafar explains, "her [Anna's] sphere is limited to the private, his [Douglass's] encompasses the public."[17] This strict delineation of sex and gender roles protects Anna's reputation as chaste—and Douglass's as well.[18] In other words, Douglass's silences about his marriage uphold the idealization of the true woman associated with the cult of domesticity and evade the stereotypical sexualization of the black body.[19] Douglass's omission does suggest that he adhered to the standards of domesticity of the era, and those standards enabled him to distinguish his public and private lives very clearly. To this end, he may have been encouraged by Anna herself. In contrast to her ambitious and accomplished husband, Anna remained illiterate throughout her life and, in William S. McFeely's words, "shunned public life."[20] The disparity in the pair's abilities and interest, not to mention the heavy demands of motherhood and domestic responsibility on a woman whose husband could be absent for long stretches, inevitably strained the Douglasses' marriage. No matter the personal motivations for his silence, the omission of details of Douglass's marriage and family life is notable only by modern standards. These few hints and rumors of life in the Douglass household are titillating, but Douglass's silence regarding his family and marriage is part of a larger effort to claim the privileges of privacy both for Douglass's life in slavery, when he and Anna courted, and in freedom. However difficult it may be to define "privacy," the intimate relationships of courtship and marriage are unquestioningly associated with the private sphere. Weddings, however, are the public ceremonies that sanction such privacy. In slavery, marriage and other intimate ties among slaves are highly scrutinized and subject to arbitrary legal and conventional proscriptions. Douglass's reference to his marriage in the *Narrative* therefore reflects his new freedom, and it entails at the same time a claim to the privileges of a private life denied him in slavery, but which he nevertheless claims retrospectively, by failing to document his courtship of Anna Murray in Baltimore.

Douglass's marriage to Anna Murray therefore indicates slavery's failure to control the private experience of slaves. Citing Orlando Patterson's concept of slavery as "social death," Milette Shamir claims that slaves experienced a "'private death,' the fact that, though limited to the private sphere, they had no proprietary claim over the space that they inhabited, nor the availability of domestic retreat from surveillance, and therefore no viable claim to full personhood."[21] Douglass's *Narrative* shows, however, that although slavery was structured in such a way as to inhibit slaves' ideas of self, they did in fact cultivate notions of selfhood. Denied the right to privacy, slaves nevertheless established among themselves intimacies and personal communities that constitute a recognizable private sphere, off limits to—beyond the recognition of—the white masters. The black private sphere was the realm of children and the very old, courtship and family life, and religious practice. Contained within the greater sphere of white privacy, however, the black private sphere of the slaves was not protected or sheltered; it was not a zone of privilege, as the master's private sphere was.[22] Those who inhabited it were subject to the surveillance of their masters and various forms of disruptions of their private affairs, including violence and the separation of families. The conditions of the slaves' tenuous privacy suggests that the distinctions between public and private are not easily drawn in slavery: the slave's privacy, like his selfhood, is always violable and never complete. It is not a zone of privilege or refuge, but a sphere of common experience that creates particular forms of knowing.

But neither is the masters' privacy complete. Douglass represents slave masters as anxious to control their reputations as honorable men and beneficent patriarchs to their slave "families," knowing that their reception among the white public will serve their private interests and give support to the institution of slavery. What is interesting is not the idea that public and private selves do not entirely agree—that is true for both the slave and the master, indeed for everyone—but that for each the idea of who or what constitutes "public" or "private" differs. For the slave, the master—and whites in general—represent the "public" for whom they must regulate their expression. But for the masters, the slaves are part of their most intimately private lives, hidden from the scrutiny of a public composed of their white peers and even the nation itself. Defenders of slavery relied on claims of its domesticity to argue it should be shielded from the scrutiny and interferences of the greater American public. This defense fed into representations of slavery as a system of patriarchal benevolence and the plantation as the grandest expression of the domestic ideal. Thavolia Glymph reminds us, however, "that the plantation household was also a workplace, not a haven from the economic world, that it was not private or made so by the nature of the labor performed within it or the sex of the managers." Glymph's concern with the interior life of the "great house" resonates across the entire plantation and throughout the slavery system. Notwithstanding claims to slavery's place in the South's private or domestic life, it was nonetheless an institution in which the claims of public matters—labor, property—and private privilege—intimacy, patriarchy—intersected one another at odd angles. Building on the work of both Elizabeth Fox-Genovese and Douglass, Glymph points out that slaves are witnesses to the "private" activities within the household and were frequently made to participate in such intimacies themselves, even as other slaves provide an "audience" for such goings-on.[23]

If slavery makes the plantation a workplace, and therefore a public space, slavery—"slavery as it is"—is nevertheless concealed from public view. This discrepancy raises questions about the viability of both "public" and "private" as categories of experience and suggests that certain activities that occur behind closed doors can in fact be public in character. They are, in other words, significant to the matters of culture and commerce that go on in the public sphere. Habermas defines the public sphere as the realm of civic affairs, and he specifies that acts such as reading are private behaviors that can affect the public sphere as they shape attitudes, opinions, and behaviors within it. Slavery is likewise something that occurs out of the public eye but affects civic life through its material contributions to the slaveholder's commercial interests and its moral resonance for the citizenry. At the same time, these definitions of "public" and "private" suggest that any behavior deemed private can be made public simply by making it visible. Certainly this is the strategy adopted by feminists and antislavery activists, who worked to bring the plights of women and slaves to public light.[24] Douglass uses this strategy liberally in his role as witness to slavery. At the same time, Douglass draws attention to the problem of distinguishing "public" and "private" within slavery, and he documents the complexity of slaves' roles as constituents of the masters' private sphere who nevertheless regard the plantation as a public realm in which all they do is subject to surveillance, yet where an action's visibility does not necessarily indicate its public or private character.

Throughout his autobiographies, Douglass provides examples of how he managed his self-presentation in slavery to generate responses especially from his masters. For instance, in the *Narrative*, Douglass explains that slaves learned never to complain about their masters to any white person for fear of reprisal: "The slaveholders have been known to send in spies among their slaves, to ascertain their views and feelings in regard to their condition. The frequency of this has had the effect to establish among the slaves the maxim, that a still tongue makes a wise head. They suppress the truth rather than take the consequences of telling it, and in so doing prove themselves a part of the human family" (*DA* 27). Douglass emphasizes the slave's human desire to protect himself against punishment and give the master no cause to separate his family. The comment also reveals the gradations of public and private experiences and relationships in slave culture. The master who initiates inquiries among the slaves seeks to protect his own public reputation by ensuring his slaves do not spread rumors about their ill treatment. The slaves themselves seek to protect the integrity of their families. The desire to maintain some semblance of a private sphere of familial relations leads the slave to play a specific public role for the master and suggests that the ultimate freedom for the slave would be to break his silence and speak the truth of his experience.[25]

In order to be left alone, slaves developed strategies of obfuscation and deception. The much-discussed example of the sorrow songs illustrates one method by which slaves negotiated their tenuous privacy. Recalling the deep pathos of the slaves' musical "prayer and complaint," Douglass acknowledges that most listeners could not recognize the "ineffable sadness" of the songs (*DA* 24). The sorrow songs represent the slaves' construction of their own private sphere in plain view but unrecognized by white onlookers. Douglass himself must be initiated into their meaning, just as he was initiated into knowledge of his own subjugation by witnessing Aunt Hester's violation: "I did not, when a slave, understand the deep meaning of those rude and apparently incoherent songs. I was myself within the circle; so that I neither saw nor heard as those without might see and hear. They told a tale of woe which was then altogether beyond my feeble comprehension" (*DA* 24). Douglass's image of the circle of slavery distinguishes between those whose experience drives them to feeling expression and those whose sensibilities enable them to comprehend the expression. His early unconsciousness of the songs' meanings reflects the fact that the songs "give voice to meaning even if no one can understand"—even, that is, if they are so shrouded in privacy as to be obscured from those who participate in their making. Douglass's position as "*both* insider and outsider" to slavery makes his work as mediator of the slave experience possible.[26] The meaning of the sorrow songs can be parsed only by Douglass, with his "peculiar doubleness, which posits deep moral value in slave culture while at the same time detaching Douglass from sympathetic immersion in it."[27] The songs' incomprehensibility both to those outside the circle and to the uninitiated means that the songs remain deeply private in character, however public or visible their expression. The certainty they offer of the slaves' humanity is ineffectual because, ultimately, it does not achieve publicity in the sense of conveying meaning beyond the circle of their production. For all their pathos, the sorrow songs are rhetorically ineffective, the polar opposite of the public expression Douglass practices.

Douglass's education in the meaning of the sorrow songs—the "first glimmering conception" they impart "of the dehumanizing character of slavery"—parallels his learning to read and write. As Douglass relates it, learning to read was the essential first step into consciousness of and participation in a world beyond slavery, but if the fruits of his efforts were a greater publicity, the effort of reading remained intensely private. In his preliterate state, Douglass lacked a coherent sense of self—like the other slave children, he was a "brute," driven by animalistic desires for food and warmth. In the language of Hugh Auld, he was a "nigger," an individual whose ignorance and lack of self-regard was the source of his value as a slave, and which was "ruined" through the acquisition of letters.[28] Pursuing literacy, Houston A. Baker argues, slaves counteract the ontological emptiness of their condition: "Only by grasping the word could [the slave] engage in the speech acts that would ultimately define his selfhood."[29] In his ignorance, the slave was confined "for life" to the private sphere. Knowing that the instruction of a slave was forbidden, Douglass turns his education into a practice not only private but also covert, all the while projecting himself as dutiful and obedient. In the private space of the Aulds' home, he needs to conceal his studies: "If I was in a separate room any considerable length of time, I was sure to be suspected of having a book, and was at once called to give an account of myself" (*DA* 40). Alternatively, Douglass's education is a private effort conducted in public spaces: "During this time," he writes, "my copy-book was the board fence, brick wall, and pavement" (*DA* 44). For the slave, the notions of "public" and "private" spaces are not available as they are among white society. Denied his humanity in so many ways, the suggestion that a slave could require protections of privacy is nonsensical, and the activities and ideas that one might ordinarily associate with the private sphere, such as cultivating family bonds or reading a book, must be hidden behind veils of deception. Thus, the fundamental distinction that Douglass establishes between white and black experience, under conditions of either bondage or freedom, is in their experiences and understanding of distinctions between public and private. For white Americans, the distinction between public and private experience is a distinction of privilege: the degree to which an individual can cordon off any aspect of his activity from the observation of others is a measure of his freedom. For the slave, the situation is more complicated. The subterfuges and deceits Douglass employs to become literate are made necessary by the racist ideology that deems his self-culture a crime, and they also reveal that ideology to be a fiction.

As portrayed in the *Narrative*, then, Douglass's secret acts expose the depths of his privacy and the eminence of his selfhood. In them he claims the right to be left alone—to do as he pleases without observation or judgment. Likewise, the ability to move at will between public and private spheres, with their associated pleasures and limitations, is fundamental to Douglass's concept of freedom, symbolized most effectively in the *Narrative* by the sloop *Sally Lloyd* and other ships on the Chesapeake. In the famous apostrophe to the ships on the Chesapeake, Douglass expresses his desire for freedom: "you are loosed from your moorings, and are free; I am fast in my chains, and am a slave! You move merrily before the gentle gale, and I sadly before the bloody whip!" (*DA* 59). Douglass's association of the ships' movement before the wind with political freedom intensifies the irony and synecdochical significance of his subsequent career as a caulker: the slave's labor ensures the freedom and financial security of the white sailors and merchants who use the ship. Through his skill at caulking, Douglass eventually earns the confidence and money to support his escape—an escape he makes in the guise of a sailor. For him, ships and shipping are rhetorically powerful figures for freedom. More than this, they provide Douglass with practical experience in the public world of labor and commerce that are essential to his successful escape. His labor at the shipyards almost cost him his life, as he was savagely beaten by white laborers who resented and feared competing with black laborers. It also instructed Douglass in the manners and idioms of public life—the "address," as Douglass puts it (*DA* 643)—that, with his borrowed protection papers, get him out of the South. As Douglass explains in *Life and Times*, his escape depended on his "knowledge of ships and sailor's talk" as well as his assessment of "the kind feeling which prevailed in Baltimore and other seaports at the time, toward 'those who go down to the sea in ships.'" (*DA* 644). This knowledge enables him to navigate the railroad and other public thoroughfares with relative confidence and to appear like one at home in the crowd. Not surprisingly, when Douglass loses his bearings and his confidence in New York City, he turns to a friendly looking sailor for assistance, who in turn leads to his benefactor David Ruggles. Douglass's experiences in the Baltimore shipyards have given him more than a "knowledge of ships and sailor's talk." Like his years running errands for Sophia Auld and playing in the streets with young white boys, these experiences add to his knowledge of the crowded world beyond the household and provide an education in the ways of urban life that enable him to assess a stranger's character effectively and recognize the risks of exposure. This knowledge allows him to navigate public life effectively—to go wherever he wants, an exercise of freedom premised on his essential selfhood.

But for Douglass and other slaves, the public world is not represented only by shipyards and city streets; it also includes their plantation workplace. Douglass's portraits of violence and cruelty tear away the veil of privacy that shrouds plantation life. In this work of exposure Douglass, like other slave narrators, objectifies his masters. The act of objectification works on the white oppressors as it does on Barnum's human exhibits: it alienates them from the audience's subjectivity, marking them as monstrous and Other. "In this respect," Leonard Cassuto argues, "fugitive slave narratives are inverted rewrites of freak show pamphlets"—souvenir texts sold alongside exhibits of human grotesques—"which are themselves hybrid adventure stories that turned people into grotesque trophy monsters to be displayed by their hunters."[30] Cassuto incorporates the slave narrative into a literary and cultural history in which human beings are displayed and interpreted for the pleasurable consumption of a colonizing power. His analysis emphasizes the definition of the grotesque as something simultaneously recognizable and alien. Seen in this way, Douglass's master retains familiar characteristics of the white citizen, but his behavior indicates a moral depravity typically associated with nonwhite savages. In this manner, Douglass demands that his audience account for his masters, tracing their social and racial taxonomies much as Barnum's patrons interrogated "What Is It?" and other human exhibits.

By contrast, Douglass represents himself in a manner that resonates with his white audience's ideals for virtue and heroism. He is the undeserving victim of his masters' cruelty, eventually "broken in body, soul, and spirit" (*DA* 58). Tellingly, Douglass uses a single incident, his punishment for the wreck of the oxcart, to represent repeated beatings (*DA* 56). The scene depicted here is one of many violent inscriptions of Douglass's "diploma" on his back, but he is unwilling to represent himself as a pupil of that school—to do so would undermine the plot of heroic self-reliance that the *Narrative* develops and that determines Douglass's public persona.[31] Douglass's reluctance to represent himself as beaten bears directly on the *Narrative*'s plot of developing manhood, which in turn is critical to his larger claim to a viable identity in the masculine public sphere. In witnessing the erotically charged assault of his Aunt Hester, the young Frederick worries that "it would be my turn next," an admission of slavery's power to effeminize its victims. Indeed, Covey demands Douglass's absolute submission and, as Douglass projects it, his unmanning.[32] But throughout the remainder of the *Narrative*, Douglass rejects this implication as he staunchly refuses to allow himself to be seen as unmanned or to risk the eroticization of his own abuse. Douglass actively resists Covey's power, not only by fighting back but also by refusing to remove his clothes and submit to the eroticized punishment. The chiasmus that structures the Covey episode refers not to man made a woman, or the man effeminized; "you have seen how a man was made a slave," he writes—brutalized and returned to his preliterate and prepubescent state of consciousness. He asserts his masculine autonomy in two ways, then, through both his violent self-defense and also his rejection of the passive feminine role.

Douglass's revisions to this episode in *My Bondage and My Freedom* go even further to specify how his expanded self-awareness leads from slavery's prison of privacy to a liberated public self: "Covey was a tyrant, and a cowardly one, withal. After resisting him, I felt as I had never felt before. It was a resurrection from the dark and pestiferous tomb of slavery, to the heaven of comparative freedom. I was no longer a servile coward, trembling under the frown of a brother worm of the dust, but, my long-cowed spirit was roused to an attitude of manly independence" (*DA* 286). The notion that Douglass is a providential figure was first imparted to him in his selection to go to Baltimore and later encouraged by his friendship with Father Lawson. Douglass's triumph over Covey affirms his sense of himself as an agent of divine will. Though his language is consistent with the evangelical Christianity of the South, Douglass's association of himself with the divine parallels the Emersonian notion of a self in communion with Spirit, and he further links the recognition of divine selfhood to masculine heroism.[33] Referring to "the Transcendentalists' endless obsession with issues of 'manliness,'" Barbara Packer argues that such gendered language was part of a recognizable "code" among contemporaries. "The opposite of 'manliness' in this code is not 'effeminacy' but 'servility,'" she writes. "To be dependent on another person for one's livelihood places the strongest possible check on freedom of thought or speech."[34] Of course, women in the antebellum period were dependent on others in exactly the ways that Packer notes here, but her emphasis on manliness as a positive expression of autonomy is very helpful in reading Douglass, whose climactic struggle with Covey does not release him from servitude but does alleviate his sense of himself as lesser, beholden, or brutish. Covey is his "brother worm," an individual equally mastered by spiritual and political forces that determine his fate. This is Douglass's transparent eyeball moment, when he is able to see past the artificial social structures to recognize the play of universal forces in the shaping of experience. The positive acknowledgment of his manhood independent of his political status as a slave enables Douglas to assume the status of personhood,[35] a selfhood that is not defined or constrained by his physical self. In fact, Douglass remained a slave, very much defined by his physical person, but the rhetorical acknowledgment of a transcendent selfhood underlines the injustice of his bondage and lays claim to the privileges of the public sphere characterized by its impersonality.

Douglass's 1855 revision of the Covey episode is of course just one of the many revisions he makes to the story of his early life in *My Bondage and My Freedom*. The book as a whole brings Douglass's story up to date, detailing his years as a paid lecturer for the AASS and his early years as a newspaper publisher in Rochester, New York. The work does not simply pick up where the *Narrative* finished, however, but provides a complete revision of Douglass's story, including reinterpretations of familiar episodes of the *Narrative*. It is, as Eric Sundquist says, "a book not just about what it means to be a slave in the South but rather what it means to be a slave in America."[36] Altogether, in *My Bondage and My Freedom* Douglass establishes a public presence that is unmediated by Garrison and the AASS and not limited to the exposure of his scars.

As David Leverenz argues, Douglass's revisions reflect the ideas of self that led to Douglass's break with the Garrisonians. Of the Covey episode in particular, Leverenz points out that the version included in *My Bondage* draws attention simultaneously to Douglass's physical power and his writerly refinement: "The revision emphasizes Douglass's discovery of manhood, which he now equates with power and moral dignity," as opposed to the drive for a personal independence that he expresses in the *Narrative*.[37] Further, I would like to suggest that as he reinterprets his personal story, Douglass refines his understanding of the relationship between his private and his public selves and explicitly denies the idea that he emerged from slavery fully formed.[38] Certainly Garrison suggests as much in his depiction of Douglass's Nantucket speech in his preface to the 1845 *Narrative*. Douglass was in fact a graduate of the peculiar institution, but, as he retells the tale in 1855, his education gave him more than the stripes on his back; it gave him an insider's knowledge of slavery's machinations that authorized his vigorous social analysis.

My Bondage aims to demonstrate that Douglass had been laboring in the fields of public advocacy long before his notable speech at Nantucket, back into his years teaching Sabbath schools on the eastern shore of Maryland. As he taught his fellow slaves to read, Douglass also hatched an escape plot that he urged on his closest friends; of those arguments, he writes, "I here began my public speaking" (*DA* 306). Douglass's new chronology of his public career requires a revision of the word "public" from a reference to the largely white assemblies Douglass addressed in the North to include black men in bondage. This usage defies the classic association of the public sphere with a privileged class of propertied white men and asserts the slave's rights to citizenship. Douglass's own publicity gives credence to his assertion, for the public presence of the eloquent black man defied conventional associations of the public sphere with white male citizens exclusively. If the black former slave could address the public, could not the black slave also participate in public life in other ways? To deny this claim was not to deny the slave's humanity, as the slaveocrats did; worse, it was to deny their very existence. To Douglass, it seemed this was in fact happening, as northerners including Garrison and his supporters argued against slavery without expressing support for racial equality. Free and slave, black people were at the very center of American public life—at the forefront of the public consciousness—but unseen by the vast majority of onlookers. To bring them into the light, Douglass worked to redefine the meaning of the "public," starting with his representation of the Sabbath schools and his first attempt to escape slavery.

Douglass's literacy enabled him to teach other slaves, and he repeatedly established informal schools that met in the evenings or on Sundays. His first effort, at Saint Michael's, was broken up by Thomas Auld and other white men who compared Douglass to Nat Turner and warned that "if I did not look out, I should get as many balls into me, as Nat did into him" (*DA* 254). This episode precipitated Douglass's rendition to the slave breaker Covey, but on his release from Covey's farm he established another, more ambitious Sabbath school at Mr. Freeland's farm. There he taught a group of about thirty men each Sunday, plus others on weeknights. Douglass and his students took pains to conceal their efforts from their white neighbors: "All were impressed with the necessity of keeping the matter as private as possible, for the fate of the St. Michael's attempt was notorious, and fresh in the minds of all" (*DA* 298). However prudent these efforts, Douglass uses his narrative to assail the hypocrisy of a slave system that rendered them necessary. As in the *Narrative*, he points out that the white southerners' professions of Christian faith contradict their actions as slave masters, and he extends his critique to the prohibitions on slave education: "Let the reader reflect upon the fact that, in this Christian country, men and women are hiding from professors of religion, in barns, in the woods and fields, in order to learn to read the *holy bible*" (*DA* 300). Douglass points out the religious hypocrisy, but he also acknowledges that southerners' fears of what education might lead to are justified. "I have met several slaves from Maryland, who were once my scholars," he writes, "and who obtained their freedom, I doubt not, partially in consequence of the ideas imparted to them in that school" (*DA* 300). Throughout his accounts in *My Bondage and My Freedom* of his time as a slave teacher, Douglass underscores the calculation with which he pressed his insurrectionist thinking on his students. Indeed, Douglass uses familiar texts to inculcate the lessons he had already taken to heart. He "tried to show the agency of ignorance in keeping men in slavery. Webster's spelling book and the Columbian Orator were looked into again" (*DA* 298). This anecdotal evidence alone supports the southerners' fears that education would undermine the slave system.

As they lead slaves to regard themselves and their circumstances in a new light, Douglass's Sabbath schools reiterate in his students the consciousness-raising process that he experienced in his own early self-schooling, and they reiterate as well the complicated dimensions of privacy and publicity that effort entailed. Douglass claims that he and his students at Mr. Freeland's took pains to "[keep] the matter as private as possible," but it was likely impossible to conceal a meeting of thirty black men among a white society already anxious about slave conspiracy.[39] Douglass's language therefore conflates the privacy of the men's reading with the secrecy of their operations. Privacy and secrecy are not synonymous, after all. Marking the distinction, Morton H. Levine argues that privacy is self-nurturing whereas secrecy is self-protective: "the aloneness of privacy both is willed by the individual and is not only voluntary but positive. For privacy is perceived by the individual as the privileged life-space within which he functions as himself, in which he experiences, exercises, and enjoys his uniqueness," but "secrecy is in essence negative. It involves keeping to oneself information which one feels would render one vulnerable to some kind of damage, either practical damage or damage to self-esteem."[40] Reading is a good example of an activity that is associated with privacy but that, under ordinary circumstances, one need not keep secret: in the nineteenth century, it is possible to read newspapers or small volumes in public spaces without sacrificing the privacy of the act. Nor would the average nineteenth-century reader, who reads in the privacy of his or her home, feel compelled to keep that fact a secret from others. For slaves, however, reading and learning to read are illicit acts that must be concealed from white people. By labeling his school "private," Douglass deliberately ignores its criminality and implicitly denies his work's transgression of the slave code, that code itself being transgressive of the slaves' humanity. Reading is widely accepted as a valuable means of cultivating the self. His "private" school, he implies, merely provides that all-important function to young men eager to improve themselves spiritually through scriptural study. His language clearly makes the case for the existence of a back private sphere, in contrast to evidence of slaves' "private death," thus asserting slaves' intrinsic humanity. At the same time, he acknowledges the white community as the slaves' public. This construction reveals the public sphere to be exclusionary and dangerous, the site not of self-abstraction and reasonable discursive exchange but of opposition, antagonism, and conflict.

Douglass's work as a teacher was therefore an important stage in his development as a public figure. His secret efforts worked to instill in his brother slaves a consciousness of the idea of slavery as a system through which their oppression served the economic, social, and political interests of their enslavers. The associations of Douglass's teaching with the insurrectionist efforts of Nat Turner and the start of his public-speaking career in *My Bondage and My Freedom* mark a radical departure from the *Narrative*. The earlier work represents Douglass's Sabbath school as a valuable example of slave community. The close ties Douglass forged with his fellow slaves, especially his students, provided necessary emotional support for the slaves and helped make up for the familial connections that slavery denied him: "We were linked and interlinked with each other. I loved them with a love stronger than anything I have experienced since" (*DA* 72). That profound sense of connectedness with his fellow slaves leads Douglass to include others in his escape effort, which he represents as an act of solidarity threatened by the fearful self-interest of Sandy, who betrays them. In *My Bondage*, Douglass gives a much fuller treatment of the first escape attempt. Although this version also emphasizes the deep friendship among the rebel band, Douglass plays up his own role in conceiving of the plot and persuading his friends to join him in it. This work is the culmination of all his self-culture to that point, and "all my little reading, which had any bearing on the subject of human rights, was rendered available" in his rhetorical efforts (*DA* 305). In *My Bondage and My Freedom*, therefore, Douglass indicates that the realization of one's selfhood, a work nurtured in private acts of self-culture, must be preserved and defended by acts of public and even violent resistance. Indeed, such resistance defines his heroism: not the noble defense of the weak, but the violent refusal to be made abject, to abandon one's selfhood.

Retelling the runaway plot in *My Bondage and My Freedom*, Douglass valorizes slaves' physical resistance of any effort to restrict their autonomy. The plot required Douglass to forge passes for himself and three others and for them to head north on the Chesapeake Bay using a stolen boat. The plan was obviously dangerous, and Douglass describes his and his companions' determination to pursue their aim at any physical cost: "It was truly felt to be a matter of life and death with us; and we fully intended to *fight* as well as *run*, if necessity should occur for that extremity" (*DA* 315). Ultimately, the plot fails, but Douglass represents the effort as a heroic act of self-redemption. In this sense, the escape attempt is the next logical step after his fight with Covey. That effort involved the master's recognition of the slave's essential selfhood, but as long as he remained in bondage, the slave was socially dead. Douglass describes escape's promise of restoration to life as a dramatic change in the slave's relationship to time and hence to his self: "The thought of only being a creature of the *present* and the *past*, troubled me, and I longed to have a *future*—a future with hope in it. To be shut up entirely to the past and present, is abhorrent to the human mind; it is to the soul—whose life and happiness is unceasing progress—what the prison is to the body; a blight and mildew, a hell of horrors" (*DA* 304–5). This is what is at stake in the escape attempt, the soul's rescue from an eternal present, and the mind's from unrelenting memory.

Eric Sundquist explains, "To have a future, as Douglass figures it, is to be free. It is thus . . . to be able to enter into the self-making process of being an American."[41] Douglass's assertion that the soul thrives in progress clearly associates him with the popular philosophy of self-culture that was rooted in Unitarianism and reaffirmed as Emersonian self-reliance. The Emersonian hero must withstand the buffets of adverse public opinion—"For nonconformity the world whips you with its displeasure," Emerson writes (*CW* 2:32)—but the slave risks actual whipping and worse punishments. Douglass chooses the revolutionary patriots, not his contemporary reformers, as the rhetorical touchstone for the band of freedom seekers: quoting Patrick Henry's "Give me liberty or give me death," he points out, "with us it was a *doubtful* liberty, at best, that we sought; and a certain, lingering death in the rice swamps and sugar fields, if we failed" (*DA* 312). In Douglass's invocation of Patrick Henry, he links his future to an American revolutionary past. This gesture, Priscilla Wald argues, is a key step in Douglass's self-positioning as an authoritative national spokesperson.[42] It also authorizes his embrace of violent resistance, even though the violence that follows as the plot unfolds tests all the participants' resolve. One participant, Sandy, gives in to his fear and betrays the group. In the event of their capture, Douglass discovers himself less brave than his companion Henry, who resists his captors and refuses to be tied up: "Henry put me to shame; he fought, and fought bravely. John and I had made no resistance. The fact is, I never see much use in fighting, unless there is a reasonable probability of whipping somebody. Yet there was something almost providential in the resistance made by the gallant Henry. But for that resistance, every soul of us would have been hurried off to the far south" (*DA* 318). Douglass represents the moment as a turning point in his thinking about revolutionary action and violent resistance. There can be value in fighting even if the result is not a triumph; the act of resistance is itself expressive of the individual's claim to his own body, and its significance extends beyond its immediate effects. This insight governs Douglass's representation of the entire escape attempt and its aftermath, which, though a failure, effectively challenged the slavers' authority and exposed the powerful self-sovereignty of the would-be fugitives.

While Henry's heroism affects Douglass strongly, the entire first escape attempt is an act of resistance that resonates beyond Freeland's farm. Just as Douglass claims his Sabbath schools were his first efforts at public speaking, he represents the escape attempt as his introduction into the white public sphere, presaging his public career in the North. In both cases, Douglass is regarded by his white audience as a spectacle of blackness: when observed in the public sphere, his physical and intellectual power are alike regarded as wondrous and disruptive of social order. This disruptive power is made abundantly clear by Douglass's mistress, Mrs. Betsey Freeland, who tells him, "but for *you*, you *long legged yellow devil*, Henry and John would never have thought of running away" (*DA* 310). Her accusation emphasizes his being "yellow," that is, a mulatto. The slur suggests that Douglass's mixed race makes him a grotesque figure, defying easy racial categorization and therefore disrupting the social order. By comparison, the blackness of Henry and John make them gullible in her eyes, easily swayed by more powerful natures. Her logic incorporates the proslavery rationale that regards black people as incapable of self-governance, Henry's heroic resistance notwithstanding. Rather than disprove or contradict Mrs. Freeland's logic, Douglass affirms it: "I gave the lady a look, which called forth a scream of mingled wrath and terror" from her (*DA* 319). He plays the part of the monster she thinks he is. In fact, his monstrous quality is really his very human rage at her usage and his situation, but this fact does not compute with her, because she has no ideological framework with which to make sense of his emotional expression. Through his look, Douglass communicates his judgment of her, and his nonverbal assertion of his intellectual and moral power angers and terrifies her because it upends white privilege.

Douglass's narration challenges the normative white view of black men not only by relating their heroic self-possession but also by challenging the authority of the evaluative white gaze. Douglass does not allow himself and his compatriots to be spectacles only; they are spectators, too, observing and judging their observers. Objectified in his glance and, more importantly, his narration of the scene, Mrs. Freeland is made to represent the arrogance, as well as the limits, of white power. In his description of the long walk to the jail at Easton, Douglass further undermines the authority of the white gaze by juxtaposing it with other interpretive perspectives. He and his fellow conspirators were led from Saint Michael's to Easton in a long march that Douglass represents as a kind of parade:

> Could the kind reader have been quietly riding along the main road to or from Easton, that morning, his eye would have met a painful sight. He would have seen five young men, guilty of no crime, save that of preferring *liberty* to a life of *bondage*, drawn along the public highway—firmly bound together—tramping through dust and heat, bare-footed and bare-headed—fastened to three strong horses, whose riders were armed to the teeth, with pistols and daggers—on their way to prison, like felons, and suffering every possible insult from the crowds of idle, vulgar people, who clustered around, and heartlessly made their failure the occasion for all manner of ribaldry and sport. As I looked upon this crowd of vile persons, and saw myself and friends thus assailed and persecuted, I could not help seeing the fulfillment of Sandy's dream. I was in the hands of moral vultures, and firmly held in their sharp talons, and was being hurried away toward Easton, in a south-easterly direction, amid the jeers of new birds of the same feather, through every neighborhood we passed. It seemed to me, (and this shows the good understanding between the slaveholders and their allies,) that every body we met knew the cause of our arrest, and were out, awaiting our passing by, to feast their vindictive eyes on our misery and to gloat over our ruin. Some said, *I ought to be hanged*, and others, *I ought to be burnt*; others, I ought to have the "*hide*" taken from my back; while no one gave us a kind word or sympathizing look, except the poor slaves, who were lifting their heavy hoes, and who cautiously glanced at us through the post-and-rail fences, behind which they were at work. Our sufferings, that morning, can be more easily imagined than described. Our hopes were all blasted, at a blow. (*DA* 319–20)

Unlike the scene of the group's capture, which took place in the privacy of the Freeland kitchen, this scene takes place "along the public highway." The presence of jeering white observers indicates that the publicity of the men's march is intended as an affirmation of white authority as well—perhaps as an example to the field slaves who also observe their passing. As Jennifer Greiman observes, the scene depicts the white crowd as "a judging, punitive public," while "Douglass also marks the limit case of inclusion in an ostensibly democratic republic."[43] Democratic spectacle generates a powerful combination of aesthetic and political elements that together render democracy an affective as well as practical experience. In democracy as in amusements, the nature of spectacle is to reinforce the subject position of the onlooker. As in the example of the freak show, where "the exhibited body became a text written in boldface to be deciphered according to the needs and desires of the onlookers," the bodies of the black prisoners are put on exhibit and subjected to the evaluative gaze of a white audience.[44] But Douglass's narration demonstrates that the public spectacle is not easily controlled—its meaning is not determined by the single, normative gaze of the white authorities, for they are part of the scene, too. The passage reverses the white onlookers' gaze, revealing them as "idle, vulgar people" and "moral vultures." As in Douglass's representations of Auld and Covey, his narration here makes an exhibit of his white captors and portrays them as monsters or human grotesques even as, perhaps because, they make a spectacle of the black bodies in their charge. Douglass shows that there is no single subject position—the spectacle is not a two-dimensional presentation of an object (Douglass) to a subject (the white crowd), but a multidimensional scene in which everyone is both observer and observed, subject and object. Yet through his claim to the authorial voice, Douglass controls this multidimensional arrangement. If he cannot eliminate or write out the judgments of the white audience, his representation of multiple audiences challenges the white audiences' assumptions of normativity and authority.

In *My Bondage and My Freedom*, Douglass uses narration of the escape attempt to compound the work of resistance. Although the first escape attempt failed, his description of the march to Easton jail demonstrates that he and his co-conspirators exemplified black resistance to white authority. The meaning of their resistance cannot be contained or controlled by their capture, as the boundaries of public and private, expression and interpretation, cannot be policed by white men on horseback. Douglass's narration, moreover, extends the episode beyond the specific time and place of its occurrence. He opens the scene of their march to Easton, for example, to yet another, larger audience of readers. Those readers, like the author himself, are able to observe the various participants and make judgments about their actions. Interestingly, Douglass's narration maintains the inscrutability of the field slaves: they observe, but remain silent. Douglass interprets their gaze as sympathetic, but its sympathy is understood only by those whose plight has earned it. Like the meanings of the sorrow songs, their glance is part of the necessarily covert expression of the black private sphere, conducted in the full exposure of the public highway, but unrecognized—probably unseen—by those who seek to control it by law and custom. The contrast between the prisoners and the slaves who observe them raises interpretive questions for the readers who observe the scene from a more critical distance outside the circle of slavery: which is less free, the slave in chains, who has been caught in the effort to escape, or the slave unchained, who looks up from his labor to observe the other as he is led past? Does the field slave consider his imprisoned counterpart a hero or a fool? The field slave is not free to express his judgment, but in depicting his silent regard of the scene, Douglass acknowledges the black readers of his narrative and invites their interpretations. Their presence in the description is important for white readers as well, a reminder that their judgment is not the only judgment, that they stand alongside black men and women in the public sphere.

In his retelling of the first escape attempt in *My Bondage and My Freedom*, Douglass conveys several ideas that are key to his political thought in the 1850s. He uses the episode to articulate the logic of violent resistance, which he associates with both masculine heroism and patriotism. Even where violent resistance fails, as it does for his coconspirator Henry, it is a necessary and powerful expression of personal agency that highlights the injustice of slavery's equally violent denial of the slave's personhood. In the years following passage of the Fugitive Slave Act, Douglass defends acts of violent resistance against slavery, as for instance in his justification for the death of James Batchelder, a guard at the Boston courthouse who was killed in the failed effort to rescue the fugitive slave Anthony Burns in 1854. In his actions, Douglass argues, Batchelder "labeled himself the common enemy of mankind, and his slaughter was as innocent, in the sight of God, as would be the slaughter of a ravenous wolf in the act of throttling an infant."[45] Violence in such instances is more than just, Douglass contends; it is a powerful statement in rejecting bondage and asserting blacks' collective manhood, and a far more reliable agent of political transformation than moral suasion.[46]

In addition to its justification of violent resistance, *My Bondage and My Freedom* offers a piercing critique of contemporary understandings of publicity and the public sphere. Throughout his career after slavery, Douglass worked to remind audiences of the black presences in a public sphere most assumed to be white. As the scene of his march to Easton jail illustrates, that assumption is not only false, but it depends on a kind of double vision among a white population that both sees and does not see the black bodies that share public spaces. Personhood follows from the abstraction of selfhood—the notion that selfhood is distinct from one's physical person and is cultivated in private experience. Contemporary thinking about race regarded black people as lacking transcendent selfhood: their identity was coterminous with their physical persons, and that fact in turn justified white America's denial of the existence of a black private sphere. It also delegitimized any public expression a black person might dare offer. Douglass shows that by denying black selfhood on the basis of physical characteristics, white America ironically rendered these highly visible bodies invisible.

Douglass's determination to participate in the public sphere challenges and is challenged by such racist thinking. At the same time, however, the public sphere is itself being transformed by a developing celebrity culture that seeks meaning in the physical person. Douglass offers a complicated and varied response to these contradictions. His embrace of violent resistance acknowledges the rhetorical power of black bodies demanding the recognition of the white public. At the same time, he mocks a white public that embraces him as a celebrity against the logic of his own racism. The final chapter of *My Bondage and My Freedom* offers numerous illustrations of these points. Douglass closes the book with a series of "Various Incidents" (as the chapter is called) from his American travels. Immediately following Douglass's account of his two years in England, where he was treated with great warmth and respect, the chapter highlights America's cultural and political failure to meet its ideals of equality. This failure is illustrated by individuals' responses to Douglass himself, as prejudiced white observers regard him at first as a representative of his race and then as somehow different, unlike the black man of their imaginations and expectations. Just as he uses the techniques of slave narrative to reverse the gaze and question the humanity of the slaveholders, Douglass uses these later incidents to expose the inhumanity of the northerners' racist policies and behaviors. The result is a portrait, or series of portraits, not of himself as autobiographer but of white America and its confusion and anxiety about the presence of blacks in the public sphere.

As they did during the civil rights movement of the twentieth century, these anxieties play out in scenes of public transport—namely, the railroad. Douglass recalls his resistance to being forced off the whites-only cars of the Eastern Railroad, on which he frequently traveled from his home in Lynn, Massachusetts. "Thus seated" in the whites-only carriage, he recalls, "I was sure to be called upon to betake myself to the '*Jim Crow car*.' Refusing to obey, I was often dragged out of my seat, beaten, and severely bruised, by conductors and brakemen" (*DA* 394). His resistance leads to even greater conflict with railway conductors. When he refuses requests to remove himself to the Jim Crow car, Douglass relates, "they clutched me, head, neck, and shoulders. But, in anticipation of the stretching to which I was about to be subjected, I had interwoven myself among the seats. In dragging me out, on this occasion, it must have cost the company twenty-five or thirty dollars, for I tore up seats and all. So great was the excitement in Lynn, on the subject, that the superintendent, Mr. Stephan A. Chase, ordered the trains to run through Lynn without stopping, while I remained in that town; and this ridiculous farce was enacted" (*DA* 394). In the passage, Douglass turns the tables on his antagonists, revealing them to be brutish in their attack on a person of character and delicacy. Physically, this is a fight Douglass is bound to lose, and he knows it. But like Henry's refusal to be tied up, his resistance expresses his manly strength of character and draws public attention to the railroad's Jim Crow policy. His act of resistance resonates as an act of civil disobedience and, Douglass further notes, contributes to the Eastern Railroad's eventual desegregation. Douglass does not take complete credit for this policy change: "The result was not brought about without the intervention of the people," he admits, and he credits also Massachusetts legislator Charles Francis Adams for his "signal service" in bringing about legislative action (*DA* 394, 395). Nevertheless, the anecdote as a whole makes clear that Douglass's physical resistance to oppression galvanized public interest—it made the issue visible, where it had before been unnoticed. The story of Douglass's defying Jim Crow parallels his resisting Covey and other instruments of white oppression. Slavery does not exist in the North, but as Douglass argues, race prejudice in social convention and legal structure forces free and fugitive blacks to endure a second slavery that restrains their freedom of movement, speech, and association. And as slaves are socially dead, Douglass suggests that segregationist policies and Jim Crow cars likewise entail the social death of black people by effectively removing them from the public sphere. In this manner, the public sphere is in fact private in character, a zone of privilege cordoned off less by money—Douglass pays for the first-class ticket—than by race.

The incident hinges on Douglass's significance, not as a black public figure but as a black man in public. Only in the retelling, in his autobiography, does his celebrity come into play, overlaying the incident with a veneer of irony. In the retelling, the incident is ironic because the readers know who Douglass is in a way that his antagonists on the train either do not know or refuse to recognize. Douglass clearly enjoys upending conventional expectations of himself based on his appearance in the public sphere. In another incident on a train, Douglass recalls white passengers' unwillingness to take the seat next to him on a crowded car until he is greeted by the governor, who promptly takes the free seat. "The despised seat now became honored," Douglass recalls. "His excellency had removed all the prejudice against sitting by the side of a negro; and upon his leaving it, as he did, on reaching Pittsfield, there were at least one dozen applicants for the place" (*DA* 396). Douglass presents the episode as a comic lesson in the folly of prejudice and the credulity of the crowd, who are easily swayed by the example of prominent men. But the episode also demonstrates the cultural use of Douglass's own celebrity. He and the governor, he explains, had no prior relationship: "I was not acquainted with him, and had no idea that I was known to him. Known to him, however, I was" (*DA* 396), and on the basis of this knowledge the governor approached the former slave. Douglass omits or chooses not to consider the question of whether the governor would have so approached an anonymous black passenger. Clearly, Douglass's celebrity paved the way for his personal acceptance in public, and his representative status in turn paves the way for more widespread acceptance of other black people.

In his acts of physical resistance on the trains, Douglass uses his body to draw attention to the presence of other black bodies in the American public sphere. His physical resistance is for him an extension of or complement to his efforts as a public lecturer, which likewise take rhetorical strength from his physical person. However uncomfortable Douglass may have been with the efforts of the AASS to draw meaning from his physical person—with their consistent sentimental association of his blackness with the abuses of slavery—he attempted to make rhetorical use of his body as well. In contrast with arguments suggesting that the focus on Douglass's body returned him to figurative slavery, Robert Fanuzzi argues that Douglass controlled his physical presence on the lecture platform in a manner that suggested his adherence to republican principles. He did so using familiar oratorical conventions gleaned from *The Columbian Orator* and other popular eloquence manuals.[47] In a sense, Douglass relied on his body to efface it: through careful and strategic presentation of his physical person, Douglass claimed the status of abstract, disembodied personhood that was the privilege of masculinity and autonomy. If this is part of his strategy on the lecture platform, where his body is visible to all onlookers, it is certainly in play in his autobiography, where his voice emerges from the page and his person is a fabrication of language and the reader's imagination only. The incidents on the train are therefore encounters between men, and while the physical action is crucial to the stories, the specifics of skin tones and scars are incidental to the issues of justice and equality that the stories develop. Interestingly, these abstractions become clearer as his physical self is itself rendered abstract.

THE CONTINUING PROBLEM, HOWEVER, WAS THAT HIS PHYSICAL PERson was not rendered entirely abstract. Throughout his career, Douglass encountered instances where his status as universal subject or juridical person was denied by a mass public mindful of his racial difference from the perceived norm. As Jeannine DeLombard has shown, reviews of Douglass's lectures consistently focused on his body rather than his oratory.[48] DeLombard concludes that this shows how Douglass's oratorical performance was impeded by persistent racism, and while this is indeed likely, it is also worth noting that such attention to a popular lecturer's person is not Douglass's lot alone. As we have already seen, Emerson's audiences also tried to "read" his body and regarded his physical appearance as a text that complemented or even superseded his oratorical one. While interpretations of Douglass's body certainly registered his audience's racial attitudes, I would argue that the tendency to interpret the public figure as a physical text is widespread and a component of celebrity culture. Douglass's career demonstrates the ways these interpretations may be inflected by or reflective of audiences' attitudes about race. In addition, the particular dynamics of Douglass's personal circumstances as a former slave-turned-celebrity make him particularly mindful of the interplay between body and publicity. As the episodes on the railroad cars demonstrate, Douglass recognizes the cultural tendency to regard him primarily as a physical text, and as he skillfully turns spectators' expectations back on themselves he encourages them to reconsider the black body—to reread it—as a mere surface masking the individual consciousness that it conceals. Emerson's trope of transparency is useful here: Douglass's public performances of selfhood aim to lead spectators to moments of transparent vision, in which they do not fail to see his blackness, but they manage to see through it to recognize the humanity, not to say the divinity, that lies within. In this way, the black body in public ceases to be a curiosity or a spectacle, and social equality emerges as a possibility if not yet a full-fledged reality.

These performances of self must occur repeatedly and in shifting contexts, however, and Douglass's later career sees him confronting the same objectifying gaze from different audiences and in different scenes. His third and final autobiography, *Life and Times* (1881, 1892), represents Douglass as a public figure and continues the work of addressing the conflicting interpretations of him. For instance, the encounter with Governor Briggs on the railway car that Douglass recounts in *My Bondage and My Freedom* parallels an incident he relates in *Life and Times*. In 1864 Douglass presented himself at the White House reception of newly reelected president Abraham Lincoln, only to be turned away by the guards, "for their directions were to admit no persons of my color" (*DA* 803). When the officers attempted to conduct Douglass and his companion out a side exit, he prevailed on another guest who recognized him: "Be so kind as to say to Mr. Lincoln that Frederick Douglass is detained by officers at the door" (*DA* 804). When at last admitted, Douglass writes, he was greeted warmly by the president, with whom he had consulted during Lincoln's previous term in office. The scene is one of two celebrities meeting on a rarefied plane, recognizing in one another their parallel stories of self-making and achievement. Asking Douglass's opinion of his inaugural address, Lincoln says, "There is no man in the country whose opinion I value more than yours" (*DA* 804). In both his appeal to the bystander at the White House and his retelling of the event in *Life and Times*, the incident reveals Douglass as more willing than ever to use his celebrity to demonstrate his public stature and innate equality. The president's compliment indicates Douglass's tremendous achievement as an orator and social critic, an identity he holds in higher regard than his past as a slave, for it is that past, and its popular associations with racial inferiority, that first bars him from the White House's East Room.

On the whole, *Life and Times* emphasizes this more mature and nuanced character. In it, Douglass emerges as a man influenced but not dominated by his experience in bondage. The work focuses on Douglass's career as a servant of public causes—it is, as Houston Baker points out, the document of a public life and career rather than an activist tale of bondage and escape.[49] But that public life derives its value—its legitimacy—from the abstract personhood that motivates it. Douglass's *Life and Times* goes even farther than his earlier books in confronting the dynamics of publicity and privacy that both enabled and impeded Douglass's public actions. The result is a book that defies the conventions of both the slave narrative and the autobiography. And whereas the first two books developed the idea of Douglass as a figure simultaneously representative and extraordinary, *Life and Times* presents him, in George L. Ruffin's words, as "*sui generis*. . . . When we bring forward Douglass, he cannot be matched" (*DA* 467). Douglass may also contain multitudes. The idea is not to catalog them but to have the depth of his subjectivity recognized. Or, to return to the Emersonian touchstone, he seeks public acknowledgment of the infinitude of his private experience. As a result, instead of a national representative of the millions who experienced slavery and racial oppression in America, the Douglass of *Life and Times* is an aspirational figure who transforms conventional understandings of race and achievement: "With this example," Ruffin writes, "the black boy as well as the white boy can take hope and courage in the race of life" (*DA* 468).

This self-consciously public stature that Douglass presumes in *Life and Times* is certainly justified by the eventful course of his life. Douglass's exposure as a celebrity contrasts starkly with the invisibility of his origins in slavery—his relegation there to the private sphere of his white master. At the same time, Douglass recognizes privacy as necessary to the cultivation of an abstract selfhood and as the privilege of citizenship. In part 2 of the book, Douglass addresses the conflicting demands of publicity and privacy by recounting the "knotty questions" he has been "pelted with" by curious observers over the years:

> There is no disguising the fact that the American people are much interested and mystified about the mere matter of color as connected with manhood. It seems to them that color has some moral or immoral qualities and especially the latter. . . . Hence I have often been bluntly and sometimes very rudely asked, of what color my mother was, and of what color was my father? In what proportion does the blood of the various races mingle in my veins, especially how much white blood and how much black blood entered into my composition? Whether I was not part Indian as well as African and Caucasian? Whether I considered myself more African than Caucasian, or the reverse? Whether I derived my intelligence from my father, or from my mother, from my white, or from my black blood? . . . Why did I marry a person of my father's complexion instead of marrying one of my mother's complexion? How is the race problem to be solved in this country? Will the negro go back to Africa or remain here? Under this shower of purely American questions, more or less personal, I have endeavored to possess my soul in patience and get as much good out of life as was possible with so much to occupy my time; and, though often perplexed, seldom losing my temper, or abating heart or hope for the future of my people. (*DA* 939–40)

This long passage—and I have omitted a fair amount in the interest of space—goes to the heart of the matter of Douglass's celebrity. It suggests that celebrity both abetted and impeded Douglass's larger social and political aims. Douglass's celebrity and public achievement provide an object on whom curious audiences quite literally project their questions about race. However intrusive these questions may be at times, Douglass recognizes that they are not personal per se. His efforts to rein in his patience and temper reflect his awareness that the questions and his responses to them are in fact part of his ongoing work toward fuller racial understanding and equality. At the same time, his need to control his temper reveals his frustration, not to say offense, at observers' pertinacity, their unconscious willingness to once again impose on his rights to private relationships of any shape or color.

Simultaneously frustrated by and sympathetic with his white observers, Douglass recognizes the significance of his life in the post-Emancipation United States. After the Civil War, Douglass sought to preserve the rights of the freedmen and promoted a philosophy of black self-reliance. His emancipationist view of Reconstruction was at odds with others as the nation struggled to remake itself. As David Blight argues, the philosophy and policies of national forgetting enabled white Americans to get beyond the traumas of war even as they overlooked or ignored slavery's role in the conflict.[50] Similarly, John Ernest claims that in the late nineteenth century, "the new visibility of the northward-bound black body marks its invisibility in the national narrative." In this context, where racism and a desire for national progress collude to erase the emancipated black population from the collective white consciousness, Douglass's renewed claims to national purpose and prominence "are examples of Douglass's attempt to transcend a cultural script beyond his control in his performance of a variety of cultural roles, and of his increasingly vexed awareness of his audience."[51] Douglass's catalog of personal questions he received takes on particular meaning in this historical context. Beyond their rudeness, the questions Douglass faces raise the question of whether, as a celebrity, Douglass is a representative figure after all, or if his value lies only in the exceptional nature of his achievements—and whether either of these possibilities reflects a hopelessly limited understanding of race and identity.

Given the tensions between the great or public man as mere spectacle or as genius, Douglass's task in *Life and Times* is a difficult one: he must use his stature as a celebrated figure to advance his emancipationist vision without becoming a distraction from that purpose. He must reinvigorate his role as a representative figure even in the full awareness of audiences' capacity to regard him as an exceptional figure—even while willing, to a certain extent, to agree with that view. To this end, *Life and Times* revisits Douglass's early years as a slave, the narrative of which establishes his representative status. In his discussions of his life after slavery, Douglass aims to situate his career in the specific circumstances of the moment to again emphasize his representative nature. As the title of his book implies, the coincidence of his exceptional character with the demands of his particular time establish him as a man of the age, representative of what might be achieved with effort, but who is nonetheless constrained by circumstance to channel his energies to specific ends. Like one of Emerson's great men, he is a man at one with his times, whose talents and efforts are attuned to the larger currents of human nature.

Douglass's recasting himself as representative not merely of his race but of larger historical forces is clearest in his representations of his post-Emancipation family life and reunions with members of the Auld family. Across all of his writings, Douglass is notoriously silent with respect to his family life. His silences about family secure for him a privileged private sphere of which he is the patriarchal head, and his absorption of domestic ideology demands that he be included in the ranks of national manhood despite his race. But Douglass's escape from the objectifying white gaze was incomplete, as is demonstrated by public reaction to his marriage to Helen Pitts in 1884. By now a prominent public figure, Douglass was subject to "intense and predictable" backlash from both black and white observers for daring to marry a white woman,[52] and it is this criticism, not the marriage itself, that Douglass describes in *Life and Times*. In doing so,

Douglass acknowledges the limitations of his achieving public acceptance—he acknowledges that his personhood, like Pitts's, remains embodied in public. At the same time, his refusal to discuss the details of his marriage reflects his continued insistence on his personhood.

In contrast with his near silence about his domestic life, Douglass provides detailed accounts of his meetings with members of the Auld family. Douglass discusses meetings with two people, Amanda Auld Sears, daughter of his former master Thomas Auld and his wife Lucretia Aaron Auld, and Thomas Auld himself. Descriptions of meetings with both these individuals bring personal detail to Douglass's story even as they serve as a parable for a nation struggling to reconcile North and South, black and white. They reveal the limits of the public language of politics and policy making, uncovering the private experience that complicates the ongoing political challenges of postbellum American society. If Douglass does not answer directly his audience's personal questions, he recognizes their need to confront and explore the deeply personal legacy of slavery in order to complete the work of Reconstruction.

Douglass's strained relationships with the Auld family had long been a focal point of his story and a cornerstone of his rhetorical method. As Douglass points out, his encounters with both Mrs. Sears and Auld himself were overshadowed by Douglass's public representations of Auld in his slave narratives, speeches, and other writings (*DA* 875). For instance, Douglass's open letter to his former master, published in the *Liberator* in 1848, accuses Auld of the most heinous crimes associated with slavery and calls Auld to moral account for his actions. Douglass asks Auld to imagine himself in the slave's position, such that he must witness the kidnapping and violation "of your own lovely daughter Amanda." This reversal of the relation between master and slave is rhetorically powerful—and also extreme, as Douglass well knows. "I intend to make use of you as a weapon with which to assail the system of slavery," he writes. "In doing this I entertain no malice toward you personally."[53] Drawing attention to the ways in which his dehumanized portrayal of Auld is contrived, Douglass underscores the artifice and effort that goes into dehumanizing Africans. And in his rhetorical reversal of the master-slave dynamic, Douglass denies Auld the shelter of privacy that has long been the refuge and the privilege of the master class.

Douglass's representations of Auld and the Auld family in his earlier writings form the backdrop for his post-Emancipation meetings with Thomas Auld and his daughter, Amanda Auld Sears. As Douglass recounts, John L. Sears, Amanda's husband, first refuses to converse with him or present him to Amanda: "Mr. Sears said that in my 'Narrative' I had done his father-in-law injustice, for he was really a kind-hearted man, and a good master. I replied that there must be two sides to the relation of master and slave, and what was deemed kind and just to the one was the opposite to the other" (*DA* 830). This exchange leads to Mr. Sears's agreeing to allow Douglass to call on his wife. In the account of the meeting, Douglass acknowledges that he sought the Aulds on friendly terms: "If any reader of this part of my life shall see in it the evidence of a want of manly resentment for wrongs inflicted by slavery upon myself and race, and by the ancestors of this lady, so it must be. No man can be stronger than nature, one touch of which, we are told, makes all the world akin. I esteem myself a good, persistent hater of injustice and oppression, but my resentment ceases when they cease, and I have no heart to visit upon children the sins of their fathers" (*DA* 832). Building on representations of Auld as a father figure that occur across his writings,[54] Douglass acts here as the representative of justice and reconciliation, and he posits the kinship between himself and his white family as indicative of the kinship binding all humanity together. Such revenge as he might once have sought he has already had, in the form of the 1848 letter and, on a larger plane, the North's ultimate triumph over the South and slavery. The encounters between Douglass and the Aulds are therefore crucial to the *Life and Times* as models of reconciliation between the aggrieved parties, slaves and slave masters, in the aftermath of their revolution in their relations to one another. Moreover, as Douglass contextualizes them in the autobiography, they are models of the kind of accepting, familial relations possible between black and white more generally in the postbellum age.

Douglass met with Amanda Sears on three occasions: first in 1859, amid the crisis caused by John Brown's raid on Harpers Ferry and the suspicion it cast on Douglass as his friend; next in 1866, in a crowded Philadelphia street; and finally in 1878, as Mrs. Sears lay on her deathbed. In *Life and Times*, Douglass carefully contextualizes discussion of his renewed ties to Mrs. Sears to support his larger argument for national racial reconciliation. He introduces Mrs. Sears in the midst of relating his involvement in the 1866 Loyalist Convention, a national convention organized in support of the Fourteenth Amendment and in reaction against the southernist and racist National Union convention meeting at the same time. Some delegates to the convention objected to Douglass's presence on the grounds that his well-publicized support for the black vote would prove divisive,[55] but Douglass highlights the racism at the heart of these objections: as the only black delegate, Douglass recalls, "I was the ugly and deformed child of the family, and to be kept out of sight as much as possible while there was company in the house" (*DA* 827). In contrast to this tension in the metaphorical family of the activist community, Douglass recognizes the affectionate embrace of his extended family, the public itself, when, during the delegates' procession to Philadelphia City Hall, he reports, he was cheered by the crowds. This warm welcome tells Douglass that "the people were more enlightened and had made more progress than their leaders had supposed" (*DA* 828). The leaders in turn were instructed by the crowds: "After the demonstrations of this first day, I found myself a welcome member of the convention, and cordial greeting took the place of cold aversion" (*DA* 829).

Douglass's meeting with Mrs. Sears occurs during the delegates' procession. He identifies her in the crowd and breaks ranks to greet her. Reporting their meeting in his autobiography, Douglass uses Mrs. Sears to exemplify the crowd's warm personal welcome, a welcome more notable because of his highly publicized use of Amanda and her father in his antislavery writings. Their brief family reunion on the Philadelphia street, noted by a crowd of onlookers that included members of the press, is for Douglass a shining example of the magnanimity and openheartedness required to heal the larger social family. Douglass extends this point by using the occasion of his public encounter with Mrs. Sears to segue into their more private meeting in 1859, which, I have noted, occurred only after a frank conversation with her husband about his representations of Thomas Auld in the *Narrative*. When Douglass does gain admission to Mrs. Sears's parlor, he is required to identify her from among a large company of women, effectively proving his right to mingle on equal terms with his former master's daughter. After he passes this test, Mrs. Sears greets him warmly and "made haste to tell me that she agreed with me about slavery, and that she had freed all her slaves as they had become of age" (*DA* 832). With this claim, Mrs. Sears establishes an intellectual equality with Douglass, whose views she acknowledges as her own. The parallels to the Loyalists' Convention and the nation at large are clear: the nation's preeminent spokesman for antislavery and equal rights must demonstrate his goodwill toward his former oppressors, but just as importantly, they must demonstrate their goodwill toward himself.

The same message comes through Douglass's remarkable meeting with Thomas Auld in 1877. Although this visit occurred in the former master's most private sanctum—he lay dying in bed—it was publicized by reporters who accompanied Douglass on his trip and called the meeting "very affecting."[56] For Douglass, the trip to Saint Michael's is a kind of homecoming. He calls Saint Michael's "the place of my home and the scene of some of my saddest experiences of slave life" (*DA* 874). In addition to his two visits with Auld, Douglass toured the Auld estate; revisited the scenes of important incidents of his early years, including Easton jail; and made at least one public speech. In that speech he denied having political intentions, but the visit with Auld, Douglass's account of it, and his public comments at the time reiterate Douglass's Emancipationist vision. Part of that vision necessarily includes Douglass's public grappling with his ambivalence about Auld and his personal past. He calls both the trip and the invitation to meet with Auld "strange" and reflects on the improbability of the situation:

"Had I been asked in the days of slavery to visit this man I should have regarded the invitation as one to put fetters on my ankles and handcuffs on my wrists," he admits (*DA* 874, 875). But the revolution wrought by the war not only put the two men "upon equal ground" (*DA* 875); it also altered Douglass's understanding of the past: "Our courses had been determined for us, not by us. We had both been flung, by powers that did not ask our consent, upon a mighty current of life, which we could neither resist nor control. By this current he was a master, and I a slave; but now our lives were verging towards a point where differences disappear, where even the constancy of hate breaks down and where the clouds of pride, passion and selfishness vanish before the brightness of infinite light" (*DA* 876). Douglass's deterministic interpretation of the past is the foundation for a new social vision: the system that made Auld a master and Douglass a slave is gone; Auld himself will soon die. His passing, and by extension the passing of the master class as a whole, augurs a new status for Douglass and all freedmen, and rather than hold on to past injuries, Douglass accepts the adjusted state of relations with equanimity. In contrast with his heavily sentimentalized rhetoric in the open letter to Auld,[57] Auld's mortality does not lead Douglass to sentimentalize or even sympathize with him. If he holds no malice toward the old master, neither does he judge him charitably. Instead, the meeting, and the transformed political reality it reflects, gains meaning as the old associations drain away and even differences as great as those of master and slave "disappear."

It is nearly impossible to imagine what the meeting must have meant to each man on a personal level. Douglass records that both men were tearful but "got the better of our feelings" (*DA* 877). Douglass asks Auld for information about his birthday, ignorance of which was "a serious trouble to me" (*DA* 877); additionally, he may have been reassured by Auld's claims that he never turned out Douglass's grandmother, as Douglass had accused him of doing in the *Narrative*. In any event, the purpose of the visit in *Life and Times* is not personal but rhetorical. Douglass uses the episode to underscore his critique of slavery as a deterministic social force, a system that controls slaves and masters alike: "I did not run away from *you*, but from *slavery*," he tells Auld, and he reiterates "that I regarded both of us as victims of a system" (*DA* 877). Douglass refuses to personalize slavery even as he addresses it in the most personal terms possible, in a confrontation with his former master, the closest thing to a father he has known. The recognition of slavery as a system enables Douglass and others to move beyond the personal injuries they suffered and into the new political and social spaces created in slavery's absence. In Auld, Douglass represents slavery's passing, not unforgotten but gone. To drive this point home, he describes the Saint Michael's estate as it appeared in 1877: "in my boyhood, sixty men were employed in cultivating the home farm alone. Now, by the aid of machinery, the work is accomplished by ten men" (*DA* 881). His implication is clear; in the absence of slavery, there is not just freedom but prosperity for those who would seek it.

The continuing debates about the rightful place of the black body in public life make Douglass's reunions with his white family especially important, and he gives them detailed attention in *Life and Times*. The meetings reflect the uneasy encounters between pro- and antislavery interests years after the national trauma of the war. Symbolically, they are reminders that the house divided was not only the North and South, but also the plantation household, whose members strained to meet one another on terms of justice in the aftermath of conflict. In representing these encounters, Douglass uses his celebrity stature to model a harmonious resolution to the nation's family feud. But the resolution he offers is not simply a restoration of the symbolic national family on newly altered terms. His own prominence, the publicity of his past use of the Aulds and of his reunions with them, contribute to his ongoing work of asserting the equality and indeed the presence of the black body in public life. If the tremendous publicity of his second marriage demonstrated that the black American remained embodied in public, his encounters with Sears and Auld suggest that circumstance will not change unless blacks' private relationships do as well. Just as the slaves' vacancy from the public sphere was created by the "private death" of bondage, their incorporation into the public sphere as juridical persons would depend on their acceptance into the parlors and bedrooms of bourgeois white society on equal terms.

IN DETAILING HIS RETURN TO SAINT MICHAEL'S, DOUGLASS MASTERFULLY balances personal detail with political philosophy. His descriptions of the Auld estate and his conversation with his old master make explicit comparisons between Douglass's boyhood in bondage and his maturity as a free man of some substance and clout. Implicitly, too, Douglass explores the transformation the nation has undergone in the same period of political and social upheaval. His account invites a reconsideration of the portrait of the slave plantation and its complicated dynamics of privacy and publicity: in the aftermath of Emancipation and Reconstruction, the plantation is still a place where public and private concerns are entangled, where a black man's bedside visit with an aged white man is an event of public significance conducted in a private setting. Having said that, Douglass's celebrity makes the meeting possible in the first place, and it secures the visit's newspaper coverage. Recognizing the power of his celebrity to gain public attention, Douglass manages his publicity to draw attention to the political significance of the apparently personal relationships at the heart of race relations in the United States.

As exposed as he is—in Saint Michael's, in his various writings, on the lecture platform—Douglass remains inscrutable. His expression is ever tuned for rhetorical resonance; his most righteous anger serves his arguments, his personal griefs represent a general condition, and he turns sentiment to public use. Douglass himself stands behind this scrim of public feeling. As an autobiographical writer, Douglass does not just project a persona, an idealized alter ego, but redirects the public gaze at a "prosthetic person"—that is, one that "takes abuse for the private person" in the full sense of the word "person" as "the unit of political membership in the American nation."[58] This technique at once conceals the veridical self from public view and also makes that self—the fact of its existence—known. And that act of consciousness making is inherently political, because it contradicts racial ideologies that deny the possibility of black selfhood.

The problem Douglass's celebrity raises is not to wonder how Douglass really felt—in calling his anger rhetorical, I do not question its authenticity—but to seek the fullness of his experience. Douglass recognizes, however, that the curiosity is also a political necessity insofar as it tacitly acknowledges the existence of a self that is affected by, if unknown to, the larger world. That recognition legitimates Douglass's participation in the public sphere. Where he was once only visible, an embodiment of blackness and oppression, he is now audible, too, and as a representative figure, he strives to make it more difficult for white America to deny the presence and voices of other black men and women in the public sphere. Douglass's celebrity by no means cured America of its racism, nor did his calls for mutual acceptance restore the American family riven by civil war. His celebrity is an important early example of the politics of presence, however—of the cultural significance of visibility, especially for minorities. As his example shows, the results of such politics cannot be measured in policies enacted or offices gained, because it seeks to influence popular feeling.

CHAPTER 5

FANNY FERN
Celebrity's Revolutionary Power

WHEN FANNY FERN BEGAN WRITING FOR ROBERT BONNER'S *New York Ledger* in 1855, she became the highest-paid newspaper writer in America—a fact known to newspaper readers in New York and elsewhere because Bonner advertised it. But readers did not know just how much Fern was earning until, in the weeks leading up to Fern's debut in the *Ledger*'s pages, Bonner confirmed that he was paying her a hundred dollars per column. After serializing her story "Fanny Ford" at that rate, in 1856 Bonner negotiated a contract to pay Fern a whopping twenty-five dollars per week to write exclusively for his paper, and he publicized that, too. The combination of high salaries and aggressive publicity paid off for Bonner: the *Ledger* drew a hundred thousand new subscribers. Fern's column was a mainstay of the *Ledger* for the next sixteen years—the rest of Fern's life—while Bonner continued to hire other celebrity writers at high rates and publish them with great fanfare.[1]

Fern's arrival at the *Ledger* exemplifies the ways celebrity culture links personality and profit. In hiring Fern, Bonner recognized not only the quality of her writing but also the marketability of Fern herself, the appeal of her personal story, curiosity about her identity, and controversy over the propriety of her writing. These same interests followed Fern from her emergence in the *Olive Branch* newspaper in 1851, but Bonner's Barnumesque embrace of aggressive promotional practices in the personal public sphere enabled him to capitalize on them as no one else had done. Both he and Fern profited by the arrangement: like Bonner, Fern recognized that her personality—her public expression of self—drove popular interest in her writing. As Brenda Weber explains, Fern's entire career hinged on her ability to feed public interest in herself while at the same time protecting herself from celebrity's voracious hunger for the public figure: she "was able to alter the signifying terms of the culture in which she resided largely by constructing various and contradictory figures of female literary celebrity."[2] Early on, Fern perfected writing strategies that both revealed and concealed the self: her first-person style affected various personas, from the sensible old maid to the practical bluestocking to the self-regarding "Miss Fan," all of which projected her unconventional thinking and masked the details of her personal background that her readers craved. In all of this, as Weber notes, Fern evades the aspects of celebrity that threaten to overwhelm or consume her, even as she continues to court public interest in and even desire for her.

From her first appearance in the *Olive Branch* in 1851, Fern encounters readers who respond to her directly, personally, and authoritatively. These letters initiate the public queries into Fern's "real" identity that persist throughout her career. Responding publicly to those queries in letters of her own, Fern actively participates in the construction of her own celebrity image. The *Olive Branch* letters reveal celebrity as a process of reading, responding to, and writing the celebrity image or personality—a process that is aptly illustrated by epistolary reciprocity.[3] At the same time, the letters show Fern's efforts not only to evade public identification—she uses the letters to establish and defend her pseudonymity—but, moreover, to reconceptualize identity itself by encouraging ongoing exchange and response that liberates identity from ideological fixtures.

Among those fixtures, the idealization of women's sexual purity is especially limiting, Fern realizes. More than any writer of the age except, perhaps, Whitman, Fern wrote about sex frankly and critically. Her critiques of gender ideologies explore the various results of a sexual double standard that granted men erotic license but bound women to notions of virtue that were personally and socially crippling. Indeed, Fern tacitly acknowledges desire, *erotic* desire, as central to her appeal. A key element of her public relations is her skillful handling of the erotic dimensions of her fame. Moreover, Fern used her own celebrity to reveal and interrogate the erotic dimensions of public life. As a woman in the public eye, Fern was keenly aware of the transgressiveness of her situation: daring to publish her views on matters of cultural and political significance, Fern claimed her right to participate in a public sphere from which women were excluded on the grounds that they lacked an abstract self. Women's identities were understood to be rooted in their bodies, in their unique biological functions that were in turn rooted in sex. Fern's celebrity reveals just how these cultural assumptions worked to silence women and exclude them from public life. Specifically, she shows that gender ideology of the time denied women the privacy men enjoyed as both a retreat from public life and also the source of abstract personhood. Like Frederick Douglass, Fern both rejected this claim and charted an alternative route to selfhood through the public sphere itself. Fern's work points out the ironies of a culture that regards women as completely present—subjects them to constant observation, surveillance, and objectification—yet fails to recognize the complexities of their experience. Those complexities, she suggests, are the basis of selfhood.

Across Fern's body of work, she aims to redefine selfhood in a manner that will accommodate women. Specifically, she encourages sympathy, the mutual recognition of other's emotional conditions, as the basis for abstract selfhood. Such sympathy promises to transform the public sphere, making it more inclusive, and it is both necessitated and challenged by celebrity culture. Fern's novel *Ruth Hall* (1855) dramatizes the situation even as it reflects Fern's own experience: as she transforms from Ruth to the popular writer "Floy," the novel's protagonist moves from obscurity to visibility. Fern shows how Ruth's years as an obscure, conventional woman in the private sphere are strangely public, while as the celebrity Floy she is at once highly visible and unrecognizable. In her depictions of Ruth in both celebrity and obscurity, Fern contrasts the interpretations of Ruth that adhere to conventional sentimental values for womanhood with those that reflect genuine sympathy for her. Fern promotes this sympathy as the corrective to a society governed by sentimental ideology because it affirms women's selfhood. At the same time, however, *Ruth Hall* shows how celebrity culture capitalizes on sentiment: the vitriolic responses to Floy's writings only inflame popular desires that consumption of her work temporarily satisfies without dictating what those desires are. In other words, Ruth's writings make readers want Floy, but they do not settle the question of what readers want her to be or who they think she is. The questions about Ruth's identity get aired in a commercial marketplace in which women participate every day as readers and consumers. Fern recognizes women's overlooked presence in the public sphere because she understands the social and political significance of consumption—hence she is well positioned to exploit her own celebrity as an agent of social change.

SARA WILLIS PARTON HAD GOOD REASONS TO ADOPT A PSEUDONYM. In the first place, she was a professional writer in an era when respectable women were restricted from public life and confined to the domestic arena. Second, her editorial essays and sketches offered unconventional views of marriage, motherhood, and the relations between the sexes in an unapologetically direct style, and they tended to arouse controversy. Finally, following the death of her first husband, she survived an abusive second marriage and divorce that brought scandal to her and her family: stung by her leaving him, her ex-husband, Samuel Farrington, spread false rumors of Fern's adultery that encouraged her relations to withhold all support from her and her two daughters. To write under her own name would only intensify the scandal and bring further hardship to her and her children. Like the protagonist of her autobiographical first novel, *Ruth Hall*, Fern turned to professional authorship out of dire economic necessity, and with her pen she remade her identity, made her fortune, and built her celebrity.

In collaboration with her editors, Fern managed to keep her identity a secret for several years despite her readers' efforts to identify her. She was exposed in 1856 by a vindictive former editor, William U. Moulton of Boston's *True Flag*, for which she wrote from 1852 to 1853. Moulton justified his revelation by citing Fern's accomplishments: "the lives of distinguished men or women have always been accounted public property," he wrote.[4] When she enters the public sphere of print, the invasive scrutiny of Moulton and others denies Fern the disembodied subjectivity that print culture privileges. As we have already seen in the examples of Emerson and Douglass, in celebrity culture the public does indeed hunger for personal information about the public figure, but to equate that desire with a right as to property is problematic. At best, it is irritating and invasive; at worst, it undermines the privacy that is essential to cultivating the self. Fern's story shows how gender plays into the dynamic issues of privacy and publicity that come with celebrity. As Fern's writings consistently point out, women are subject to near-constant surveillance by husbands, parents, neighbors, and society at large. The ideology of separate spheres consigns women to the private sphere of the home. Her actions there are invisible to others unless or until she violates the rules of domestic or social order. Women therefore experience a double status with respect to privacy and publicity: their fulfillment of conventional gender roles and duties requires women's vigilant attention to their behavior and appearance before others and subjects them to others' observations and judgment. But at the same time, these gender conventions occlude women's experience from public view. In such an environment, to call Fern a "public woman" is to invoke an array of complex claims: insofar as she states her ideas and opinions in writing, she puts herself in the public sphere, defying traditional gender roles. In Mary Kelley's words, Fern and other female writers are "displaced people" or "hybrids, a new breed."[5] But Fern's critique of traditional gender roles argues that all women are "public women" such as herself. As a celebrity she experiences a magnified version of the scrutiny all women face, yet, like other women, her public exposure does not reveal the fullness of her character and experience.

As a writer, Fern draws extensively on personal experience. Her autobiographical novel *Ruth Hall* is the most obvious example, but her newspaper writing is also heavily autobiographical—so much so that Laura Laffrado suggests interpreting it via "the poetics of women's autobiography": "The weekly publication of the newspaper essay—its scheduled, familiar discourse—promotes the woman writer's repeated redefinitions and reconfigurations of the self."[6] In Laffrado's analysis, Fern's autobiographical self emerges through analysis of her various historical personas. As autobiography, Fern's newspaper pieces work indirectly, casting a self-portrait that is refracted by the contours of her fictive persona. Fern's episodic, variegated, and revisionist approach to self-representation relates to the "fissures" and "displacements" that Shari Benstock claims characterize women's autobiography, which is not beholden to linear chronology or even a cohesive idea of self.[7] These features differentiate women's autobiography from the works that shape a masculine autobiographical tradition. These strategies of self-representation in women's autobiography respond to an ideology of self that excludes women. As Sidonie Smith explains, autobiography involves the articulation of a disembodied, abstract self capable of higher reasoning and intellectual transcendence, all qualities that nineteenth-century America naturalizes as masculine. By contrast, women's selfhood is determined by their bodies—their biological function as mothers, their sexuality, and the "encumbrances" of family and domestic responsibilities that these require: "In thrall to her body and to the affections and behavior associated with her encumbrances, 'woman' remains 'naturally' less rational than man. Rather than working logically, her mind works from the margins of logic: her way of knowing and interpreting is less abstract, less integrative, less transcendent, less impartial, and less self-conscious than the interpretive mode of 'metaphysical man.'"[8] For Fern (or indeed any woman writer) to write autobiography is to break with the conventions of gender ideology, defy recognizable and legible patterns of social behavior, and appear before the public as "a monster."[9] Granting this inevitability, Smith explains, the persevering woman writer can find freedom in her unmooring from conventional identity and "experiment . . . with the discursive elasticities inherent in self-imagining."[10]

Fern does both of these things. Her writings invite outraged responses from readers who deem the outspoken woman monstrous, a traitor to her sex. In the very acts of writing and publishing, she breaks out of the restricted zone of action permitted her as a woman and enters the masculine public sphere. And in her assumption of a pseudonym and creation of various, quasi-autobiographical personas, she occupies different subject positions and social roles that are nevertheless tethered to her as they express her views. Fern's playful self-representations—and sometimes deliberate misrepresentations—purposely challenge her readers' assumptions about her and about women in general. Stylistically, her writing combines techniques of fiction and nonfiction, sentiment and satire. This famously mixed style is surely one source of Fern's early celebrity, inasmuch as it delivered mixed signals about the writer's identity; for instance, one early reader queried whether she were "Jack or Gill."[11] Modern critics have been just as perplexed, wondering that Fern's deployments of sentiment hinted at her allegiance to conservative ideological values even as her more "acerbic" writings attacked the conservative mainstream views associated with sentiment.[12] But Fern's mixed style makes sense in light of Smith's claims about women's autobiography: "In daring to write about herself for public consumption, the autobiographer already transgressed cultural boundaries, straying beyond the boundaries of a 'selfhood' situated at the very margins of cultural action, meaning, and discourse into another's territory at the center of culture. As she wrote, she traveled discursively between these two territories, sometimes straying further into one territory, sometimes staying longer, but always weaving in and out of them in the complex dance of displacement and redeployment."[13] Representing herself in a culture ideologically unequipped to recognize or accept women's autobiographical writing, Fern "weaves" between spheres ideologically coded masculine and feminine, in the process generating a portrait of a self that is shaped simultaneously by conservative claims for womanhood and her own recognition of the insufficiency of those claims to account for her experience. This view of Fern's newspaper writing meshes with Susan K. Harris's persuasive analysis of Fern's elastic technique as a novelist. She notes, "the dual narrative voices of *Ruth Hall* indicate a writer trying to transcend the language and references that had already created her heroine.... The work is structured to show, first, how Ruth is defined by the voices of her culture; then, to suggest what kind of voice she might have when she finally begins speaking and writing for herself."[14] In both the novel and newspaper writings, the upshot of Fern's discursive strategy is to claim a self that is not limited by her body. The result is, necessarily, to enter into a public sphere that is not accepting of women's presence, in which the "public woman" is always a contradiction, always controversial—always a celebrity.

I emphasize Fern's celebrity rather than her notoriety, although that term too is apt. Chris Rojek points out that celebrity and notoriety are often linked, and he suggests that because "celebrity divides the individual from ordinary social life," it is itself a transgressive condition. Notoriety, a form of mass publicity that results from explicitly transgressive actions, "is often associated with shifts in aesthetic culture."[15] Certainly that is the case with Fern, the pathbreaking woman journalist with the revolutionary style and message. To call Fern notorious is to accept, as some of her contemporaries did, that her presence in public life crosses moral boundaries and reveals a degraded character. Celebrity, on the other hand, has a more positive connotation. Even as the celebrity's meaning is unsettled and subject to controversy, in general celebrity suggests the public's embrace of the popular figure by means of capitalist consumption. As Rojek explains, celebrity culture is one of the most important mechanisms for mobilizing "abstract desire" in the mass public, and the mechanisms by which celebrities' images are projected before the collective consciousness serve to "compel consumption."[16] Certainly this process is evident in Robert Bonner's heavy promotions of Fern, which I described at the start of this chapter; similarly aggressive advertising strategies made Fern's *Ruth Hall* a best-seller.[17] Fern's celebrity reveals the dimensions of consumers' desire.

While the economic model of celebrity registers desire in dollars, Fern herself registers affect as publicity's recompense. Exploring her aims to her earliest readers, Fern writes, "I always contrive to make people to love, or hate me, *with a VENGEANCE. I* don't care *which*; anything but a milk-sop indifference!" (*OB*, March 13, 1852). While it is true that Fern's readers expressed their sentiments economically, by buying a copy of the paper or one of her books, she clearly imagines their sentimental expression as part of a reciprocal or dialogic exchange with herself and other readers. Therefore, Fern's celebrity might be said to mobilize a desire to see and hear others, to be seen and heard—to participate in a personal public sphere. Fern's model of publicity acknowledges that the public sphere is the site not of reasoned debate but of the emotive expression mediated through a commodified print culture. And as she embraces sentimental discourse as a means of participating in the personal public sphere, she claims space there for herself and other women who are understood to lack the disembodied selfhood that is the ticket to the impersonal, or masculine, or reasoned, public sphere.

Accounting for Fern's celebrity, Joyce Warren has said that Fern produced "uncommon discourse"—discourse "that threatens the status quo"—even as she spent her career writing for periodicals that courted "the common people."[18] But what is it exactly that makes Fern's discourse uncommon? In many respects, Fern's work is conventional and highly professional. Known for her vernacular style, Fern was an able participant in the personal public sphere of the newspaper press. Her conversational vernacular style invites and elicits responses from her readers. Like her contemporary and sometime-friend Walt Whitman,[19] she uses her first-person writing style to create a recognizable persona. She calls out to other public figures in her newspaper sketches, and she uses the position of newspaper columnist to editorialize on ideas and events of public relevance—the significant difference being that, unlike most newspaper writers, she does not imagine "public" to be a synonym for "masculine." Fern's writing is unconventional not because she uses a satirical vernacular style or even because she is a woman, but because she dares to challenge conventional assumptions that the public is an abstraction of the idealized masculine ethos. She criticizes the assumption that the publicity men enjoy elevates them or transforms them into civic paragons, the models of classical democratic virtue. On the contrary, the assumption of a disembodied masculine public sphere provides men cover from which they may indulge physical pleasures, from tobacco use to sexual dalliances, which negatively affect others with whom they share both public and private spaces. At the same time, Fern uses her own celebrity to draw attention to the presence of women in public and to reveal the doctrine of separate spheres as a fiction. Her observational sketches of city life often focus on the hardships women endure as they navigate a public that devalues, objectifies, or ignores them: the petty abuses of female shop clerks, for instance, who are insulted and degraded by both their customers and their employers. Fern is also critical of middle-class women's blind acceptance of gender hierarchies and sentimental ideology that gives them petty social power exercised through conventional etiquette and regulation of social appearances.

These concerns are evident in Fern's writings from the start of her professional career. Indeed, Fern is the unique writer who seems to burst forth a fully formed artist, although her career had a long foreground in a household of privilege and literary achievement. Fern first began writing professionally in 1851, publishing in Boston's *Olive Branch* and later in *The True Flag*. As she represents it in *Ruth Hall*, and as confirmed by her biographer, Fern turned to professional authorship as a last resort: lacking an income and refused the assistance of her family, she needed to support herself and her children. If she was new to publishing, however, Fern was a gifted writer from her girlhood. She drew on knowledge she gained as a child reading copy for her father. Nathaniel Willis Jr. was the founder and editor of the prominent Calvinist periodicals the *Boston Recorder* and the *Youth's Companion*. In addition to any exposure to periodical publishing that Fern received at home, she was an avid newspaper reader, as many of her sketches suggest. The first sketch she published, "The Model Husband," references newspaper reading as an index of a healthy marriage. She imagines the "model husband" as one who "never takes the newspaper and reads it, before [his wife] has a chance to run over the advertisements, deaths, and marriages, etc."[20]

Fern's representation of women as newspaper readers is consistent with the developments of the early nineteenth-century newspaper industry. With the advent of the penny dailies, publishers needed to expand their coverage beyond the traditional matters of politics and mercantile notices that supplied the weekly papers' contents. The penny press is infamous for its sensational crime reporting, an innovation that certainly attracted readers, but equally important to their healthy circulations was wider coverage of cultural events and social notices such as marriages and deaths.[21] This broader content helped make newspaper readers of women, who had no direct interest in the newspapers' traditional topics and who were restricted from the male social spaces—coffeehouses and taverns—where newspapers were read. At the same time, because penny papers were not supported by subscription as the partisan weeklies were, they depended heavily on advertising revenues to stay afloat. Advertisements were not typographically distinguished from news copy as clearly as they are in modern newspapers, and contemporary readers read them with the same avidity as they did the editorial content. The growth of newspaper advertising is directly related to the growth of the commercial marketplace as capitalist models of manufacture and distribution replaced traditional home industries in supplying basic needs from clothing to food.²² Commercial advertisements were therefore particularly interesting reading for women, who were largely responsible for managing the household economy. Shopping provided an important means by which women participated in public life, and newspaper advertisements helped them negotiate the movement from the private sphere of the home to the public sphere of commerce. Taken together, these changes in newspaper contents widened the definition of "news" and redefined the boundaries between public and private spheres at the same time as they catered to a female readership.

Fern's depiction of the housewife as newspaper reader registers these cultural transformations ushered in by the expansion of the press, and it further implies that associations of the public sphere with republican masculinity do not hold up. To be sure, women continued to face severe restrictions on their participation in public life, but they were not completely absent from it; indeed, they never were.²³ The newspaper-reading wife of Fern's "The Model Husband" encourages readers to reconsider what constitutes public and private matters, just as the newspaper itself does. For Fern and the female newspaper readers she creates, reading the newspaper is a means of public participation that relieves women of the burden of a completely domestic existence. The husband who fails to pass the paper to his wife may be comically discourteous, but he is also cruel: he fails to recognize his wife's need for fuller human experience beyond the home, and he does not recognize that her isolation deprives her of mental stimulation.

Fern's exposure to the newspapers acquainted her with the personal style that permeated the day's journalism. As I have already argued, that style is a feature of the antebellum press, particularly the penny press, as it revives and reappropriates the civic journalism of an earlier period. The technique makes it possible for the newspaper to draw on two different forms of expression, the voice and print, that convey authority in different ways. The vernacular qualities of the newspaper's personal style create a sense of proximity between writer and reader that is similar to the immediacy of oral expression. In this way, the newspaper—or the individual journalist—is able to address many readers conversationally, as if addressing a single person. In the culture of separate spheres, conversation was understood primarily as a private form of communication heavily associated with the feminine domestic sphere and distinguished from oratory. Fern's writings in particular capitalize on the conversational qualities of the newspapers' personal style. Just as Margaret Fuller's staged "Conversations" allowed her to bridge the gap between the female private sphere and the lyceum, Fern's use of the newspaper's personal or conversational style enables her to participate in the masculine public sphere of print while adhering (however loosely) to conventions for women's discourse.

Fern's newspaper sketches, especially her satiric pieces, exhibit her tendency to draw on elements of both printed and oral forms of communication. The paper's print format conveys the authority of a wide dissemination and influence, while her manipulation of typefaces takes advantage of both the orality and printedness of the newspaper. She uses italics, capitals, and punctuation to indicate oral inflections, such as dialect and emphasis. She often presents her satires as responses to epigraphs that she reproduces at the head of the column. The overall effect is to create a kind of dialogue between writers through the medium of print. The strategy enables Fern to take on some of the apparent monoliths of her culture. She is especially keen to respond to truisms about such gendered topics as woman's nature or married life, sentimental expressions whose wide dissemination in print gives them authoritative power. She does not habitually cite her epigraphs' sources, but some come from mainstream periodicals such as the *New-York Tribune* or *Punch*, and many from advice manuals and familiar proverbs. In all cases, Fern uses these authoritative pronouncements as a jumping-off point for her own criticism of specific issues. For instance, in a piece titled "Mr. Punch Mistaken," Fern responds to a line from that famous publication: "A man will own that he is in the wrong—a woman, never; she is only *mistaken*." The piece that follows disputes this "incendiary paragraph," saying the man who admitted to being wrong is "an animal which has never yet been discovered, much less captured" (*RHOW* 254). Fern's rejoinder carries the doubled weight of rebutting the epigraph's claim and challenging the masculine cultural authority of *Punch*. Presenting her critique of "Mr. Punch" as a dialogic response to the epigraph, Fern talks back to the magazine in her own printed column much as any reader might disagree with an item she read in her own home. Fern's conversational style effectively extends to the public sphere the conversations that one imagines occur in parlors everywhere *Punch* is read, and because her statement is printed, it makes a greater claim to authority. Her use of epigraphs incorporates the masculine voice of print-based authority into the comparatively feminized form of conversation.

An 1852 piece from the *Olive Branch*, the frequently anthologized "Sunshine and Young Mothers," develops the strategy of using epigraphs in a manner that fully expresses Fern's use of the conversational style to develop a bold critique of the sentimental representation of woman. The piece takes a quotation idealizing motherhood as its point of departure: "If you wish to look at melancholy and indigestion, look at an old maid. If you would take a peep at sunshine, look in the face of a young mother," the epigraph concludes (*RHOW* 231). Fern then launches into a caustic deconstruction of motherhood and marriage from the point of view of a self-confessed "old maid":

> Now I won't stand that! I'm an old maid myself; and I'm neither melancholy nor indigestible! . . . I never want to *touch* a baby except with a *pair of tongs!* "Young mothers and sunshine!" Worn to fiddling strings before they are twenty-five! When an old lover turns up he thinks he sees his grand-mother, instead of the dear little Mary who used to make him feel as if he should crawl out of the toes of his boots! Yes! my mind is *quite* made up about *matrimony;* but as to the *"babies,"* (sometimes I think, and then again I don't know!) but on *the whole I believe* I consider 'em a d——ecided humbug! It's a *one-*s*ided* partnership, this marriage! the *wife casts up all the accounts!* (*RHOW* 231)

Fern discourages the notions that in the married state, domestic women maintain their ideal beauty and goodness and that they are kept apart from the public sphere. Engaging the language of business and finances, the passage conveys the sense of marriage as a social institution carried out in private settings. In this understanding, privacy is less an idealization of domestic seclusion or romantic solitude than enforced exile or house arrest. In labeling babies a "humbug" and marriage an uneven partnership, Fern asserts that women are tricked into sacrificing personal health and comparative freedom while men enjoy both the pleasures of domestic comfort their wives' hard work provides and the liberty of a life abroad from home. By claiming that domestic and maternal labors ruin women's youthful good looks, Fern touches lightly on the erotic dimensions of closely regulated gender relations: confined to domestic life, still-young women no longer encourage men's desires. In the piece, the husband "gets into the omnibus, looks *slantendicular* at the pretty girls, and makes love between the pauses of business during the forenoon *generally*" (*RHOW* 231). Fern uses the omnibus as a vehicle of physical and erotic freedom, but she shows that freedom is a privilege for men and a burden to women, who are subjected to erotic speculation every time they leave the house. These are highly charged topics generally off limits to public discussion. Fern's particular writing style suits her interpretation of marriage and enables her to offer her critique: adapting the conversational style to the printed page, Fern enacts a semiprivate expression in the pages of the *Olive Branch*, which in its regular printed appearance and formal ties to Methodism assumes quasi-institutional authority.

The notion of a female writer stripping the varnish from marriage and motherhood proved extremely controversial among *Olive Branch* readers. In 1852 the *Olive Branch* published a handful of letters from readers responding to Fern's writing. While the letters offer no unified perspective on her and her work, all share an interest in her identity, and most share the assumption that her identity is shaped by her sex and sexuality. From asking for Fern's real name and particulars of her life, the letters develop into a multivoiced discussion of her ideas that incorporates highly personal judgments of Fern herself.[24] Her informal style and straightforward social criticisms, not to mention her humor, contradicted some readers' judgments of appropriate women's writing. Responding to these letters in her vernacular style, Fern combines the conversational style of her sketches with an epistolary form of writing. Fern's use of the epistolary form takes advantage of its centrality to both newspapers and a tradition of women's writing;[25] in both contexts, letters approximate spoken dialogue. Elizabeth Hewitt explains that "insofar as the letter approximates conversation, it offers something like the Arendtian model of the public sphere with its accent on agonistic relations; and insofar as it is a written mode, it serves as a paradigmatic genre for describing the ties that bind a nation too large to be present to itself."[26] This comment aptly describes the frequently heated exchanges between Fern and her far-flung readers over the role of women in contemporary society. Fern's readers understand that her public presence in the *Olive Branch* grants her an authoritative air, and they debate whether or not she represents American women. With her distinctive style, however, Fern stands out as a singular figure. Hence, readers' letters reflect Fern's double status as both representative and unique. This simultaneous meaning likewise emerges from the epistolary form, which "offers a template for a central problem of democratic politics, which is the reconciliation between individual liberty and public solidarity."[27]

Fern's reader correspondence in the *Olive Branch* shows both the specific ways that public and private concerns are interrelated and also the ways in which men and women worked to maintain the fiction of separate spheres. Exposing the intersections of private and public is crucial to Fern's emerging project in the *Olive Branch*, the rethinking of identity, especially as it is inflected by gender and shaped by ideology. Using pseudonyms, Fern and her readers both conceal and reveal the self. On the one hand, this dual tendency suggests a model of the self as "ambiguous."[28] But Fern's model of selfhood actually sought clarity. It sought a means of assessing the authentic elements of individual character, which is to say, the aspects of the individual that were uninfluenced by ideology or social convention. The use of pseudonyms was important in this effort, as it unmoored the writer from biographical and social particulars that might prejudice readers and facilitated complex performances of irony and affect. At the same time, personal correspondence provided a model for individual expression that was understood to be true to the writer. For this reason, Fern's most vehement correspondents should be understood as emulating her practice of self-identification even when they stridently oppose her views or portray her as an aberration of womanhood—or even when they claim to love her.

For Fern, self is the transcendent core of one's being, whereas identity is the particularized description of the individual shaped by circumstance, custom, and ideology. It is clear from Fern's use of pseudonyms that she sought to protect her identity, at least at the start of her career.[29] Nonetheless, her earliest *Olive Branch* writings assume a distinctive, first-person point of view and a lively conversational style in an epistolary form that invites identification. Because letters are one genre of writing that traditionally has been deemed acceptable for women, it is significant that Fern uses the letter form, which enables her to offer trenchant criticism of social life as nothing more than the casual claims of an isolated if outspoken individual. For instance, in an early piece that takes the form of a letter to her editor, Fern asserts that the failure to live up to the popular ideals of femininity leads to a kind of death sentence for women—an idea that becomes a motif in her early writing: "Between you and I, and the door-post, Mr. Editor, a woman might as well cut her throat at once, if she isn't *pretty*," she writes as "Tabitha" (*OB*, August 2, 1851). Indicated by the conventional figures of speech, grammatical improprieties, and italics, the conversational qualities of Fern's writing are consistent with conventions of letter writing. In addition, by transmitting the qualities of everyday speech to writing and even print, Fern takes advantage of the malleability of the letter as a genre.[30] Throughout the *Olive Branch* correspondence, Fern uses the formal qualities of the letter and the associations of letter writing with women's expression to her rhetorical advantage.

Because readers readily associated her writing voice with her personal voice, Fern's dexterous movement between satire and sentiment within the pages of the *Olive Branch* creates the appearance of an unstable identity. If the two modes seem incompatible to some critics, the published responses from readers suggest that her sentimental and satirical work was equally provocative to readers. The exchanges follow a pattern whereby a reader's letter to the newspaper—often via the editor, Reverend Thomas Norris—elicits a response either from Norris or Fern or both. While they ostensibly respond to a specific reader's letter, once published in the pages of the *Olive Branch* these exchanges appealed to an even wider audience, the newspaper's general readership. In this way, Fern's correspondence reflects epistolarity's ability to embrace plural audiences and resonate on both the personal and public levels.[31]

Olive Branch readers' curiosity about Fern's identity peaked in 1852, following an exchange between Fern and a reader "Eva" who expressed romantic interest for another contributor, provocatively named "Jack Fern." In her letter to "Eva," Fern not only addresses the original questions about her sex but also extends that response into a more general reflection on the social conventions that pressure women's identities. Revealing that she was no "Jack," Fern provides a satirical self-portrait: "I'm a poor, long-faced, draggle-skirted, afflicted, downtrodden female.... Can't do anything I want to cause it 'never'll do.' Have to laugh when I feel sober, cry when I'm merry, and be as artificial as a waxdoll, for fear 'somebody will say something'" (*OB*, January 17, 1852). This darkly humorous letter marks the origins of Fern's signature satirical mode, the "female complaint." Lauren Berlant defines the complaint as "an international mode of public discourse that demonstrates women's contested value in the patriarchal public sphere by providing commentary from a generically 'feminine' point of view."[32] Fern draws attention to the artificiality of women's behavior as a performance of selflessness and a denial of their physicality. More specifically, as she represents herself as a woman in absolute control of her physical responses to pleasure and pain, Fern satirizes the self-erasure and masochism inherent in the doctrine of true womanhood. Referring to another passage in Fern's writing, Marianne Noble explains that "a woman was to negotiate the contradiction between her own embodiment and the ideal of bodilessness through a self-effacing form of presence, acting *as though* she lacked a body."[33] If women's biology ensures the impossibility of their possessing an abstract self, ideological insistence on women's moral and religious purity required them to deny their physical needs, transcending the body. Caught in this impossible position, Fern, like all women, is nothing but a wax doll, a selfless idol contained in a negligible frame, utterly inconsequential and socially dead.

It is important to note that Fern's complaints originate in a context of correspondence with a reader. As in her previous letter as "Tabitha," Fern uses the context of semiprivate exchange between two women as a premise for her pointed social critique, which she expresses in a conversational tone. Although Fern claims that the masculine pseudonym grants her license to express her views more completely, ironically it is the letter that liberates Fern from the restrictions on women's expression that she complains about. Thereafter Fern is able to use the female pseudonym while maintaining the satirical writing style that so many of her readers identify as unfeminine. Yet Fern's satire catches her in a double bind: she can publicly claim her sex, but she cannot escape the gender stereotypes that affect public perception of her status as a woman. The dilemma induces her to attempt to redefine "woman" itself. Berlant identifies Fern as one practitioner of the complaint who "developed a counterstrain, which aimed critically to distinguish 'women' in their particularity from 'woman' in her generic purity."[34] Berlant's discussion of Fern's complaint literature suggests that Fern brings together discourses on women's sentimentalized, social identities and individualism. Fern's response to "Eva" excoriates the generic version of woman as "waxdoll"—a pretty but passionless objectification of femininity. Subsequently, Fern develops an even more particular identity by explaining her dark humor: "it's a way I have, when I can't find a razor handy to cut my throat!" (*OB*, January 31, 1852). In this instance, her "black humor . . . was not supposed to exist in women"[35]—again, Fern is no "waxdoll"—but her defiance cuts in two directions. A poor substitute for the razor, her self-expression is also a form of suicide, but so would be the choice to live in the self-denial required of conventional women. Her satiric honesty cost Fern nothing less than her identity as a woman. In owning her feelings about social and gender roles while admitting her female sex, Fern gives up any claim for acceptance, and she demonstrates that the attainment of individualism comes at the cost of established gender identity. Henceforth she seeks a new articulation of selfhood in which her sex is a contributing but not a limiting factor. Controversy, provocation, and the verbal exchange modeled in correspondence are critical to her identity-formation project.

Apparently, Fern's letter to "Eva" did little to satisfy readers' curiosity. In March 1852 the *Olive Branch* published a letter to the editor asking, "Who is Fanny Fern? pray tell me. I almost tear the *Olive Branch* in pieces in my eager haste to read the productions of her magic pen." Signed "Jack Plane" of Groton, the letter was printed above the editor's reply: "Friend Jack,—you may as well keep quiet, for Fanny utterly refuses to allow us to use her true name. She is not ambitious of notoriety. We will inform Jack and others, however, that the lady belongs to one of our most respectable families, and is very highly esteemed in a wide circle of friends, in and out of our good city. But Jack, you need not tease her for her name, for you should know, that if a woman won't, then she won't, and there's an end *on't*" (*OB*, March 6, 1852). In its authoritative air, playful repetitions, and ironic language, this letter comes across as a little too pat. It would be easy to dismiss the letters the *Olive Branch* printed concerning Fern, considering the possibility that they were manufactured either by Fern or her editors for publicity's sake, but I think we should take these letters seriously for a couple of reasons. First, Warren reports that Fern received quantities of mail from readers, and she answered some privately and others in her *New York Ledger* column.[36] It is not implausible that reader correspondence began while she still lived in Boston. Second, even if the letters are fabrications for the sake of publicity, the correspondence between "Jack Plane" and editor Norris models the epistolary expectations the paper's producers and readers could bring to the paper, the site of their mutual interaction. Significantly, Norris publishes Plane's letter as a letter—he does not incorporate it into an editorial statement about Fern's identity, for instance, but represents the issue as one of exchange between himself and a reader. At the same time, however, he maintains his authority as both the author of the letter and the editor of the *Olive Branch*. In spite of the letter's apparent openness, Norris's response really says very little about Fern. Reverend Norris leads readers to see Fern primarily as a woman, with all the stereotypical qualities that implies: respectability, esteem, and stubbornness masked as resoluteness.

A few days later, Fern uses the letter form to provide another self-portrait that contradicts Norris's suggestions that she is resolute. This self-portrait is the cornerstone of Fern's public persona. Titled "To Jack Fern," the letter demonstrates that her primary stance as a writer is reactive and contrarian, and more than that, it incorporates those qualities into a philosophy of individuality and personal identity:

> I'm a regular "Will o' the Wisp;" everything by turns, and nothing long. Sometimes I'm an old maid, sometimes a wife, then a widow, now a Jack then a Gill, at present a "Fanny." If there's one thing I abominate it's *sameness*; no article of furniture in *my* premises stands in the same spot two days in succession. If I'd been born a *twin*, I should have *poisoned t'other* one. . . .
>
> I always contrive to make people to love, or hate me, *with a VENGEANCE*. *I* don't care *which*; anything but a milk-sop indifference! . . . That's *what* I am, and as to the "*who*," I'm rather mystified *myself*, on *that* point. Sometimes I think, and then again I don't know!! (*OB*, March 13, 1852)

Her own pseudonym enclosed in quotation marks, Fern does not yet fully associate her private self with her public moniker, as she eventually would do.[37] The claim of a changeable nature challenges the categories of identification that are governed by gender ideologies, categories that are moral and sexual—a wife, an old maid—and also literary. Claiming "I am everything by turns and nothing long," Fern explicitly links her individual identity to the model of romantic temperament popularized by the British poet Lord Byron, suggesting that however radical her writing may appear, she seeks to represent herself in a manner that has a foreground in literature, as distinguished from the more popular traditions of either familiar letters or newspaper writing.[38] Byron's apparently diverse sexual experience—allegations of hetero- and homosexual liaisons, his incestuous relationship with his sister, and his dissolute marriage—appealed to audiences as the ultimate expression of autonomous individualism even as it appalled as a transgressive form of otherness. Like Fern, Byron comes across as so various a character that modern critics wonder at times whether he possessed a "self" at all, or if he lived entirely through his creations. It is plausible that he used his reputation for changeableness to insulate himself from the exposure of celebrity.[39] Such volatility also evokes Emerson's insistence that the self-reliant individual should not be bound by his previous thought: "why drag about this corpse of your memory, lest you contradict somewhat you have stated in this or that public place? Suppose you should contradict yourself; what then?" (*CW* 2:33). Emerson can embrace inconsistency and nonconformity because he distinguishes the self on which he relies from the person who makes public statements. The self is impersonal, disembodied, and hence free. Fern claims similar freedom in full awareness that her culture will recognize the woman's license as licentiousness. She therefore uses her self-portraits to spur readers' curiosity and fuel debates over her identity that in fact engage larger cultural questions about gender, selfhood, and freedom. She prompts fuller consideration of whether the selfhood acknowledged in the context of celebrity culture is the real self, impersonal and transcendent.

Seen through the framework of romantic individualism, Fern risks being interpreted as a grotesque "other." As I have detailed in previous chapters, popular exhibitions of human grotesques, such as those promoted by Barnum, tend to concentrate on representations of racial or physical deviance from a perceived white, able-bodied norm. Fern's publicity suggests an analogy with representations of transgressive gender identity in light of the clearly defined and recognizable norms of true womanhood. Fern knowingly challenges and disrupts those gender norms by crafting a persona who is open to a range of friendships, intimacies, and associations; expression is not constrained by social decorum, because any utterance can be justified by a changeable character—which is to say, a character unconstrained by gender, political association, or social status. Fern seeks readers who will regard her for "what," not "who," she is, because, she suggests, selfhood arises from the exercise of an autonomous will, not arbitrary categories or socialized decorum. Likewise, she seeks an emotional response borne of analytical interpretation that, in its intensity, challenges conventional affective expression: she wants her audience to love or hate her "with a vengeance." In contrast with her self, then, which is unfixed from convention, Fern crafts an identity through the engagement of her public expressions of her ideas and feelings with a reactive audience. As a public phenomenon, her identity is enhanced by the readers' responses to her expression. And, in turn, those responses, publicly expressed, reveal the identities of individual readers.

Residing in the intersections of expression and intense emotional response, therefore, identity emerges in sentimental relation to other selves such as those developed through letters. In this construction, indifference to others is self-effacement. Fern seeks to turn the tables on a gender-based identity that destroys women who diverge from the ideological norm. As with Byron, however, Fern was reviled as much as loved for her changeability and passion. *Olive Branch* readers emphasize the grotesque character of a woman who defies entrenched expectations of feminine thought and behavior. Their letters engage a give-and-take of authority and judgment, particularly where claims of selfhood are seen to reverberate in the social or public realm as suggestions of sexual liberty. For instance, "Eliza" contributes a four-stanza poem dedicated to the puzzle of Fern's identity. I quote two verses, first and last, in full:

> Oh mirth-provoking Fanny,
> Pray tell me if you will,
> What sort of being you really are,
> And whether a Jack or a Gill;
> And much I wonder Fanny,
> If you are maid or wife;
> On the shady side of forty,
> Or in the bloom of life.
> . . . .
> The ideal picture I have sketched,
> Is a being kind and true,
> And all that's good in womankind
> I've credited to you.
> Oh mirth-provoking Fanny,
> If the genius of your pen
> Can stir the heart of woman thus,
> How is it with the men?
> (*OB*, April 10, 1852)

In its second-person address to Fern, the poem builds on the letter's mode of reciprocal expression. Like the subject of her poem, "Eliza" takes advantage of the letter's tendency for shape shifting to generate her own literary performance. Even as she writes in praise of "the genius of [Fern's] pen," "Eliza" makes the sentimental claim to have been touched at the heart by Fern's wit and humor. Her ability to stir such affect among women, however, raises the question of whether she can translate feminine affect into heterosexual desire. "Eliza" recognizes that the womanly goodness manifest in Fern's irreverent mirth may keep her out of the heterosexual economy that governs women's social livelihoods. Fern's willingness to write like a man, represent herself as either "a Jack or a Gill," and even to "stir the heart of woman" with her phallic pen all point to a potential sexual deviance.

By combining tactics of sentimental appeal to womanly virtues and ironic portrayal of deviance from social norms, the poem imitates and competes with Fern herself. Imitation is flattery, but also critique and, potentially, theft—of Fern's style and her very persona.[40] If "Eliza" gets away with encroaching on Fern's territory, it may be because "Eliza" engages Fern's tactics in a dialogue with Fern herself that continues a week later in Fern's response to "Eliza."[41] Her letter answers "Eliza's" direct questions about her appearance and even gives a hint of how it is for her with the men: "I'm a *female woman!* and I wish the day had been blotted out of the calendar, that wrote me down one. Such a '*Jack*' as I might have been! It makes me mad to think of it. No help for it *now*. I shall know better next time. It's my present intention to get married as soon as I can get a chance. I have black eyes and hair, and am very *petite*, please your ladyship. I am as sensitive as the 'Mimosa,' spirited as an eagle, and untamable as chain lightning. Can make a pudding or write a newspaper squib, cut out a child's frock or cut a caper, and crowd more happiness or misery into *ten minutes* than any Fanny that ever was christened" (*OB*, April 17, 1852). The letter echoes the self-portrait Fern previously directed to "Jack Plane," emphasizing Fern's changeability, energy, and power. But here she is powerful despite the limitations on her sex, not merely by working around them. This significant shift positions Fern for a more pointed critique of gender ideology. Aware that her behavior transgresses gender categories, Fern turns to images from the natural world to describe herself; if she is a nearly superhuman power, no human imagery applies.

This very superhuman capability comes under fire from another reader, "S," in the same issue of the paper. "S" reacts to an earlier, contradictory claim of Fern's: having received a marriage proposal from "Bachelor M.O.," Fern declares, "I won't say '*obey*' for any priest in the land; no! not if *you held a pistol to my head!*" (*OB*, February 28, 1852). In this claim and in other instances, "S" argues, Fern portrays women as rather too capable, and she criticizes Fern for failing to take sides in the gendered power struggles being fought out in the nation's parlors and bedrooms:

> By and by, I dare say you will make a call upon some woman, who does all her drudgery without a single domestic, and after you have painted her to her arm-pits in soap-suds, and the same afternoon in a corn-colored bonnet, as brisk as a bee, making calls before she takes in her clothes, every man will imagine his wife *can* or *ought* to follow the same recipe. Your lessons are not at all palatable, Fanny—but then you have no sort of mercy on either sex.
>
> ... Talk about your *obeying* [a husband]—such a will-o'-wisp, helter-skelter, jack-o'-lantern creature! Why, your husband would unite with the choice spirits at a club house before you had been married twenty-four hours. Men won't be caudled as they once were—there are amusements now away from home, when the wife flies off the handle. (*OB*, April 17, 1852)

In her response to Fern's comments on matrimony, "S" reveals that Fern's claims for herself have a much wider significance for women in general and their security within the heterosexual economy of marriage. For this writer, Fern's efforts to bring women recognition for their domestic labors does not advance women's cause, because Fern encourages men to see women as endlessly energetic. The letter writer hints that a wife's sexual relationship with her husband would suffer when he expects her to possess endless energy. Not limiting herself to a critique of Fern's arguments, however, "S" indicts Fern personally. She insinuates that her hypothetical husband would become unfaithful, since his staying out of the house implies his rejecting the "amusements" offered by his wife. The bottom line for this writer is that Fern assumes too much power for her sex in a culture that grants men a wide array of privileges, including sexual license. Fern's dissent therefore does not indicate her progressivism so much as her difference. Having "no sort of mercy on either sex," Fern is portrayed here as crossing categories of gender that are marked by sympathy. As a result, the writer implies, she identifies as neither female nor male. Hence she is a "jack-o-lantern creature," a figure of grotesque distortion and fun that frightens.

This interpretation is amplified four months later in a letter from "Francesca Lowell": "Well, Miss Fan, it seems we have found you out. A *female woman!* What made you tell? we might, perhaps, have imagined you a mermaid, or a fairy with *invisible green eyes*. . . . My husband thinks you have been disappointed in love, and that is what makes you so flighty" (*OB*, August 28, 1852). "Female woman" was a term Fern coined to designate women who identified with the patriarchal ideals of femininity.[42] The term satirizes them by combining their biological sex (female) with their ideological identity (woman), suggesting that they fuse, or confuse, two distinct aspects of their selfhoods. For Fern to call herself a "female woman" is then ironic, much like her referring to herself earlier as a "waxdoll." In her reaction to Fern, however, "Francesca Lowell" accepts "female woman" as a positive, conventional construction of femininity, and she scoffs that Fern could claim to embody it. Interestingly, it is the very absence of irony in "Lowell's" response that indicates the success of Fern's satire: prompting her readers to "hate her with a vengeance," Fern elicits a judgment that reveals "Lowell's" values and locates her in the social and ideological landscape.

In attributing Fern's otherness to failed romance, "Lowell" reveals her inability to see Fern as anything *except* a woman, however failed. This double vision is consistent with Leonard Cassuto's dialectic of the human grotesque: observers of the grotesque, he argues, are never able to separate the human from the inhuman; the very duality of the subject's identity renders her grotesque. Moreover, the letter writer (and her husband) accuses Fern of being "flighty," a term meant to diminish Fern's grandiose claims for exemption from social categories. Criticizing Fern as both intellectually and morally inconstant, "Lowell" upholds the feminine virtues of fidelity, piety, and submissiveness. In addition, by attributing Fern's inconstancy to failed romance, the writer strikes even lower, suggesting Fern is unable to get or keep a man—she is, frankly, undesirable. Clearly the ideal of womanhood to which "Lowell" adheres associates women's moral consistency with her "virtue" or sexuality. In this construction, the woman who withholds herself ultimately finds sexual fulfillment. Fern stands accused of the twin transgressions of her gender, being both unvirtuous and sexually cold, and is doubly monstrous.

Thus, Fern is not a "female woman" but "a mermaid with invisible green eyes," a physical oddity such as P. T. Barnum exhibited at his American Museum. The cultural lines are clear: a woman's attitude may be explained by her level of participation in the heterosexual economy, or else she may be deemed a freak of nature. Freaks such as Barnum's Feejee Mermaid appealed to audiences because they combined biological species, such as a fish and a human, and challenged observers to confront the categories of life that structured their thought. The possibility of difference might tantalize the imagination, but the dominance of the observer's judgment over the object is always affirmed: the freak is a passive object on which the viewer exercises interpretive and intellectual authority. An object of spectatorship and judgment, the human grotesque is likewise the object of interpretation that ultimately affirms both the intellectual and the social superiority of the observer. "Lowell's" letter claims similar intellectual and social authority. It attempts to redesignate Fern as a freak and diminish any social authority that goes with her role as a published author in the public sphere.

"Lowell" can never have the last word, however, because unlike the freak or grotesque, Fern is not a passive object on display, and the correspondence between a newspaper writer and her reader is not an exhibit by Barnum. The newspaper does not presume from the outset that its author is a freak or grotesque as a freak show does, so it does not lend institutional sanction to the observer's judgment. As a genre, moreover, letters tend to be "sites of contestation," where author and readers grapple over issues of social authority and relations based on class, gender, and race.[43] The genre's expectations of response naturally limit any one letter's authoritative claims. Publication of letters opens up the possibility for multiple points of view and suggests they are equally valid. Just as the reader's judgment acts as a check on Fern's authority to speak for all women, the newspaper's publication of the correspondence provides only a limited power for readers. Hence in the same issue of the paper, reader "Fanny Dade" writes, "About your identity, as to the *who* or the *where*, has troubled me very little. I know very well *what* you are to *me* in the weekly visits of the Olive Branch—a kind, loving sister, with a flashing smile that breaks through the drolleries, making me long to shake hands with you" (*OB*, August 28, 1852). Juxtaposed with the accusatory letter from "Francesca Lowell," "Dade's" letter embraces Fern as part of the sorority of women who are sympathetic to the trials each faces as a wife and mother and equally vulnerable to loss. It is significant that "Dade" responds explicitly to Fern's sentimental pieces—she alludes to the sketch "Incident at Mt. Auburn," in which a mother spends all her time by the graveside of her very young child, only to be brought back to reality by the ghostlike presence of her other, living child. The pairing of "Lowell's" and "Dade's" letters points out the mixed effects of Fern's blended styles. She challenges as well as comforts, willfully resisting readers' categorization. In this sense, even her style is grotesque.

Most of the letters I have examined so far are from women. But the *Olive Branch*'s letters from male readers demonstrate that women's social status reverberated in male as well as female identity. Two letters demonstrate this point—both, interestingly, from men claiming to be from Alabama. First, "Albert" addresses his impassioned declaration to editor Norris, like a lovestruck young man asking for a father's permission to marry his daughter:

> but the fact is, unless I find out something about Fanny, I shall go crazy, commit suicide, or do some other desperate act that will cast a shadow of gloom over the enlightened millions of our happy and prosperous country . . .
>
> Born and reared amid the wilds of Alabama, the genial warmth of her Southern sun has infused into my nature a fiery, impulsive temperament; and basking amid the shades of her pine-clad forests and magnolia groves, have I been taught to love. Does Fanny know what it is to love—to hope? Don't think me crazy, Mr. Norris. Who is Fanny Fern? Does such a being exist? or am I worshipping at the shrine of some imaginary divinity, of whom I shall never know aught save the weekly pencillings that have so maddened my fiery brain? (*OB*, June 19, 1852).

This letter portrays "Albert" as a man of feeling whose emotional effusiveness indicates the depth and genuineness of his ardor. In his efforts to identify as unconventional a woman as Fern, "Albert" relies on conventions of southern masculinity and romance, as well as of nationalism. Transcending regional boundaries and sectional differences, "Albert" claims, Fern's appeal also threatens to undermine national peace. Deeply entrenched social and ideological conventions clearly provide a stability that Fern's vigorous difference threatens, yet Fern's influence affirms "Albert's" masculinity and virility: even in erotic dissolution, he continues to exert a far-reaching male power by creating in his letter an ironic comedy of gender equal to Fern's.[44]

Another male reader from the South provides a different interpretation of Fern's influence. "Harry" reflects that Fern threatens masculinity by advocating women's potential independence from men. Specifically, he worries that by advocating the single life for women, Fern would reduce men's chances for happy marriage—an idea that is comical in its exaggerated sense of one writer's influence, but deadly earnest in the letter writer's expression. By addressing his concerns to Norris, "Harry" appeals to the wider privilege of male authority. In this way, he attempts to put Fern in her place as a woman, circumventing any social authority she may claim as a writer with a public voice:

> We want you to tell Fanny Fern to hush her palavering about marrying. She is corrupting the minds of the "fair sex." She'll ruin all our prospects for doubling. . . . It don't concern her who marries. She thinks because she's an "old maid," and don't (?) want to marry, and hates "babies," and "don't want to touch them except with a pair of tongs," no one else wants to marry. She thinks because her little bit of an odd heart is cold, *every* body's is so. Why, Fanny, ain't you ashamed? What, a woman take hold on a baby with a pair of tongs? Fy! fy! I know *now* you *are* a soulless old maid, or you are no woman at all. I know you *can't* be a *man*. Nor you can't be a *"mother."* Nor you can't be any "of the girls." No, you *are certainly* an old maid. And because you couldn't marry, you are just talking as you are, to keep the girls from marrying. *But you can't come it*. For we intend to expose your designs. And if we can't we'll just petition Mr. Norris not to let you write in the Olive Branch any more. (*OB*, July 24, 1852)

As he purports to speak for all men, "Harry" assumes the masculine role of disciplinarian, castigating Fern for her defiance and calling on Reverend Norris to do likewise.[45] In contrast, he regards Fern as an idiosyncratic figure, whose access to the public forum raises the worrisome prospect that her oddball views will gain traction. "Harry's" real worry, then, is that women may in fact come to recognize their potential power—that they may opt out of the ideological structures of marriage and separate spheres altogether. "Harry" argues that Fern's rejection of conventional gender roles shows she is not "one of the girls." In criticizing Fern, he evokes one of the most persistent and damning judgments available to him: if she is biologically female, he asserts, Fern is by no means a true woman.

Letters from both "Albert" and "Harry" indicate that Fern wields a power out of balance with that of ordinary women. That power comes from her having a public voice. And in both cases, her power is threatening: either she causes erotic dissolutions that wreak social havoc, or she causes similar empowerment in other women, which also wreaks social havoc. As with the female letter writers, admissions of love and hate for Fern identify the letter writers according to their ideas, expectations, and desires regarding women. They represent different versions of Fern's public identity, thus affirming that in interpretation, at least, her identity is constant. But at the same time the men clarify their own public identities through letters giving voice to those interpretations. This epistolary use of interpretation as self-expression is entirely in keeping with Fern's reciprocal process of self-identification.

A final sample demonstrates the range of readers' letters as rhetorical performances. For several weeks in April and May 1852 the *Olive Branch* published a flurry of reader correspondence. Reader "Nick Notion" defends Fern against "S's" criticism with a fantasy of marrying her (*OB*, April 24, 1852). "Patience Pepper" shares her own story as a wife whose husband deserted her because she was too outspoken, and she encourages Fern to stay single (*OB*, May 1, 1852). "Jenny Jessamine" reflects on the economic advantages she could glean from the knowledge of Fern's identity: "It's not out of curiosity that I wish to find out . . . but you see I intend to sell *Fanny Fern Bonds* to the *anxious ones* at a dollar a-piece" (*OB*, May 15, 1852). In a letter to Norris, "Dorcas Dandelion" claims Fern's writing proves she is not a single but a married woman: "I don't believe her knowledge of hu————*brutish* nature (she calls men *brutes*) was all picked up by *observation*. It must have been by *experience*" (*OB*, May 22, 1852).

All of these letters help feed curiosity about Fern among the *Olive Branch*'s readership, and hence they work to Fern's and the paper's advantage. In their responses to Fern, moreover, the writers use letters to stake out their own positions in debates over the significance of sex and gender in social life and relations. Fern herself is the ostensible subject of their letters, but in fact she provides the occasion, not the substance, for readers' discussion. As Fern's reader correspondence indicates, that discourse involves active and ongoing acts of reading or interpretation of Fern, the celebrity, that occur simultaneously with the reading of the *Olive Branch* and the letters it publishes. The publication of individual reader correspondence provides a compellingly dramatic representation of that reading act. Taken together, the letters model reading and writing as acts of critical interpretation. These critical acts, moreover, closely imitate Fern's epistolary style, including the conversational italics and the use of sentimental pseudonyms. Reinventing herself as "Fanny," Fern makes her own critical intervention into sentimental gender ideology. Her claims to have a variable character draw on recognizable romantic models of autonomous selfhood that directly challenge conventional expectations of women's constancy. Fern uses correspondence with *Olive Branch* readers to reformulate identity as a matter of individual judgment and expression that is often at odds with others' values and sensibilities. Following her lead, readers use her own tactics to parse and critique her methods and conclusions as well as establish their own identities, however masked.

THE *Olive Branch* CORRESPONDENCE SHOWS FERN ATTEMPTING TO establish a public identity divorced from her personal circumstances. The effort marks her as monstrous or grotesque—a spectacle such as Barnum might exhibit. Indeed, her effort to sequester her personal life from her professional life parallels patterns in his own celebrity, yet whereas Barnum's reticence about his family led critics to question whether he possessed a private self, Fern's defensive reticence prompted even greater interest in her life. Such protections as her pseudonym provided were fragile at best, and Fern's practice of writing autobiographically was undeniably provocative. When her defenses were breached and her private identity exposed, Fern did not have to hide or take a new pseudonym; she actually inhabited her pseudonym more securely by integrating it into her private life. As Robert Gunn explains, Fern's pseudonymity is not part of a strategy of anonymity but "an artifact of publicity, a print-level staging of the dynamics of veiling and spectatorship that construes the ordinary protocols of public life as forms of exposure." Importantly, Gunn links Fern's use of the pseudonym to the gaze that both exposes the public woman and renders her meaningful: "Seemingly paradoxically, pseudonymity thus promotes the gaze as the governing protocol of public life even as it works to mitigate its effects."[46] Not unlike Whitman, Fern desires to be seen—she seeks publicity—but she also desires autonomy. She resists the objectifying power of the gaze by deflecting it from the details of her personal experience to larger issues of gender and identity. To develop my comparison of Whitman and Fern further, I would suggest that, for Fern, the apt Lacanian analogue is not his theory of the gaze but his concept of the mirror stage. According to Benstock, the mirror stage informs much of women's autobiographical writing in that it reveals "the measure to which 'self' and 'self-image' might not coincide, can never coincide in language."[47] Fern's writings describe a world where women rarely see themselves depicted accurately or realistically. She therefore attempts to particularize women's experiences, resisting the cultural tendency to see woman as a generic type. Her fictionalizations of her own life transform the particularity of her lived experience into a representation of the complex realities of women's diverse circumstances.

Still, for a woman such as Fern, the risks of crossing the culturally sanctioned bounds of gender identity are high. As Fern quickly rose to celebrity, she made business decisions that challenged the gendered norms of the publishing industry, and in the process she angered one former editor. In 1853 Fern left Boston for New York and began publishing her sketches for more money with the *Musical World and Times*. She continued to send original material to the *Olive Branch* and *True Flag*, where she had experienced her first successes, but her relationship with *True Flag* editor William Moulton was damaged. According to Joyce Warren, Moulton was "angry at having to pay her more money under the threat that she would no longer write for him."[48] In 1855 Moulton got his revenge in the form of *The Life and Beauties of Fanny Fern*, in which he exposed her personal background, uncovered the autobiographical origins of the just-published *Ruth*

Hall, and repeated the scandalous rumors of adultery and sexual freedom first promulgated in Boston by Fern's ex-husband, Samuel Farrington. Moulton's personal style implies intimate knowledge of Fern and presumes to interpret her character for an interested audience of strangers:

> To have her sit by your side one hour, and——sparkle, (*talk* don't express the idea,) is worth all the Fern Leaves and Ruth Halls in the world. Witty and pathetic by turns; now running over with fun, and now with tears; always sprightly, always plain and terse in her language, she is sure to entertain you for one hour at least, as no other woman can. She will entertain you another hour, some time, if you choose. But the probability is, you don't choose. Such women don't wear well. Their conversations are like "Fern Leaves"— brilliant enough at first, but presently wearisome, and insipid. . . .
>
> Fanny's words are the least of her fascinations. Her manner is that of a consummate actress. And it is not long before you discover that she is little else than an actress.[49]

Purporting to offer a biography of a notable public figure, Moulton portrays Fern as feckless. If his reference to her changeable character seems to confirm her 1852 description of herself as a "will of the Wisp," his emphasis on her gender reveals that such inconstancy marks her lack of virtue. His criticism taps into the cultural distrust of artifice and performance as unnatural and fraudulent. If pseudonymity enables Fern to occupy multiple subject positions to critical and aesthetic effect—"she could be anybody," Lara Langer Cohen puts it[50]—that variability is the most unsettling element of her publicity for Moulton, particularly because it alters her private behavior as well. Considering the long-standing restrictions on the theater in Moulton's hometown of Boston, his calling Fern an actress is particularly damning. It suggests that her expressions and behavior cannot be trusted as reliable markers of her actual feelings. The ultimate public women, actresses were thought to defy conventions of modesty and chastity that restricted women to the private sphere. On stage, they were subject to the unchecked male gaze; this fact, combined with their ability to feign emotions such as love on cue, gave them a reputation for sexual promiscuity. To call Fern an actress is to imply not only that she was available for men's sexual speculation (if not more), but also that she enjoyed and encouraged their objectifying glances.

Moulton makes this insinuation clear elsewhere in the book, imagining men in the street observing and commenting on Fern's appearance: "What a figure!" one exclaims; Moulton writes, "Does she care? She looks as if she liked it!"[51] The scene reverses a similar moment in *Ruth Hall* in which Ruth, a stand-in for Fern, is observed by two rakish characters in her boardinghouse: "'Deuced nice form,' said Jim, lighting a cheap cigar, and hitching his heels to the mantel, as he took the first whiff; 'I shouldn't mind kissing her'" (*RHOW* 73). Fern uses this scene to highlight Ruth's modest character and to illustrate the readiness with which men objectify women. Ironically, Moulton's depiction of Fern affirms the novel's social critique: the woman in public—whether she is a "public woman" or not—is subject to men's objectifying gaze and speculation about her sexual availability.

The Life and Beauties did not diminish Fern's popular success; if anything, the exposure of her novel's autobiographical details fueled readers' curiosity. As a personal attack, however, the book made a direct hit. Both Fern and Robert Bonner denounced the work, but it "caused Fern so much pain that, given the emphasis on retiring womanhood that the century demanded, it is a mark of Fern's unusual courage that she did not wholly withdraw from public life."[52] Indeed, as Warren details, perceptions of Fern as an insufficiently modest and chaste woman tainted many of her personal relationships long after her break with her family following her divorce from Farrington in 1851. In 1856 Fern married James Parton. His sister was sensitive to the public insinuations about Fern's character, and she refused to accept the match. Relations between Fern and her husband's extended family remained difficult throughout their long marriage. That Fern sometimes used their feuds as the basis for columns likely confirmed her relations' judgments of her impropriety. But for Fern, public expression was an important antidote to personal trials.

As these details show, Fern's popular success was by no means an unambiguous triumph. It came at some personal cost. But if her writings invited harsh judgments of her personal life and character, that was no worse than anything she had already heard from her own relations; moreover, expressing herself opened her experience beyond the comparatively small social sphere in which she moved and forged connections among anonymous sympathetic readers. Her experience illustrates the complex ways that the personal and the public are intertwined in celebrity and that the personal is always public for women. That is, because she enters the public sphere, Fern's personal traits are magnified even to the point of distortion. Even behind various screens of pseudonym and personas, her so-called transgressions of cultural norms are particularly acute examples of women's publicity.

Fern's embrace of a personal public sphere entails, therefore, a complicated negotiation with a diverse, mass audience. Her experience demonstrates that the public is not a monolithic, single-minded entity—nor is Fern. Fern resists to a point of defiance cultural tendencies to generalize, and she attempts to unify her audience in its recognition and acceptance of its pluralism. As a celebrity, she was subject to near-constant speculation about her life, and she mastered a style of writing that created the illusion that she was revealing it. The truth was harder to find, however, especially in the absence of genuine sympathy between the onlookers and their object. Fern makes this point in an 1879 *Ledger* column, "How I Look," where she depicts two strangers claiming to identify her among the spectators at an opera: "'You know her, then?' asked the lady.—'Intimately,' replied this strange gentleman—'*intimately*. Observe how expensively she is dressed. See those diamonds, and that lace! Well, I assure you, that every cent that she has ever earned by her writings goes straightway upon her back'" (*RHOW* 368). Of course, the gentleman describes someone other than Fanny Fern. Laughing at his preposterous and presumptuous claims to know her "*intimately*," Fern describes herself in the negative, as the opposite of the flashy woman he observes. Suggesting that she does not pour her earnings into diamonds and fine clothes, Fern indicates her frugal and modest character and indirectly responds to detractors, from Moulton forward, whose opinions of her character rest on prejudices against women in the professional public sphere. She aligns herself instead with the conventions of middle-class, true womanhood.

Like Whitman in the "Calamus" poems, Fern responds to popular views of her by attempting to correct them. "How I Look" turns the tables on the gossips and social gadflies who assume a measure of social and cultural authority by speculating about public figures. Such speculation is inevitable in celebrity culture—but, Fern points out, it is baseless: despite the illusions of intimacy in the personal public sphere, celebrities such as Fern remain strangers to most. Fern reveals that the kind of staring that dominates celebrity culture is a form of social power through which spectators exert their dominance over their subjects.[53] As in the case of the freak show, staring reinforces the observer's subject position as normative, authoritative, and inherently masculine, and whether the observer deems the subject erotically desirable, morally derisible, or something in between, the gaze determines the object's meaning and significance in a manner that reinforces the subject's values and interests. But Fern "reversed the concept of the controlling gaze.... In her fiction and in her newspaper articles the gaze is aggressively feminine: a woman looking *at men*, appraising, sometimes admiring—Fern was even unusually frank in her appreciative comments about the male body—in a way that was thought to be the prerogative of the male gaze."[54] Fern responds to a masculine discourse of gender based on sexual status and subject positioning. In her manipulations of those discourses, she controls the language of gender representation, and she occupies the subject position that objectifies the male other. Fern's inversion of the power dynamic is incomplete, however. As she assumes the empowered position of observer and critic of (male) social life, Fern actually enhances her own objectified status. She draws attention to herself as an unconventional woman, an iconoclast, a celebrity—interest in whom is intensified by her position not alongside male figures of cultural authority, but outside of the cultural norm.

"How I Look" therefore highlights Fern's predicament, as a public woman and as a woman. Her presence in the public sphere of print opens her to the harsh and prejudicial judgments of those who associate the public sphere with certain masculine freedoms. Under these circumstances, her celebrity magnifies her public presence even as her self remains unacknowledged, hidden in the shadows of her own celebrity, unlooked for in a public world she, as a woman, is thought not to inhabit. Fern's celebrity shows not just how ingrained such views were, but how the society policed women's behavior in service of those views. Under the conditions of sentimentality and the culture of separate spheres, the private sphere is not a refuge for women but a kind of prison, a panopticon. In celebrity, however, Fern both anticipates and, through strategic artistic choices, evades scrutiny. She does not set the terms of her celebrity so much as she participates in the negotiations over her meaning that celebrity entails. She thereby embraces the personal public sphere as a site that is, for all its imperfections, inclusive of those who are excluded from the traditional public sphere—and, in doing so, she asserts her claim to an abstract selfhood that legitimates her controversial intervention into public life.

Fern understands this ephemeral existence to be the lot of all women. Seemingly every gesture and word is carefully policed by others who nevertheless fail to see—that is, sympathize with—them. In *Ruth Hall* she develops sympathy as an idealized response to others that marks a full recognition of their nature. The novel illustrates the distance between women's objectified status, in which they are regarded primarily in terms of their embodiment, and their actual selves. Another way of looking at this is to say that *Ruth Hall* reflects on its protagonist's public life, which as Fern illustrates, begins long before she becomes a published author. In Ruth Hall Fern constructs not only a protagonist, the center of the novel's action and its readers' attention, but a focal point for most of the novel's other characters as well. This near-constant observation of Ruth is most damaging when conducted by female characters, such as Ruth's mother-in-law or society ladies, who wield social power that parallels men's economic power. Subject to nearly constant observation, interpretation, and criticism even before she becomes the celebrity writer "Floy," Ruth never occupies a truly private space. Ruth attracts attention in part because she is unusual, unconventional. At the same time, that attention singles her out, marking her as different—and, as different, also by turns attractive, desirable, curious, peculiar, marketable, or threatening. Other characters' objectification of Ruth not only denies her privacy; it makes her life public. Fern's fiction challenges the prevailing assumption that domesticity protects women from the rough-and-tumble of the public sphere. In her depictions of city life especially, Fern reveals a keen perception of the relationships between private or domestic life and the public sphere. Her critiques of the gendering of space and domestic labor and of sexual double standards points out not only the hypocrisy of a philosophy of separate spheres but also its fraudulence. Moreover, the male interests that govern the public sphere objectify women—all women—who venture into public space.

Just as Fern's *Olive Branch* correspondents' criticism of her hinges on claims about her sexual behavior and availability, observers of Ruth judge her character according to their perceptions of her physical appeal and sexual availability. As a girl at boarding school, "Ruth's schoolmates wonder[ed] the while why she took so much pains to bother her head with those stupid books, when she was every day growing prettier, and all the world knew that it was quite unnecessary for a pretty woman to be clever." Even her brother notes her physical development, remarking, "You've positively had a narrow escape from being handsome" (*RHOW* 16). Fern's narrative reveals how such speculations are intertwined with the sentimental fantasies about marriage, motherhood, and sex that guide girls' steps into womanhood. Ruth herself recognizes the possibility of sympathetic union in marriage—the possibility that "her twin-soul existed somewhere"— are tied up with her own sexual self-awareness: "Eureka! She had arrived at the first epoch in a young girl's life,—she had found out her power!" That power is her ability to attract "glances of involuntary admiration from passers-by," to "inspire love!" or at least erotic attraction (*RHOW* 15).

As a married woman, Ruth enjoys an affectionate intimacy with her husband, and their caresses and pet names suggest to Ruth's Calvinistic mother-in-law an indecent sexual expressiveness. Ruth is affectively generous even to the point of wastefulness, whereas her mother-in-law is affectively frugal,[55] and their conflict yields outcomes that are both economic and affective: the elder Halls withhold both affection and money from Ruth. And whereas Ruth's affective openhandedness brings her the bounty of her daughters, her miserly in-laws must procreate on the cheap, emotionally speaking, by seizing Ruth's daughter as a kind of collateral. Yet Mrs. Hall justifies her behavior as virtue, compared with Ruth's license. Mrs. Hall's near-constant surveillance of Ruth focuses on her carefree manners, which suggest an insufficient virtue: Ruth tramps over the countryside looking for wildflowers, she climbs trees, she lets her curly hair flow freely "like a wild Arab's," and she even addresses the minister while perched on a stone wall (*RHOW* 38–39). On one furtive inspection of Ruth's things, Mrs. Hall soliloquizes, "I've been peeping into her bureau drawers to-day. What is the use of all those ruffles on her under-clothes, I'd like to know? Who's going to wash and iron them?" (*RHOW* 18). In contrast to the invasive watchfulness of Mrs. Hall, the novel imagines Ruth's happy inspection of the space she shares with her husband:

> How odd to see that shaving-brush and those razors lying on *her* toilet table! then that saucy looking smoking-cap, those slippers and that dressing gown, those fancy neckties, too, and vests and coats, in unrebuked proximity to her muslins, laces, silks and de laines!
> Ruth liked it. (*RHOW* 18–19)

In her ideologically informed understanding of Ruth's role as wife and housekeeper, Mrs. Hall regards all physical pleasures, from a country ramble to sex, as a failure of domestic responsibility. In these separate appraisals of Ruth's personal possessions, the novel illustrates both the extent of the scrutiny women endure and observers' limited ability to comprehend their subject.

Fern suggests that the publicness of Ruth's existence is a defining quality of sentimental womanhood. Privacy is just one of the sacrifices that the pious, submissive, domestic woman makes, along with physical health and various freedoms. Fern is especially alert to the ways women police one another and uphold the cultural values that subordinate them to men. These "female women," as Fern calls them, betray other women and support the hegemonic ideals of masculinist culture. In *Ruth Hall* Fern uses Mrs. Hall's invasive examinations of Ruth's domestic arrangements to illustrate this point. Mrs. Hall's judgmental gaze follows Ruth through her kitchen to the quasi-public space of the parlor and even upstairs to rooms reserved for the immediate family circle: "Well, we'll see how the *kitchen* of this poetess looks. I will go into the house the back way, and take them by surprise; that's the way to find people out. None of your company faces for me" (*RHOW* 32). She understands that the parlor is the site in which a housewife might craft a public identity; her intrusion through the back door seeks a less contrived picture of Ruth.[56] But Mrs. Hall is not the only character who imposes on Ruth's private spaces: Mrs. Jiff, Ruth's nurse after her first child's birth, invades Ruth's bedroom, "opening drawers and closets 'by mistake'" and hovering nearby "whenever dear Harry came in to her chamber to have a conjugal chat with her" (*RHOW* 25, 26). Figures such as Mrs. Hall and Mrs. Jiff scrutinize not just Ruth's domestic arrangement but her marriage as well in the effort to ascertain whether her public persona—her company face—agrees with her private character.

Women such as Mrs. Hall claim power for themselves by enforcing dictates of domesticity that lead to exactly the kind of surveillance of women that Ruth experiences. But such women tacitly understand that their own privacy is likewise constrained: observing others, they know themselves to be observed as well. In *Ruth Hall* Fern represents gossip as a tool women use to police one another's behavior. Mrs. Hall gossips about Ruth with neighbors and even her dressmaker, debating Ruth's character and actions; following Harry's death, Mrs. Hall and her husband discuss a course of action with respect to Ruth that will save face in their social circle (*RHOW* 69). Later, two of Ruth's friends from her married days debate whether to visit her in her tenement flat and consider her social decline: "I declare, Mary," one of them says. "If Ruth Hall has got down hill so far as this, *I* can't keep up her acquaintance. . . . Come, come, Mary, take your hand off the knocker; I wouldn't be seen in that vulgar house for a kingdom" (*RHOW* 81). The two women continue to speculate about why Ruth's family refuses to help her: "Hyacinth [Ruth's brother] has just married a rich, fashionable wife, and of course he cannot lose caste by associating with Ruth now; you cannot blame him" (*RHOW* 82). In their cruelty, these women reveal that neither Ruth nor her extended family can expect any measure of privacy in their affairs. They live in a community where every action is observed and interpreted by their social peers. Ruth's fall puts her far enough outside her social circle that these women decline to associate with her, but not so far out that they fail to talk about her. Her family connections to a socially prestigious man such as Hyacinth make her situation noteworthy. Such gossip reveals women's tenuous position in a society organized to reflect the financial and social interests of men. Their actions are measured by their effects on the men whose interests they touch.

Ruth Hall is structured to reinforce this message about women's publicity. Fern herself points out her novel's interest in privacy's limitations: in her preface, she claims the work is "entirely at variance with all set rules for novel-writing. . . . [I] have entered unceremoniously and unannounced, into people's houses, without stopping to ring the bell" (*RHOW* 3). This is an apt summary of the novel's organization into short, sketchlike chapters that focus on different characters. Ruth remains the novel's subject, however; as Susan K. Harris observes, the language of the many different characters in the novel defines Ruth's character in relation to their own values.[57] This technique reinforces the notion that Ruth's life—and by extension all women's lives—is subject to constant scrutiny.

As Ruth transforms into a writer, she learns to assume the role of observer as well. Looking out from her rented room, she observes the inhabitants of the tenement opposite; each window reveals a tableau of poverty, hard work, and suffering: "tier above tier the windows rose, full of pale, anxious, care-worn faces—never a laugh, never a song—but instead, ribald curses, and the cries of neglected, half-fed children" (*RHOW* 90). Unlike her former friends, who shun Ruth and others who live in the slums, Ruth regards her neighbors with sympathy and Christian charity. Ruth's view of the tenement shows just how rare privacy is, especially for the urban poor, and Ruth's sympathy for her neighbors recognizes the similarity of their circumstances. Karen Waldron argues that Ruth's experiences in the city intensify the publicness Ruth has known throughout her life: "Ruth's city life . . . finally articulates what she has been experiencing all along, the voyeuristic invasion and language which prove there is no protected private sphere. The result is authorship." Waldron sees Ruth's turn to authorship as a reaction to the intensified pressure of the male gaze in the city—as a response to her need to "move out of her subject position" and develop a "private-public" voice of her own.[58]

As closely as Ruth is observed, few people really see her. Fern represents sympathy as a rare but necessary emotional connection between Ruth and the few characters who comprehend her nature. Her husband Harry is the first and most important person with whom she experiences sympathetic union: "But was Harry blind and deaf?" the narrator asks rhetorically. "Had the bridegroom of a few months grown careless and unobservant? Was he, to whom every hair of that sunny head was dear, blind to the inward struggles, marked only by fits of feverish gaiety?" (*RHOW* 23). Of course the answer to these questions is "no," and Fern's repeated use of the word "blind" reinforces the idea that his sympathy registers as an ability to properly see Ruth. The crisis of the novel is therefore not simply her grief in widowhood or her economic decline, but the loss of such sympathy and the intimacy that comes with it. She finds some comfort in friends such as Mrs. Leon, with whom she shares an aversion to superficial society and whose unhappy marriage is the inverse of her ideal one; in her editor Mr. Walter she finds a brotherly love and support that compensate for the harsh treatment she receives from her actual brother Hyacinth. In these relationships Fern charts alternatives to conventional social and familial relationships. Moreover, in Mr. Walter Fern promotes an idealized version of the gentleman editor who combines sound business sense with genuine concern for the writer he shepherds.

In these sympathetic friendships, Fern promotes an ideal of reciprocal vision of others that replaces the domineering, one-directional gaze in structuring social relationships. Fern's reciprocal vision makes affect something to be exchanged rather than expended, and it is paralleled by renovated economic relationships that replace exploitative self-interest with transactional exchange. In the course of the novel, Fern's father and in-laws portray family as an expense, as they squabble over their financial responsibilities to her in her widowhood: "when a man marries his children, they ought to be considered off his hands," Ruth's father argues to Mr. Hall's retort that after a lifetime of working for his money, "he don't feel like throwing it away on other folks' children" (*RHOW* 71). Bereft of her husband, Ruth no longer has an ideologically sanctioned place in her society, and therefore she loses the economic support marriage once provided her. As Jennifer Harris astutely observes, Ruth has no economic value of her own, thanks to the sentimental gender ideologies that structure her life. As a result she is subject to the machinations of avaricious relatives who not only deny her necessary financial support but even cheat her out of her husband's possessions, to which she is legally entitled. But as she remakes herself as an author and businesswoman, Ruth learns "not only to evaluate her worth, but also to speak on her own behalf, thereby establishing the terms of that worth."[59]

In contrast to the novel's exploitative family relationships, Ruth's relationship with Mr. Walter epitomizes the affectively and economically reciprocal relationships the novel idealizes. He champions her both because he sees the market value of her writing and because he sympathizes with her plight. Fern uses a language of kinship to express Ruth and Mr. Walter's connection: she regards him as "a brother; a—*real, warm-hearted, brotherly brother*, such as she had never known" (*RHOW* 144). In this respect, Mr. Walter is an obvious contrast to her cruel brother Hyacinth as well as Ruth's father and in-laws. Mr. Walter is also a foil for the conniving editor Mr. Lescom, who excuses his taking advantage of Ruth with the maxim "*business* is one thing—*friendship* is another" (*RHOW* 147). As David Dowling notes, Walter's business model breaks with the prevailing gentlemanly code among editors, under which they abstain from poaching one another's writers. Walter's system privileges and rewards the authors themselves in recognition of their value in creating marketable work.[60] In other words, he puts capitalism before gender, to the mutual benefit of himself and Ruth. In Mr. Walter's partnership with Ruth, Fern envisions the ideal editor who chivalrously protects his female writer; he is both a business partner and a friend. Through Mr. Walter, Fern makes the case that friendship ought to contribute to one's emotional and material welfare. In this respect, Fern shows what friendship might look like in the context of marketplace capitalism.

Fern uses Ruth's relationship with Mr. Walter to reimagine women's place in the literary marketplace. Likewise, in Floy's relationships with her readers, she envisions her ideal readership as one that is emotionally responsive to her work. Indeed, her most fulfilling relationships are those she establishes with her readers. As "Floy," Ruth is able to generate strong emotional connections with individual readers whom she never meets in person. The letters from these sympathetic readers are remarkably similar to those included in the *Olive Branch*. In the novel, the letters counterbalance the harshly critical letters she also receives, just as Ruth's relationships with Mary Leon and Mr. Walter outweigh the fraught ties of family and social acquaintances. In both cases, Fern privileges relationships formed independently of conventional ties, and she shines a spotlight on friends whose judgment of Ruth's character is not distorted by social prejudice. Moreover, letters from Floy's readers point to a new definition of self, one that is determined not by circumstance, person, or biology, but by the capacity for sympathy. As one reader puts it, "I address a stranger, and yet *not* a stranger, for

I have read your heart in your many writings. In them I see sympathy for the poor, the sorrowing, and the dependent; I see a tender love for helpless childhood" (*RHOW* 165). Drastically unlike any of the other interpreters of Ruth's character, the letter writer assumes that the goodness and compassion contained in Floy's public expression reflects a genuineness of feeling—a self—that transcends the particulars of circumstance and experience. Fern's idealized reader therefore articulates an idea of self as an affective center, a capacity for feeling and its expression through the individual.

Although this seems to reinforce the sentimental trope of nurturing womanhood, I'd argue that it is much closer to the "law of love" advocated by Lydia Maria Child in her *Letters from New-York*. A pioneering woman journalist, Child anticipates Fern in the journalistic use of the letter form to address an array of issues of public import. She uses a digressive, personal style that is far less colloquial than Fern's but just as significant as a model of women's social discourse. Like Fern, Child expresses a commitment to gender equality; both writers, moreover, reject the sexual double standards that criminalize women's sexual freedom while indulging men's so-called passions. Philosophically, Child is closely allied with the transcendentalists, and while she criticizes Emerson's betrayal of women's rights, she shares his interest in "the stern old conflict between Necessity and Freewill." Unlike the former minister, Child is perfectly willing to ground her idealism in Christian belief, particularly a view of God as "the Heavenly *Father*" rather than "the Almighty": she moves away from an authoritarian, Calvinistic theology. Her paternalistic God requires that "the highest ideal of Justice is perfect and universal Love." In opposition to the morally pure law of love, Child recognizes "a *false* necessity . . . the pressure of public opinion; the intolerable restraint of conventional forms."[61] Like Emerson, Child is skeptical of mass culture as a force that undermines individual critical insight and that compels conformity. Public opinion exercises a lawlike compunction but prevents the union, or communion, that love promises.

In her commitment to the law of love—to sympathy—in the midst of a crowded, acquisitive urban center, Child "models a sympathetic alternative to the detached voyeurism of the traditional urban flaneur," even as she records the emotional toll of so extensive a sympathy.[62] Although Fern is less critical of capitalism and mass culture than Child is, she shares Child's vision of love and sympathy as the keys to social improvement if not thoroughgoing social reform. The comparison to Child reinforces Carole Moses's argument that Fern's work expresses a "domestic transcendentalism."[63] Insofar as Fern claims sympathy as constitutive of self, she promotes an understanding of the self that includes women irrespective of physiognomy, biology, and other "encumbrances." The several scenes of Ruth's reading and responding to letters from her readers emphasize sympathy as a recognition of selfhood that is situated in but transcendent of particular circumstances. But taken as a body, the letters raise questions about sympathy's economic value and the relationship between abstract selfhood and capitalism. For instance, Ruth/Floy might dismiss a letter asking for money or other material support (*RHOW* 153–55, 164). But when Mary Andrews writes that she senses she will die in childbirth and asks Floy to care for her infant, Ruth responds, "Poor Mary! that letter must be answered" (*RHOW* 166). In each of these examples, a reader imagines the author as a particular type of person able to provide services beyond the literary; their requests, and Floy's responses to them, extend the marketplace for goods and services in which both parties already participate as suppliers and consumers of popular literature. By choosing whether and how to extend that marketplace, Floy and Fern suggest values for that marketplace at each stage. In other words, Fern invigorates the literary marketplace with qualities of affect and compassion that are specifically linked to sympathy and that are exchanged reciprocally.

Other responses to Floy corroborate this reading, engaging the compassion of Ruth/Floy without requiring material exchange from her. In many of these instances, the letter writers project their own strongest needs or desires onto Floy. For instance, a child writes that her mother often reads Floy's columns to her and asks, "How do you look? I guess you look like mamma" (*RHOW* 189). She associates Floy with the maternal kindness that is central to her sense of personal security. Another writer offers Floy the highest praise of positive influence: "I am a better son, a better brother, a better husband, and a better father, than I was before I commenced reading your articles" (*RHOW* 183). Letters such as these repay the author's work with their own expressions of affect. Significantly, their expressions engage values of family feeling and kinship ties, suggesting that Floy's influence over individuals in fact reinforces the values of family life associated with domestic happiness. The effect is not limited to the private sphere, however, and not only because the individuals are influenced by Floy's very public writings. In responding to Floy as they do, the writers indicate that her public influence over private feeling flows back outward again, instilling the values of compassion, love, and honesty into all of their expressions and actions.

Floy's writings instigate a reciprocal exchange of sympathies among her readers. Through her celebrity, then, Floy becomes the center of a national community whose membership is determined by sympathy. Critics note that, in *Ruth Hall*, Fern critiques the hypercompetitive, hypermasculine world of commercial publishing; through her portrayal of Mr. Walter as a business partner with "brotherly" feelings for Ruth, Fern advocates a model of literary professionalism that is both ethical and friendly to women writers. The novel's apparent domestication of the publishing business extends to the reading public as well:

as Floy's male readers become more sympathetic to the subjects she publicizes in her newspaper sketches, they are liable to become better sons, brothers, and husbands. Glenn Hendler argues that Fern consistently critiques men as "simultaneously too 'effeminate' and too 'public'" in their rejection of domesticity.[64] *Ruth Hall* idealizes men, such as Mr. Walker and Floy's best male readers, who successfully integrate domestic roles with their public selves. Similarly, Fern's model community does not fail to acknowledge women but brings their intense privacy, isolation, and suffering to sympathetic light. Through Ruth's celebrity, Fern models a sympathetic community that is an attractive alternative and corrective to prevailing models of sociability and belonging.

Doubtless, this idealized, sympathetic community yields Ruth tremendous financial benefits. Her success as a writer is not merely a triumph of sympathy in an unsympathetic society, but an integration of sympathy into a commercial marketplace. As Jennifer Harris puts it, Ruth's/Floy's popularity registers as a market value determined by the mutual sympathy she exchanges with her readers. Sympathy in the novel is a "currency" that accompanies Ruth's growing material wealth.[65] Put another way, as a commercial commodity, Ruth mobilizes abstract desires in her readers that can be satisfied only by the marketplace, and *Ruth Hall* shows that for Fern the most important, and lucrative, desire among her readers is their desire for sympathy. That particular combination of sympathetic appeal and commercial success is the cornerstone of Fern's success as well, but in neither Ruth's nor Fern's case does it tell the whole story of celebrity. As letters from Floy's readers show—letters we may understand as representations of those Fern herself received—not all readers responded to her sympathetically. Ruth also reads letters that criticize her writing as "unmitigated trash," ask her to ghostwrite a popular story, and solicit money (*RHOW* 166, 164, 182). Fern sums up the range of responses to Floy in a passage that could well describe popular reaction to Fern herself:

> All sorts of rumors became rife about "Floy," some maintaining her to be a man, because she had the courage to call things by their right names, and the independence to express herself boldly on subjects which to the timid and clique-serving, were tabooed. Some said she was a disappointed old maid; some said she was a designing widow; some said she was a moon-struck girl; and all said she was a nondescript. Some tried to imitate her, and failing in this, abused and maligned her; the outwardly strait-laced and inwardly corrupt, puckered up their mouths and "blushed for her;" the hypocritical denounced the sacrilegious fingers which had dared to touch the Ark; the fashionist voted her a vulgar, plebian thing; and the earnest and sorrowing, to whose burdened hearts she had given voice, cried God speed her. (*RHOW* 133)

The passage encapsulates the wide-ranging responses to Fern's own newspaper columns in the early days of her career, when readers questioned the identity behind the pseudonym. It also demonstrates Fern's/Ruth's gift for observing her observers: here she categorizes her critics—the hypocritical, the "fashionist"— just as they attempt to categorize her. But whereas she claims to see her readers clearly, they are unable to discover her. The public is unable to locate the woman writer along the continuum of ideological norms, and as a result, "all said she was nondescript." The word "nondescript" recurs in nineteenth-century usage to designate persons or things whose categorical evasiveness is their chief point of interest. The word carries connotations of exhibitionism, spectacle, and indeterminacy that are especially useful in relation to celebrity figures such as Floy. Fern's use of the word was probably influenced by P. T. Barnum, to whom she makes reference in many of her newspaper pieces as a purveyor of public curiosities. Barnum used the word frequently to classify his most puzzling exhibits, especially his displays of human curiosities. Exhibits such as his displays of "savage" Indians and "exotic" beauties adhere to the logic behind his notorious "What Is It?" exhibit—a man dressed in furs and skins who ran about erratically, hollering and grunting. According to James W. Cook, the purpose of such a character was "to create a fundamentally *liminal* creature . . . onto which numerous geographic, racial, and cultural templates could be applied."[66] These cultural values and interpretations often carry erotic dimensions, and Fern's passage alludes to the ways the public woman's status as "nondescript" registers popular assumptions about female sexuality. As in both Fern's and Ruth's experience, Floy is subject to speculation about her sexual availability and her coherence with normative gender ideologies. In privileging the sympathetic responses to Floy, Fern proposes an alternative set of responses to women in public—one that is informed by sympathy rather than ideology. Fern builds her case for an ideal readership and attempts to restructure the public sphere in a manner that is more receptive to her and other women in public. But overall, her value in the marketplace accounts for the diverse responses, even the controversies, that follow her. If Fern herself values sympathy and uses her work didactically to promote it, *Ruth Hall* indicates that the market as a whole values sentiment: readers' attempts to make sense of Floy are shaped by ideologically inflected gender norms and express their views in emotionally charged language.

Fern rejects the sentimental ideals of womanhood that inform most readers' responses to her and favors a public reception based on sympathy. She attempts to create a model of public engagement, of community, that includes women through fuller recognition of their experiences. She uses that personal sympathy to promote sympathetic relations among both men and women as an alternative to the combative personal public sphere. Many readers, including Fern's best reader, Joyce Warren, emphasize Fern's championing of women's financial independence. The bank note that Ruth receives in the novel's closing pages symbolizes her independence, a feminist victory over the protectionist attitudes toward women that restricted their freedom. The fact of Ruth's wealth should not be overshadowed by the means by which she attains it: her celebrity enriches her by mobilizing desires for womanhood that are in conflict with one another and that are all answered, apparently, by her public expressions of selfhood. That celebrity capitalizes on controversy over the public person's significance is clear. She recognizes the public sphere is not homogeneous, and she knows the diversity of responses she elicits is fundamental to her success. In authoring *Ruth Hall*, Fern knowingly elicits controversy: her autobiographical novel represents the same public interest in and confusion about the star author's identity that Fern herself experienced, and the caricatures of family members and editors practically invite speculations about their real-life counterparts. She does not, therefore, reject the personalization of public life; rather, she attempts to refine or redirect the personal response characteristic of the public sphere and celebrity culture. Her purpose is as much rhetorical as it is personal. On the one hand, she seeks to preserve her own selfhood from the invasive consumerism that she understands to be necessary to her success. On the other hand, she recognizes the cultural value of that effort—its relevance in renovating the public sphere in a manner that is amenable to women. Fern thus engages celebrity to expand women's participation in public life by providing a means of recognizing their intrinsic selfhood.

NOTES

INTRODUCTION

1. Henry James, "Emerson," in James, *Partial Portraits*, 32, 22, 33.
2. Ibid., 25.
3. Leon Edel, introduction to James, *Partial Portraits*, xv.
4. James, *Partial Portraits*, 32.
5. Dyer, "Stars as Images," 153.
6. Dyer, *Heavenly Bodies*, 4.
7. Tompkins, *Reader-Response Criticism*, xv. Tompkins is commenting here on Wolfgang Iser's idea of the reader's role in constructing meaning.
8. Tompkins, *Sensational Designs*, xi.
9. In their introduction to *Materializing Democracy*, Russ Castronovo and Dana D. Nelson ask, "How central are materials such as public space, novels, advice manuals, celebrities, mass communication technology, classrooms, or prisons to the building of democracy?" (10).
10. On the relationship between celebrity and politics, see Marshall, *Celebrity and Power*; Blake, *Walt Whitman and the Culture of American Celebrity*, 54–58.
11. Braudy, *Frenzy of Renown*, 38, 29.
12. Ibid., 371, 372.
13. Mole, *Byron's Romantic Celebrity*, 1, 3.
14. Mole, *Romanticism and Celebrity Culture*, 12.
15. The association of professional authorship with entrepreneurship is from Dowling, *Capital Letters*, 2. The characterization of authorship prior to the market revolution as a gentlemanly pursuit is informed by Buell, *New England Literary Culture*, 58–59. In addition to these works, the key texts on the professionalization of authorship include Charvat, *Profession of Authorship in America*; Coultrap-McQuinn, *Doing Literary Business*; Brodhead, *Cultures of Letters*; Zboray, *Fictive People*; and Newbury, *Figuring Authorship in Antebellum America*.
16. On the emergence of the best-seller, see Mott, *Golden Multitudes*; Geary, "Domestic Novel."
17. McGill, *American Literature*, 17.
18. Roland Barthes, "The Death of the Author," in Barthes, *Image, Music, Text*, 147.
19. Ibid., 143.

20. Lehuu, *Carnival on the Page*, 4.

21. Warner, "Mass Public," 381.

22. The persuasive power of physical proximity between orator and audience is a central idea in Gustafson, *Eloquence Is Power*.

23. One might make the case that in our current moment, audiences have greater access to celebrities thanks to the preponderance of social media, which enable celebrities to address audiences directly. A fuller consideration of these questions requires analysis of new media and the rhetorics they generate. As a starting point see Jenkins, *Convergence Culture*. Jenkins defines convergence culture as the place "where old and new media collide, where grassroots and corporate media intersect, where the power of the media producer and the power of the media consumer interact in unpredictable ways" (4). This media environment is far different from what I describe in this book, and it discourages simple comparisons between nineteenth-century celebrity culture and twenty-first-century celebrity culture. See also Marwick and boyd, "To See and Be Seen," as well as Page, "Linguistics of Self-Branding."

24. Elmer, *Reading at the Social Limit*, 7.

25. Warner, "Mass Public," 386.

26. Adorno and Horkheimer, "Culture Industry."

27. Boorstin, *Image*, 49, 57.

28. Smith, "Resisting the Gaze of Embodiment," 80.

29. Sorisio, *Fleshing Out America*, esp. chap. 1. See also Sanchez-Eppler, *Touching Liberty*.

30. See Dillon, *Gender of Freedom*.

31. Warner, "Mass Public," 383.

32. On the presence of women in public life, see Dillon, *Gender of Freedom*. See also Ryan, "Gender and Public Access," and Ryan, *Civic Wars*.

33. Nelson, *National Manhood*, 17.

34. Garvey, *Creating the Culture of Reform*, 14–19.

35. Castiglia, *Interior States*, 102.

36. Nelson, *National Manhood*, 34.

37. Goldsmith, "Celebrity and the Spectacle of Nation," 22.

38. Rojek, *Celebrity*, 14–15.

39. Anderson, *Imagined Communities*.

40. Jefferson, *Papers of Thomas Jefferson*, 148–52.

41. Tocqueville, *Democracy in America*, 263, 264.

42. Greiman, *Democracy's Spectacle*.

43. Marshall, *Celebrity and Power*, 57–58, 65.

44. For the view that the celebrity projects a stable self, see Dyer, "Stars as Images," 162–75. Of equal interest, John Langer's study of television personalities also emphasizes the stability of the celebrity's projected self. See Langer, "Television's 'Personality System.'"

45. Elmer, *Reading at the Social Limit*, 29.

46. Mouffe, *Democratic Paradox*, 103.

47. Emerson, *Collected Works*, 1:168.

CHAPTER 1. P. T. BARNUM

1. On Barnum's role in the history of advertising, see Applegate, *Personalities and Products*, 60. Jennifer Wicke discusses Barnum's self-referentiality as authorship in the Foucouldian sense of the creation of a new discourse. See Wicke, *Advertising Fictions*, esp. 63–64. David Haven Blake discusses Barnum's importance to the language and aesthetics of advertising in his *Walt Whitman and the Culture of American Celebrity*, 98–137.

2. P. T. Barnum, *Struggles and Triumphs*, 161. Subsequent citations will be cited parenthetically within the text as *ST*.

3. Adams, *E Pluribus Barnum*, 43.

4. Scholarship on Barnum's audiences is somewhat mixed. In *Struggles and Triumphs*, Barnum himself emphasizes the mixture of social classes in his audiences. Since his museum was located on the fringes of New York's rough Bowery neighborhood, he tended to draw local working-class patrons. But the museum's prosperity resulted from Barnum's efforts to attract middle-class audiences from the city and, with the growth of the railroad, tourists from outside the city. He was especially keen to attract women, his target audience for lecture room performances. Barnum critics emphasize his efforts to attract a middle-class clientele, and considering his lifelong appeals for respectability, I am inclined to agree that Barnum's core audience was middle class. But in terms of social values, the middle class is far from homogenous. Adams supports a reading of Barnum's clientele as "middle- and working-class 'respectables,'" and he notes the widening of the American Museum's patron base after the Jenny Lind tour (*E Pluribus Barnum*, 76, 74). See his chapter 3 for a fuller account of Barnum's attempts to attract different social groups. On the racial composition of audiences, James W. Cook points out that Barnum "did not regularly welcome African Americans until after the Civil War." See his *Arts of Deception*, 24.

5. Adams, *E Pluribus Barnum*, 18.

6. See Rourke, *Trumpets of Jubilee*.

7. Roland Barthes, "Rhetoric of the Image," in Barthes, *Image, Music, Text*, 39.

8. Neil Harris, *Humbug*, 61–74.

9. Barnum, *Life of P. T. Barnum, Written by Himself*, 154. Hereafter cited parenthetically within the text as *Life*.

10. Reiss, *Showman and the Slave*, 6–7.

11. Thomson, *Extraordinary Bodies*, 59.

12. Cook, *Arts of Deception*, 16.

13. Neil Harris, *Humbug*, 77.

14. Cook, *Arts of Deception*, 17.

15. On nineteenth-century American preoccupations with confidence, see Halttunen, *Confidence Men and Painted Women*, and Lindberg, *Confidence Man in American Literature*.

16. "Barnum's Autobiography," 2.

17. Eddy, "Barnum," 175.

18. On Barnum and hype, see Blake, *Walt Whitman*, 105–8.

19. On Barnum's Circassian Beauty and the erotic, white gaze, see Frost, *Never One Nation*, esp. chap. 3.

20. On Barnum's use of the ideology of True Womanhood in marketing the Jenny Lind tour, see Adams, *E Pluribus Barnum*, chap. 2.

21. Barnum, *Humbugs of the World*, 20. Hereafter cited parenthetically within the text as *HW*.

22. Neil Harris, *Humbug*, 217.

23. Thoreau, *Walden and Resistance to Civil Government*, 66. It is likely that Barnum read Thoreau: according to A. H. Saxon, Barnum read widely, especially in history and travel, and Thoreau's name is included in a list of famous men whose biographies Barnum donated to the Bridgeport, Connecticut, public library in 1882. See Saxon, *P. T. Barnum*, 279.

24. Reese, *Humbugs of New-York*, 151.

25. Neil Harris, *Humbug*, 216.

26. Croly, *Miscegenation*, 16. In *Humbugs of the World*, Barnum credits George Wakeman and E. C. Howell as Croly's coauthors, although their names do not appear in the modern reprinted edition of the pamphlet.

27. Ibid., 27.

28. Lemire, *"Miscegenation,"* 4.

29. Croly, *Miscegenation*, 60, 11.

30. On the significance of the term "preference" in miscegenation debates, see Lemire, *"Miscegenation,"* throughout.

31. Frost, *Never One Nation*, 6.

32. On the prevalence of representations of nonwhites as savage, see Frost, *Never One Nation*, esp. chap. 1.

33. Barnum, *Selected Letters*, 35.

34. Quoted in Neil Harris, *Humbug*, 65.

35. Quoted in Saxon, *P. T. Barnum*, 99.

36. Adams, *E Pluribus Barnum*, 161.

37. Strong, *Diary of George Templeton Strong*, 12. See also Saxon's reading of this passage in *P. T. Barnum*, 99.

38. Thomson, *Extraordinary Bodies*, 63–70.

39. Cook, *Arts of Deception*, 138.

40. Barnum, *Selected Letters*, 22.

41. The group also included two unidentified women, probably wives of delegates, and one child. Details of the delegation are scant. Barnum himself misremembers the year of the exhibit—he says it occurred in 1863 instead of 1864. His account of the exhibit focuses especially on the Kiowa Yellow Bear, but the Kunhardts claim he erred and that the correct name is Yellow Buffalo; see Kunhardt et al., *P. T. Barnum*, 176. Most scholarly accounts follow Barnum's lead in identifying the delegates, however, and in lieu of sufficient evidence supporting an alternative, I do, too. See esp. Mayhall, *Kiowas*, and Hoig, *Kiowas*.

42. P. T. Barnum and Samuel G. Colley, "Visit of Indian Chiefs," *New-York Daily Tribune*, April 7, 1863, 2.

43. Rockwell, *Indian Affairs*, 10–15.

44. "Visit of Indian Chiefs."

45. Ibid.

46. Frost, *Never One Nation*, 25.

47. For interpretations of the business arrangement as bribery, see Wallace, *Fabulous Showman*, 206, and Mayhall, *Kiowas*, 203, which largely follows Wallace's reading.

48. "Local Intelligence: A Tragic Affair in the Bowery. A Visit of the Indians to Public School No. 14," *New York Times*, April 11, 1863.

49. Berkhofer, *White Man's Indian*, 27.

50. For an overview of the delegation's visit to Washington, D.C., see Hoig, *Kiowas*, 71–74.

51. "Amusements," *New York Times*, April 13, 1863.

52. On the tropes of Indians as torturers and baby killers, see Derounian-Stodola et al., *Indian Captivity Narrative*, 70–73, as well as Ramsey, "Cannibalism and Infant Killing."

53. In fact, the Indians did not deceive Lincoln but were apparently appeased by their brief meeting with him. In his address to the delegation, Lincoln emphasized the importance of treaties in keeping the peace between whites and Indians. See Hoig, *Kiowas*, 71–72.

54. Frost, *Never One Nation*, 24.

55. Greiman, *Democracy's Spectacle*, 21.

56. Rojek, *Celebrity*, 12.

57. Dyer, *Heavenly Bodies*, 7.

58. Marshall, *Celebrity and Power*, 47.

59. Rojek, *Celebrity*, 11.

60. Hamilton, *Impersonations*, 190.

61. Kunhardt et al., *P. T. Barnum*, 84.

62. The critical literature on commercial leisure skews toward the late nineteenth and early twentieth centuries. See, for example, Gleason, *Leisure Ethic*, and Nasaw, *Going Out*. Greater context for Barnum's work can be gleaned from studies of the history of dime museums, the freak show, and popular theater. On dime museums, see Dennett, *Weird and Wonderful*, as well as articles by John C. Ewers and Louis Leonard Tucker in Bell, *Cabinet of Curiosities*. On the freak show, see Bogdan, *Freak Show*. On popular theater, see Butsch, *Making of American Audiences*.

63. Adams, *E Pluribus Barnum*, 30.

64. Kunhardt et al., *P. T. Barnum*, 84.

65. On the use of home architecture to delineate public and private spaces within the domestic realm, see Shamir, *Inexpressible Privacy*, as well as Halttunen, *Confidence Men and Painted Women*.

66. Neil Harris, *Humbug*, 4–5.

67. Fretz, "P. T. Barnum's Theatrical Selfhood," 99. Similarly, Braudy, in *Frenzy*

of Renown, claims that Barnum "illustrates the increasingly elaborate sense of being in public that characterized the American performer and the American audience of the later nineteenth century" (499).

68. Quoted in Saxon, *P. T. Barnum*, 16.

69. Adams details Barnum's early adoption of the persona of a Yankee slaveholder, Bartleby Diddleum, as well as his strategically mounting pro- and antislavery dramas in his lecture room. On Diddleum, see Adams, *E Pluribus Barnum*, 5–8; on the lecture room dramas, see Adams, *E Pluribus Barnum*, chap. 4.

CHAPTER 2. WALT WHITMAN

1. Whitman, *Prose Works 1892*, 712–13. Hereafter cited parenthetically within the text as *PW*.

2. Rojek, *Celebrity*, 106.

3. In keeping with such an interpretation, his brazen promotional efforts reveal Whitman's "absorption" of the strident self-promotion of a commercialized public life. For a full discussion of Whitman's self-promotions in the context of the emerging advertising culture, see Blake, *Walt Whitman*, chap. 3, as well as Francis, "Outbidding at the Start."

4. Whitman, *Leaves of Grass 1860: The 150th Anniversary Facsimile Edition*, 363. Hereafter cited parenthetically within the text as 1860 *LG*.

5. Burroughs, *Walt Whitman*, 94.

6. Brown, "Young Editor Whitman."

7. On artisan republicanism in general, see Wilentz, *Chants Democratic*. On the artisan republican politics of the penny press, see Schiller, *Objectivity and the News*, esp. chap. 1.

8. Whitman, *Journalism*, 13. Hereafter cited parenthetically within the text as WJ.

9. See Vincent J. Bertolini, "Fireside Chastity: The Erotics of Sentimental Bachelorhood in the 1850s," in Chapman and Hendler, *Sentimental Men*, 19–42.

10. Several critics trace the personal style of Whitman's poetry directly to the personal style of contemporary journalism. See, for instance, Brown, "Young Editor Whitman," 143; Fishkin, *From Fact to Fiction*, 5, 18; Greenspan, *Walt Whitman*, 109; Noverr, "Journalism," 31. The idea of a personal style of journalism is also implicit in histories of the newspaper, particularly in their tracing specific newspapers' contents and styles to their prominent editors. See especially Schiller, *Objectivity and the News*.

11. "Fact-based reporting" is not a synonym for "objectivity." Michael Schudson claims that while objectivity was an ideal of reporting from the 1830s, it "did not become the chief norm or practice in journalism in the late nineteenth century when the AP was growing"; see *Discovering the News*, 5. However, in *Objectivity and the News*, Schiller counters that objectivity is a matter more of style than attitude, and he claims that the inclusive coverage of the penny press constituted a form of objectivity.

12. Cmiel, *Democratic Eloquence*, 58–70.

13. Nord, *Communities of Journalism*, 9.

14. On the importance of reciprocity to letters as a genre, see Altman, *Epistolarity*, 88. Also, Eve Tavor Bannett connects the reciprocal expectations of letter writing with models of conversation; see *Empire of Letters*.

15. Larkin, "Inventing an American Public," 254.

16. Habermas, *Structural Transformation*, 19, 169.

17. See Schiller, *Objectivity and the News*; Fanuzzi, *Abolition's Public Sphere*; Castiglia and Hendler, introduction to *Franklin Evans*.

18. See, for instance, essays by Nancy Frasier and Mary Ryan in Calhoun, *Habermas and the Public Sphere*; Stansell, *City of Women*.

19. Ronald J. Zboray points out that the presence of newsboys and book vendors on railways encourages changing habits of reading, particularly reading in public spaces. See *Fictive People*, esp. chap. 5. See also David M. Henkin's discussion of the penny press in *City Reading*.

20. Loughran, *Republic in Print*, 27.

21. Henkin, *City Reading*, 15–16.

22. Looby, *Voicing America*, 4.

23. Warner, *Letters of the Republic*, 40.

24. In November 1842 the *Aurora*'s daily circulation was 5,000, according to Hudson, *Journalism in the United States*. Notwithstanding the probable inaccuracy of this figure, Whitman's success in overseeing higher circulations has been accepted at face value. See the introduction to WJ, liii, and Brown, "Young Editor Whitman," 141.

25. Noverr, "Journalism," 37.

26. Whitman was likewise fired from the *Brooklyn Daily Eagle*, which he edited from 1846 to 1848, over political differences with publisher Isaak Van Anden. In both cases, his former editors claimed he had been dismissed for laziness, but the political causes have been widely accepted. See the introduction to WJ, as well as Noverr, "Journalism."

27. Noverr, "Journalism," 35.

28. My understanding of Whitman's parallels to Paine owes much to Loughran's chapter on the material history of *Common Sense* in *The Republic in Print*. Cmiel discusses Paine's vernacular strategies as a key example of the middling style (*Democratic Eloquence*, 50).

29. On the expressions of authority inherent to correspondence, see Hewitt, *Correspondence and American Literature*, 7–8, and Theresa Strouth Gaul, introduction to *To Marry an Indian*, 1–76.

30. According to Krieg, *Whitman and the Irish*, the legislature's compromise "did not allow public funding of religious schools but did proscribe all sectarianism in the public schools and made the city schools part of the state system with a board of education to oversee them" (42).

31. Krieg argues that Whitman's apparent anti-immigrant stance is really anti-Catholicism, "for he viewed their [the Irish immigrants'] church not only as undemocratic but as antidemocratic" (*Whitman and the Irish*, 33; see also her discussion of the schools question and Whitman's *Aurora* coverage of it, 37–46). By contrast, in *Walt Whitman: The Song of Himself*, Jerome Loving rejects the notion that Whitman shares the anti-Irish sentiments of the *Aurora* editorials and argues that his attempts to "soften" the paper's anti-Irish rhetoric "may have led him to the voluntary conclusion of his duties there" (65). In *Walt Whitman's America*, David S. Reynolds points out that Whit-

man "resisted thoroughgoing nativism" and "denounced the emerging Native American Party" (99).

32. Nord points out that in times of crisis, the forum-function of the newspaper may create more confusion than clarity (*Communities of Journalism*, 211).

33. Marshall, *Celebrity and Power*, 6.

34. Blake, *Walt Whitman*, 49.

35. Marshall, *Celebrity and Power*, 47.

36. The key text in discussions of the flâneur is Walter Benjamin, "On Some Motifs in Baudelaire," in Benjamin, *Illuminations*, 155–200. For discussion of the flâneur in American literature, including in Whitman, see Brand, *Spectator and the City*. On the flâneur as a reader, see Hayes, "Visual Culture."

37. For discussions of the panorama and its influences in Whitman, see Brand, *Spectator and the City*, 158–59, and Dougherty, *Walt Whitman*, 139–71. For a discussion of panoramic representations of New York, see Bergman, "Panoramas of New York."

38. Quoted in Brasher, *Whitman as Editor*, 42.

39. For sentimentality's role in answering such questions, see Halttunen, *Confidence Men and Painted Women*. On the significance of parades and other street festivals in crafting a participatory spirit of nationalism, see Waldstreicher, *In the Midst*, and Newman, *Parades*.

40. I am drawing here on Charles Altieri's idea of "anti-spectacle." Altieri is particularly interested in methods of creating ideas of national identity and collectivity that do not depend on public ceremonies of state or metonymic signifiers (such as flags), which, he argues, "serve to stabilize existing authority in order to displace other, more local vehicles for imagining social bonds." See "Spectacular Anti-spectacle," 290.

41. Brand, *Spectator and the City*, 159; Greenspan, *Walt Whitman*, 108.

42. Like much of Whitman's journalism, the review of Emerson's lecture was unsigned. In accepting it as Whitman's work, I follow the lead of editors of his journalism who determine Whitman's authorship through clues of publication date and style. On the question of authorship, see the introductions to the various editions of Whitman's journalism, especially Rubin and Brown, *Walt Whitman*.

43. Greeley, "Mr. Emerson's Lectures."

44. Erkkila, *Whitman the Political Poet*, 93–94.

45. Larson, *Whitman's Drama of Consensus*, 23.

46. Whitman, *Leaves of Grass: The First (1855) Edition*, 9. Hereafter cited parenthetically within the text as 1855 *LG*.

47. Blake, *Walt Whitman*, 63, 101.

48. "Walt Whitman's Dirty Book," *Cincinnati Daily Commercial*, November 29, 1860, 3; "'Leaves of Grass'—Smut in Them," *Springfield Daily Republican*, June 16, 1860, 4, Walt Whitman Archive, ed. Ed Folsom and Kenneth M. Price, www.whitmanarchive.org.

49. As I discuss, the idea of a "homosexual utopia" comes from Thomas Yingling, "Homosexuality and Utopian Discourse in American Poetry," in Erkkila and Grossman, *Breaking Bounds*. On the political significance of Whitman's representation of homosex-

uality in the public sphere, see also Erkkila, *Whitman the Political Poet*; Moon, *Disseminating Whitman*; Martha Nussbaum, "Democratic Desire," in Seery, *Political Companion to Walt Whitman*, 96–130.

50. Blake, *Walt Whitman*, 163.

51. Vendler, *Invisible Listeners*, 56.

52. Ibid., 5. Other notable criticism that links the "Calamus" poetry to Whitman's personal experience includes Loving, *Walt Whitman*; Pollak, *Erotic Whitman*.

53. Yingling, "Homosexuality and Utopian Discourse," 144.

54. Larson, *Whitman's Drama of Consensus*, 166.

55. Lauren Berlant, "Intimacy: A Special Issue," in Berlant, *Intimacy*, 2.

56. Elmer, *Reading at the Social Limit*, 7.

57. Rojek, *Celebrity*, 196.

58. Richard Dyer discusses the function of images in mediating knowledge in popular culture in *Matter of Images*, esp. introduction.

59. Lacan, *Four Fundamental Concepts of Psychoanalysis*, 80–81.

60. Žižek, *Looking Awry*, 6.

61. Folsom, *Walt Whitman's Native Representations*, 137.

62. See Nussbaum, "Democratic Desire," 113.

63. Ibid., 123.

64. Bunker, *From Rail-Splitter to Icon*, 9.

65. Holzer et al., *Lincoln Image*, 27.

66. Ibid., 14–15.

67. Bunker, *From Rail-Splitter to Icon*, 9.

68. Holzer, *Lincoln Seen and Heard*, 9, 36.

69. On painters' difficulty with Lincoln as a subject, see Holzer et al., *Lincoln Image*, 21–23. On Lincoln's indifference to his likenesses, see both *Lincoln Image* and Holzer, *Lincoln Seen and Heard* throughout.

70. Reynolds, *Walt Whitman's America*, 440.

71. Loving, *Walt Whitman*, 285.

72. Walt Whitman, *Drum-Taps and Sequel to Drum-Taps*, xviii–xix. Hereafter cited parenthetically within the text as *SDT*.

73. Pollak, *Erotic Whitman*, 159.

74. Barthes, *Camera Lucida*, 14.

75. Folsom, "Whitman's 'Calamus' Photographs," in Erkkila and Grossman, *Breaking Bounds*, 205–6.

76. Lincoln, "Address at Gettysburg, Pennsylvania," 536.

77. Castronovo, *Necro Citizenship*, 4.

78. Holzer, *Lincoln Seen and Heard*, 53, 55.

CHAPTER 3. RALPH WALDO EMERSON

1. Emerson, *Journals and Miscellaneous Notebooks of Ralph Waldo Emerson*, 14:335. Hereafter cited parenthetically within the text as *JMN*.

2. Emerson, *Collected Works of Ralph Waldo Emerson*, 2:31. Hereafter cited parenthetically within the text as *CW*.

3. Braudy, *Frenzy of Renown*, 445.

4. Marshall, *Celebrity and Power*, 8.

5. Bosco and Myerson, *Emerson in His Own Time*, 174–75.

6. Ibid., xvii.

7. Augst, *Clerk's Tale*, 135–36.

8. In labeling the print marketplace "carnivalesque," I have in mind Isabelle Lehuu's work *Carnival on the Page*.

9. In a very striking example, Mary Kupiec Cayton contrasts Emerson's lectures on "Wealth" with P. T. Barnum's lectures on "The Art of Money-Getting," which often occurred in the same venues during the same lecture season. See "Making of an American Prophet," 614–15.

10. Stadler, *Troubling Minds*, 18, 19.

11. Cayton, "Making of an American Prophet," 597–620.

12. Wider, "What Did the Minister Mean."

13. On the Divinity School "Address" controversy, see the selection of reviews in Myerson, *Emerson and Thoreau: The Contemporary Reviews*, 33–54 (hereafter cited parenthetically within the text as *ETCR*).

14. Emerson, *Letters of Ralph Waldo Emerson*, 2:166–67. Hereafter cited parenthetically within the text as *Letters*.

15. Bishop, *Emerson on the Soul*, 147.

16. Augst, *Clerk's Tale*, 87, 118.

17. Ray, *Lyceum and Public Culture*, 7. See also Bode, *American Lyceum*.

18. See Ray, *Lyceum and Public Culture*, chap. 1.

19. Museum theaters such as Kimball's in Boston made efforts to attract audiences with sentimental melodramas whose themes of moral reform aided the "sentimental education" of the nineteenth-century New England's new middle class. See McConachie, "Museum Theater."

20. Channing, *Self-Culture*, 78–79, 60.

21. Robinson, introduction to *William Ellery Channing*, 30.

22. Milder, "Radical Emerson?" 56.

23. *Cincinnati Gazette*, January 28, 1857, quoted in Mead, *Yankee Eloquence*, 42–43.

24. *Cincinnati Times*, quoted in Mead, *Yankee Eloquence*, 43.

25. Ellen Tucker Emerson, "What I Can Remember about Father: Manuscript, 1902," MS Am 1280.227, Ralph Waldo Emerson Memorial Association deposit, Houghton Library, Harvard University.

26. Bosco and Myerson, *Emerson in His Own Time*, 81.

27. Stadler, *Troubling Minds*, xvii (italics in original).

28. Willis, *Hurry-Graphs*, 170.

29. Ibid., 170–71.

30. Ibid., 172.

31. Emerson, *Later Lectures of Ralph Waldo Emerson*, 101–6.

32. Willis, *Hurry-Graphs*, 175.

33. Bosco and Myerson, *Emerson in His Own Time*, 197. The quotation is from William Dean Howells's retrospective on Emerson's early reception among a certain segment of the popular audience.

34. Willis, *Hurry-Graphs*, 177.

35. Lowell, *My Study Windows*, 377.

36. Holmes, *Ralph Waldo Emerson*, 376, 379.

37. George Santayana, "Emerson," in Santayana, *Essays in Literary Criticism*, 224.

38. Stallybrass and White, *Politics and Poetics of Transgression*, 57.

39. See Sorisio, *Fleshing Out America*, 38.

40. On a related point, Christopher Newfield associates Emerson's distrust of the masses with homophobia, seeing in it the fear of unchecked eroticism among crowds of men. See *Emerson Effect*, 91–128.

41. Elmer, *Reading at the Social Limit*, 7.

42. Barbara Packer argues that Emerson adhered to views of "racial physiognomy" that believed in inherent differences between the races. See her "Historical Introduction." See also Sorisio, *Fleshing Out America*, 104–42.

43. Rojek, *Celebrity*, 58.

44. See, for instance, Baudrillard, *Simulacra and Simulation*, and Debord, *Society of the Spectacle*.

45. Ron Bosco and Joel Myerson, introduction to Emerson, *Later Lectures*, xix, xviii.

46. The connection between the eighteenth-century man-of-feeling and oratorical practice is explored in Fliegelman, *Declaring Independence*. Emerson's trope of electricity may reflect his interests in scientific advances in electricity and galvanism, which are traced in Eric Wilson, *Emerson's Sublime Science*. In addition, in a chapter on Walt Whitman, Alan Ackerman Jr. explores the idea of oratory as "electric" in ways that help contextualize the kind of eloquence Emerson might have sought. See Ackerman's *Portable Theatre*, esp. 51.

47. Kateb, *Emerson and Self-Reliance*, 5, 10.

48. Cameron, *Impersonality*, 85, 86.

49. On the connections between Unitarianism and the self-culture movement, see Robinson, *Apostle of Culture*, 11ff.

50. Sloan, "The Miraculous Uplifting," 12.

51. Bosco and Myerson, introduction to Emerson, *Later Lectures*, xxvii. See also Buell's discussion of Emerson's lecturing in *New England Literary Culture*.

52. Other children in the community eventually also sought Emerson's tutelage in these recitations, too. See Ellen Tucker Emerson, "What I Can Remember about Father: Manuscript, 1902," MS Am 1280.227, Ralph Waldo Emerson Memorial Association deposit, Houghton Library, Harvard University, and Edith Emerson Forbes, [Memories of Ralph Waldo Emerson and of Home Life in Concord] MS Am 1280.235, Ralph Waldo Emerson Memorial Association deposit, Houghton Library, Harvard University.

53. Railton, "Seeing and Saying." For a discussion of Emerson's rhetorical techniques

in the sermons, see the introduction by Arthur Cushman McGiffert Jr. to his *Young Emerson Speaks*.

54. Cheyfitz, *Trans-Parent*, esp. 109, 121.

55. On Emerson's disdain for feminized domestic life, see Leverenz, *Manhood and the American Renaissance*, 65ff, as well as Cheyfitz's chapter on the "house-hero" in *Trans-Parent*.

56. See Felluga, *Perversity of Poetry*, on the link between the "nervous temperament" and notions of genius among romantic poets.

57. For a more detailed account of Emerson and Fuller's intellectual and erotic relationship, see Buell, *Emerson*, 87–90; Crain, *American Sympathy*, 177–237; Zwarg, *Feminist Conversations*.

58. Halttunen, *Confidence Men and Painted Women*, 59. See also Milette Shamir's discussion of the gendering of household spaces, which draws on Halttunen's study, in *Inexpressible Privacy*, esp. 32–40.

59. On a related point, Stadler notices the scopophilia of Emerson's descriptions of "great men" and suggests that in light of Emerson's powerful visual descriptions of these men's bodies, we might reconsider "any overly hasty reading of the famous 'transparent eyeball' figure as an exemplary instance of a definitive Emersonian association between vision and disembodiment" (*Troubling Minds*, 17).

60. Leverenz, *Manhood and the American Renaissance*, 54.

61. Quoted in Bosco and Myerson, *Emerson in His Own Time*, 138–39.

62. Ibid., 138.

63. Milder, "Radical Emerson?" 77.

64. Newfield, *Emerson Effect*, 7.

65. Cameron, *Impersonality*, 107.

66. See McFeely, *Frederick Douglass*, 166.

CHAPTER 4. FREDERICK DOUGLASS

1. In *Frederick Douglass: Freedom's Voice*, Gregory P. Lampe details the importance of oral culture within slavery, particularly the tradition of slave preaching (3–4), as well as Douglass's experience in New Bedford as a lay preacher with the New Bedford AME Zion Church prior to his emergence in the Garrisonian movement (28–42).

2. Douglass, *Autobiographies*, 3, italics added. Hereafter cited parenthetically within the text as *DA*.

3. Sanchez-Eppler, *Touching Liberty*, 15, 18.

4. At the same time, his canny use of photographs and author portraits suggests his unwillingness to abandon an identity rooted in his physical person. For a discussion of Douglass's use of authorial photography, see Stauffer, *Black Hearts of Men*, 46–56. On the disembodied authorial self, see Warner, *Letters of the Republic*.

5. On the antislavery movement's influence on the slave narrative genre in general and Douglass's 1845 *Narrative* in particular, see Sekora, "Black Message/White Envelope."

6. Newbury, "Eaten Alive."

7. Ernest, *Resistance and Reformation*, 15.
8. Ernest, *Liberation Historiography*, 157.
9. Douglass, *Frederick Douglass*, 39.
10. Martin, *Mind of Frederick Douglass*, 271.
11. For a discussion of Douglass's use of the heroes of the American Revolution and his casting himself their heir, see Robert S. Levine, "Slave Narrative," 99–114. Rafia Zafar discusses the parallels between Douglass and Benjamin Franklin. See *We Wear the Mask*, 106–7. In *To Wake the Nations*, Eric J. Sundquist offers an extended discussion of Douglass's rhetorical use of revolutionary figures, including examples from the American Revolution, Nat Turner, and Toussaint (30–36).
12. Wilson J. Moses, "Writing Freely?" 68–69.
13. Warren and Brandeis, "The Right to Privacy."
14. See "Right to Privacy in Nineteenth-Century America."
15. Arendt, *Human Condition*.
16. "Right to Privacy in Nineteenth-Century America," 1895n26.
17. Zafar, *We Wear the Mask*, 109.
18. McFeely, *Frederick Douglass*, 66.
19. Beyond these ideological considerations, Douglass may have had personal motivations: his oldest child, Rosetta, was frequently teased with rumors she had been conceived out of wedlock. See McFeely, *Frederick Douglass*, 70.
20. Ibid., 103.
21. Shamir, *Inexpressible Privacy*, 102.
22. In *Keywords*, Raymond Williams defines "private" in part as "a record of the legitimation of a bourgeois view of life: the ultimate generalized privilege, however abstract in practice, of seclusion and protection from others (*the public*); of lack of accountability to 'them'; and of related gains in closeness and comfort of these general kinds" (243).
23. Glymph, *Out of the House of Bondage*, 3, 43.
24. On the political significance of publicizing facts and behaviors otherwise kept private, especially in the women's movements, see Ryan, *Civic Wars*; Benhabib, "Models of Public Space"; Sanchez-Eppler, *Touching Liberty*; Shamir, *Inexpressible Privacy*.
25. Jeannine DeLombard, "Eye-Witness to the Cruelty."
26. Ernest, *Resistance and Reformation*, 146, 143.
27. Sundquist, *To Wake the Nations*, 91.
28. See Houston A. Baker, *Journey Back*, 33–34, on how Auld's use of the word "nigger" reveals its inapplicability to Douglass.
29. Ibid., 31.
30. Cassuto, *Inhuman Race*, 117.
31. Douglass's refusal to portray himself as beaten corresponds with his role as witness to slavery. In several "witnessing scenes," DeLombard argues, Douglass "shifts the metonym of authorship from the vulnerable, corporal eyeball to the unassailable, immaterial voice, a shift that corresponds with the text's overall progression from slavery to freedom and from South to North" ("Eye-Witness to Cruelty," 246).

32. Both DeLombard, "Eye-Witness to Cruelty," and David Leverenz make this point; see Leverenz's chapter on Douglass in *Manhood and the American Renaissance*.

33. On Douglass's sense of his sacred mission as an abolitionist crusader, and its parallels with other forms of romantic prophecy, including the Emersonian version, see Stauffer, *Black Hearts of Men*, 33–41.

34. Packer, *Transcendentalists*, 100.

35. Or, to use DeLombard's phrase, he claims the position of the "universal subject." In "Eye-Witness to History," DeLombard explicitly associates this position with the Emersonian notion of self-erasure that comes with the attainment of the ideal state of transparency.

36. Sundquist, *To Wake the Nations*, 90.

37. Leverenz, *Manhood and the American Renaissance*, 109.

38. In his critique of Douglass's biographies, Peter Walker points out that the tendency to see Douglass as a "unified" or fully formed person from the time of his escape overlooks the personal crisis of familial identity that plagued Douglass throughout his adulthood and that registers in his autobiographical writings in various ways. See *Moral Choices*, 211–61.

39. McFeely, *Frederick Douglass*, 50.

40. Morton H. Levine, "Privacy," 10, 19.

41. Sundquist, *To Wake the Nations*, 125.

42. See Wald, *Constituting Americans*, 91–92.

43. Greiman, *Democracy's Spectacle*, 7.

44. Thomson, *Extraordinary Bodies*, 60.

45. Douglass, *Frederick Douglass*, 279.

46. On the growing appeal of violent resistance to Douglass and others following passage of the Fugitive Slave Act, see Von Frank, *Trials of Anthony Burns*, 315–16. This claim runs throughout Stauffer's discussion of Douglass's increasing radicalism in the 1850s, and he points out the connection between passage of the Fugitive Slave Act and Douglass's decision to regard the Constitution as a proslavery document, freeing himself to use political means of pursuing abolition (*Black Hearts of Men*, 164).

47. Fanuzzi, "Trouble with Douglass's Body."

48. DeLombard, "Eye-Witness to Cruelty," 271.

49. Houston A. Baker, *Journey Back*, 45–46.

50. Blight, *Race and Reunion*.

51. Ernest, *Resistance and Reformation*, 171, 173.

52. Martin, *Mind of Frederick Douglass*, 99.

53. Douglass, *Frederick Douglass*, 116.

54. On Douglass's representations of Auld as a father figure, see Sundquist, *To Wake the Nations*, 98–108.

55. McFeely, *Frederick Douglass*, 250.

56. "Frederick Douglass at His Old Home," *Baltimore Sun*, June 19, 1877, 1.

57. Sundquist, *To Wake the Nations*, 108.

58. Warner, "Mass Public," 381; Berlant, "National Brands/National Body," 112.

CHAPTER 5. FANNY FERN

1. For details of Bonner's hiring of Fern and other celebrity writers, see Warren, *Fanny Fern*, 144–49, as well as Dowling, *Business of Literary Circles*, 61–88.

2. Weber, *Women and Literary Celebrity*, 100.

3. Altman, *Epistolarity*, 88.

4. Moulton, *Life and Beauties*, iii.

5. Kelley, *Private Woman, Public Stage*, 111.

6. Laffrado, "I Thought from the Way You *Writ*," 82.

7. Benstock, "Authorizing the Autobiographical." For a study of women's autobiography and psychoanalytic theories of ego-formation, see Susan Stanford Frieman's essay "Women's Autobiographical Selves: Theory and Practice," in Benstock, *Private Self*, 34–62.

8. Smith, "Resisting the Gaze of Embodiment," 81. Also, Karen Sanchez-Eppler develops these ideas in her discussion of the women's rights and abolitionist movements in *Touching Liberty*.

9. Smith, "Resisting the Gaze of Embodiment," 83. Weber develops this idea at length and explores Fern's handling of her own "monstrous" status in her excellent chapter "'A Sort of Monster': Fanny Fern, Fame's Appetite, and the Construction of the Multivalent Famous Female Author," in Weber, *Women and Literary Celebrity*, 73–100.

10. Smith, "Resisting the Gaze of Embodiment," 85.

11. *Olive Branch* (Boston), April 10, 1852, American Antiquarian Society, Worcester, Massachusetts. Subsequent citations will be given parenthetically within the text, using the abbreviation *OB* and the date of publication.

12. Anxiety about Fern's mixture of sentiment and satire in *Ruth Hall* has a long critical history; for an overview of critical reception of the novel in the twentieth century, see Susan K. Harris, *19th-Century American Women's Novels*, 111–13. More recent criticism has sought to reconcile the two styles and the two ideologies they seem to represent; in particular, in *The Fabrication of American Literature*, Lara Langer Cohen associates her pluralistic style with her "literary irreducibility" and "suggest[s] that Fern's relation to the marketplace might be as constitutive as it is antagonistic" (150).

13. Smith, "Resisting the Gaze of Embodiment," 85.

14. Susan K. Harris, *19th-Century American Women's Novels*, 114.

15. Rojek, *Celebrity*, 177, 176.

16. Ibid., 189, 190.

17. For an excellent analysis of the marketing of *Ruth Hall*, see Geary, "Domestic Novel."

18. Warren, "Uncommon Discourse," 51.

19. Fern and Whitman became social acquaintances in early 1856, and Fern wrote a

laudatory review of *Leaves of Grass* in May of that year. But in February 1857 Fern and her husband James Parton fell out with Whitman over a $200 loan that Whitman failed to repay. For a full reading of this episode, see Warren, *Fanny Fern*, 160–78.

20. Fern, *Ruth Hall and Other Writings*, 215. Subsequent citations of this volume will be given parenthetically within the text as *RHOW*.

21. On the penny papers' transformation of news coverage—and, indeed, popular understanding of what news is—see Baldasty, *Commercialization of News*, and Schudson, *Discovering the News*, 22–30. See also Schiller, *Objectivity and the News*, esp. chap. 2.

22. Baldasty discusses the importance of advertising in *Commercialization of News*, chap. 3.

23. On the presence of women in the nineteenth-century American public sphere, see, for instance, Dillon, *Gender of Freedom*; Ryan, *Women in Public*; Stansell, *City of Women*. See also the vigorous feminist responses to Habermas by Nancy Fraser and Seyla Benhabib in Calhoun, *Habermas and the Public Sphere*.

24. While it is well known that Fern received copious amounts of mail from readers throughout her career, none of the other periodicals for which she wrote published a comparable selection of reader correspondence. I hesitate to draw too-broad conclusions about Fern's relationship with her readers from the *Olive Branch* correspondence alone; however, I do think it yields important insights into her celebrity at the moment of its formation.

25. On letters as an acceptable form of writing for women, see Brandt, *Eighteenth-Century Letters and British Culture*, 18. On the other hand, in *Epistolary Histories*, Amanda Gilroy and W. M. Verhoeven argue that the popularity of epistolary novels written by women leads to the association of epistolarity with women's writing.

26. Hewitt, *Correspondence and American Literature*, 12.

27. Ibid., 8.

28. Laffrado, "I Thought from the Way You Writ," 87.

29. See Warren, *Fanny Fern*, 102.

30. Bannet, *Empire of Letters*, xvii–xviii.

31. Ibid., 281.

32. Berlant, "Female Woman," 433.

33. Noble, *Masochistic Pleasures of Sentimental Literature*, 37, emphasis in original. For an explanation of the ideology of true womanhood, see Welter, "Cult of True Womanhood"; Kerber, "Separate Spheres," 159–99.

34. Berlant, "Female Woman," 434.

35. Warren, *Fanny Fern*, 100.

36. Ibid., 258–60.

37. Ibid., 103.

38. Commonplace throughout the century, the quote "I am everything by turns and nothing long" is first attributed to Byron by his friend the Countess Marguerite Blessington, who published her *Conversations with Lord Byron* in *The New Monthly Magazine and*

Literary Journal, July 1832–December 1833. It is also published in a modern edition as *Conversations of Lord Byron*, edited by Ernest J. Locall Jr.

39. See Frances Wilson, *Byromania*; Jay A. Ward, "The Gloomy Vanity of 'Drawing from Self'": Byron and Romantic Self-Fashioning," in Peer, *Inventing the Individual*.

40. Later in her tenure with the *Olive Branch*, Fern responds angrily to writers whose imitations of her style she sees as a direct threat to her intellectual property. See Homestead, "Every Body Sees the Theft"; Newbury, *Figuring Authorship in Antebellum America*, 186–99.

41. That dialogue apparently continues in Fern's sentimental sketch "A Peep Behind the Scenes" in the same issue of the paper (*OB*, April 10, 1852). There, two young women, Kitty Fay and Nellie, discuss Kitty's willfulness. Nellie worries that Kitty is altogether too outspoken and bound to be the target of gossip and scandal (frequent topics of Fern's). Kitty, however, thrives on "astonishing people." Like Kitty, Fern clearly values the impulse to break with convention, even to astonish.

42. Berlant, "Female Woman," 429–54.

43. Gaul, introduction to *To Marry an Indian*, 29.

44. My reading of "Albert" is in keeping with Vincent J. Bertolini's argument that the culture "domesticates" the bachelor in an effort to curtail or contain his threat to the heterosexual social structure. See Bertolini, "Fireside Chastity."

45. On the male disciplinarian of women as a staple of sentimental discourse, see Noble, *Masochistic Pleasures of Sentimental Literature*, 39, and also chap. 2.

46. Gunn, "How I Look," 27.

47. Benstock, "Authorizing the Autobiographical," 15.

48. Warren, *Fanny Fern*, 112.

49. Moulton, *Life and Beauties*, 32–33.

50. Cohen, *Fabrication of American Literature*, 155.

51. Moulton, *Life and Beauties*, 52–3.

52. Warren, *Fanny Fern*, 180.

53. Thomson, *Staring*, 40–44.

54. Warren, *Fanny Fern*, 309. See also Mulvey, "Visual Pleasure and Narrative Cinema."

55. See Wilhelm, "Expenditure Saved."

56. I am especially interested here in the relationships between and among women that Fern depicts throughout *Ruth Hall*, but it should not be overlooked that Harry and his father, Dr. Hall, engage a similar dynamic of transparency and watchfulness, in which Dr. Hall challenges his son's authority in managing his business affairs and paternal duties. Taken together, the actions of both Dr. and Mrs. Hall can be read as attempts to reinscribe the younger couple in a gendered ideology of duty and authority.

57. Susan K. Harris, *19th-Century American Women's Novels*, 116.

58. See Waldron, "No Separations in the City," 98.

59. Jennifer Harris, "Marketplace Transactions," 349.

60. Dowling, *Capital Letters*, 65–81.

61. Child, *Letters from New-York*, 133, 134.
62. Roberts, "Public Heart," 752.
63. See Carole Moses, "Domestic Transcendentalism of Fanny Fern."
64. Hendler, *Public Sentiments*, 153–54.
65. Jennifer Harris, "Marketplace Transactions," 354.
66. James W. Cook, "'Of Men, Missing Links, and Nondescripts: The Strange Career of P. T. Barnum's 'What Is It?' Exhibition," in Thomson, *Freakery*, 145.

BIBLIOGRAPHY

Ackerman, Alan J. *Portable Theatre: American Literature and the Nineteenth-Century Stage*. Baltimore: Johns Hopkins University Press, 1999.
Adams, Bluford. *E Pluribus Barnum: The Great Showman and the Making of U.S. Popular Culture*. Minneapolis: University of Minnesota Press, 1997.
Adorno, Theodor, and Max Horkheimer. "The Culture Industry: Enlightenment as Mass Deception." In *The Dialectic of Enlightenment*. New York: Continuum, 1972. 123–71.
Altieri, Charles. "Spectacular Anti-spectacle: Ecstasy and Nationality in Whitman and His Heirs." In *Ceremonies and Spectacles: Performing American Culture*. Ed. Teresa Alves, Teresa Cid, and Heinz Ickstadt. Amsterdam: V.U. University Press, 2000. 289–312.
Altman, Janet Gurkin. *Epistolarity: Approaches to a Form*. Columbus: Ohio State University Press, 1982.
Anderson, Benedict. *Imagined Communities: Reflections on the Origin and Spread of Nationalism*. London: Verso, 1983, 1991.
Applegate, Edd. *Personalities and Products: A Historical Perspective on Advertising in America*. Westport, Conn.: Greenwood, 1998.
Arendt, Hannah. *The Human Condition*. Chicago: University of Chicago Press, 1958.
Augst, Thomas. *The Clerk's Tale: Young Men and Moral Life in Nineteenth-Century America*. Chicago: University of Chicago Press, 2003.
Baker, Houston A., Jr. *The Journey Back: Issues in Black Literature and Criticism*. Chicago: University of Chicago Press, 1980.
Baker, Thomas N. *Sentiment and Celebrity: Nathaniel Parker Willis and the Trials of Literary Fame*. New York: Oxford University Press, 1999.
Baldasty, Gerald. *The Commercialization of News in the Nineteenth Century*. Madison: University of Wisconsin Press, 1992.
Bannet, Eve Tavor. *Empire of Letters: Letter Manuals and Transatlantic Correspondence, 1688–1820*. Cambridge: Cambridge University Press, 2005.
Barnum, P. T. *Humbugs of the World*. New York: Carleton, 1866.
———. *The Life of P. T. Barnum, Written by Himself*. 1855. Urbana: University of Illinois Press, 2001.
———. *Selected Letters of P. T. Barnum*. Ed. A. H. Saxon. New York: Columbia University Press, 1983.

———. *Struggles and Triumphs; or, Forty Years' Recollections of P. T. Barnum*. 1869. Ed. Carl Bode. New York: Penguin, 1981.

Barthes, Roland. *Camera Lucida: Reflections on Photography*. Trans. Richard Howard. New York: Hill & Wang, 1981.

———. *Image, Music, Text*. Trans. Stephen Heath. New York: Hill & Wang, 1977.

Baudrillard, Jean. *Simulacra and Simulation*. Trans. Sheila Faria Glaser. East Lansing: University of Michigan Press, 1995.

Bell, Whitfield Jenks, Jr., ed. *Cabinet of Curiosities: Five Episodes in the Evolution of American Museums*. Charlottesville: University Press of Virginia, 1967.

Benhabib, Seyla. "Models of Public Space: Hannah Arendt, the Liberal Tradition, and Jürgen Habermas." In Calhoun, *Habermas and the Public Sphere*, 73–98.

Benjamin, Walter. *Illuminations*. Ed. Hannah Arendt. New York: Schocken, 1968.

Benstock, Shari. "Authorizing the Autobiographical." In *The Private Self: Theory and Practice of Women's Autobiographical Writings*. Ed. Shari Benstock. Chapel Hill: University of North Carolina Press, 1988. 10–33.

Bergman, Hans. "Panoramas of New York, 1845–1860." *Prospects* 10 (October 1985): 119–37.

Berkhofer, Robert F., Jr. *The White Man's Indian: Images of the American Indian from Columbus to the Present*. New York: Knopf, 1978.

Berlant, Lauren. "The Female Woman: Fanny Fern and the Form of Sentiment." *American Literary History* 3, no. 3 (Autumn 1991): 429–54.

———, ed. *Intimacy*. Chicago: University of Chicago Press, 2000.

———. "National Brands/National Body: *Imitation of Life*." In *Comparative American Identities: Race, Sex, and Nationality in the Modern Text*. Ed. Hortense J. Spillers. New York: Routledge, 1991. 110–40.

Bertolini, Vincent J. "Fireside Chastity: The Erotics of Sentimental Bachelorhood in the 1850s." In Chapman and Hendler, *Sentimental Men*, 19–42.

Bishop, Jonathan. *Emerson on the Soul*. Cambridge, Mass.: Harvard University Press, 1964.

Blake, David Haven. *Walt Whitman and the Culture of American Celebrity*. New Haven, Conn.: Yale University Press, 2006.

Blight, David. *Race and Reunion: The Civil War and American Memory*. Cambridge, Mass.: Harvard University Press, 2002.

Bode, Carl. *The American Lyceum: Town Meeting of the Mind*. New York: Oxford University Press, 1956.

Bogdan, Robert. *Freak Show: Presenting Human Oddities for Amusement and Profit*. Chicago: University of Chicago Press, 1988.

Boorstin, Daniel. *The Image; or, What Happened to the American Dream*. New York: Atheneum, 1962.

Bosco, Ronald A., and Joel Myerson. *Emerson in His Own Time: A Biographical Chronicle of His Life, Drawn from Recollections, Interviews, and Memoirs by Family, Friends, and Associates*. Iowa City: University of Iowa Press, 2003.

Brand, Dana. *The Spectator and the City in Nineteenth-Century American Literature*. Cambridge: Cambridge University Press, 1991.

Brandt, Clare. *Eighteenth-Century Letters and British Culture*. London: Palgrave Macmillan, 2006.

Brasher, Thomas L. *Whitman as Editor of the Brooklyn Daily Eagle*. Detroit: Wayne State University Press, 1970.

Braudy, Leo. *The Frenzy of Renown: Fame and Its History*. New York: Oxford University Press, 1986.

Brodhead, Richard H. *Cultures of Letters: Scenes of Reading and Writing in Nineteenth-Century America*. Chicago: University of Chicago Press, 1993.

Brown, Charles H. "Young Editor Whitman." *Journalism Quarterly* 27 (Spring 1950): 141–48.

Buell, Lawrence. *Emerson*. Cambridge, Mass.: Harvard University Press, 2003.

———. *New England Literary Culture from Revolution through Renaissance*. Cambridge: Cambridge University Press, 1986.

Bunker, Gary L. *From Rail-Splitter to Icon: Lincoln's Image in Illustrated Periodicals, 1860–1865*. Kent, Ohio: Kent State University Press, 2001.

Burroughs, John. *Walt Whitman: A Study*. Boston: Houghton Mifflin, 1902.

Butsch, Richard. *The Making of American Audiences from Stage to Television, 1750–1990*. Cambridge: Cambridge University Press, 2000.

Calhoun, Craig, ed. *Habermas and the Public Sphere*. Cambridge, Mass.: MIT Press, 1992.

Cameron, Sharon. *Impersonality: Seven Essays*. Chicago: University of Chicago Press, 2007.

Cassuto, Leonard. *The Inhuman Race: The Racial Grotesque in American Literature and Culture*. New York: Columbia University Press, 1997.

Castiglia, Christopher. *Interior States: Institutional Consciousness and the Inner Life of Democracy in the Antebellum United States*. Durham, N.C.: Duke University Press, 2008.

Castiglia, Christopher, and Glenn Hendler. Introduction. *Franklin Evans; or, The Inebriate*. By Walt Whitman. Ed. Christopher Castiglia and Glenn Hendler. Durham, N.C.: Duke University Press, 2007. ix–lvii.

Castronovo, Russ. *Necro Citizenship: Death, Eroticism, and the Public Sphere in the Nineteenth-Century United States*. Durham, N.C.: Duke University Press, 2001.

Castronovo, Russ, and Dana D. Nelson. *Materializing Democracy: Toward a Revitalized Cultural Politics*. Durham, N.C.: Duke University Press, 2002.

Cayton, Mary Kupiec. "The Making of an American Prophet: Emerson, His Audiences, and the Rise of the Culture Industry in Nineteenth-Century America." *American Historical Review* 92 (1987): 597–620.

Channing, William Ellery. *Self-Culture*. 1838. New York: Arno, 1993.

Chapman, Mary, and Glenn Hendler, eds. *Sentimental Men: Masculinity and the Politics of Affect in American Culture*. Berkeley: University of California Press, 1999.

Charvat, William. *The Profession of Authorship in America, 1800–1870*. Ed. Matthew J. Bruccoli. Columbus: Ohio State University Press, 1968.

Cheyfitz, Eric. *The Trans-Parent: Sexual Politics in the Language of Emerson*. Baltimore: Johns Hopkins University Press, 1981.

Child, Lydia Maria. *Letters from New-York*. Ed. Bruce Mills. Athens: University of Georgia Press, 1998.

Cmiel, Kenneth. *Democratic Eloquence: The Fight over Popular Speech in Nineteenth-Century America*. New York: William Morrow, 1990.

Cohen, Lara Langer. *The Fabrication of American Literature: Fraudulence and Antebellum Print Culture*. Philadelphia: University of Pennsylvania Press, 2012.

Cook, James W. *The Arts of Deception: Playing with Fraud in the Age of Barnum*. Cambridge, Mass.: Harvard University Press, 2001.

Coultrap-McQuinn, Susan. *Doing Literary Business: American Woman Writers in the Nineteenth Century*. Chapel Hill: University of North Carolina Press, 1990.

Crain, Caleb. *American Sympathy: Men, Friendship, and Literature in the New Nation*. New Haven, Conn.: Yale University Press, 2001.

Croly, David G. *Miscegenation*. 1863. Upper Saddle River, N.J.: Literature House, 1970.

Debord, Guy. *The Society of the Spectacle*. Detroit: Black & Red, 1983.

DeLombard, Jeannine. "'Eye-Witness to the Cruelty': Southern Violence and Northern Testimony in Frederick Douglass's 1845 Narrative." *American Literature* 73, no. 2 (June 2001): 245–75.

Dennett, Andrea Stulman. *Weird and Wonderful: The Dime Museum in America*. New York: New York University Press, 1997.

Derounian-Stodola, Kathryn Zabelle, and James Arthur Levernier. *The Indian Captivity Narrative, 1550–1900*. New York: Twayne, 1993.

Dillon, Elizabeth Maddock. *The Gender of Freedom: The Fictions of Liberalism and the Literary Public Sphere*. Stanford, Calif.: Stanford University Press, 2004.

Dougherty, James. *Walt Whitman and the Citizen's Eye*. Baton Rouge: Louisiana State University Press, 1993.

Douglas, Ann. *The Feminization of American Culture*. New York: Knopf, 1977.

Douglass, Frederick. *Autobiographies: Narrative of the Life of Frederick Douglass, an American Slave, My Bondage and My Freedom, Life and Times of Frederick Douglass*. New York: Library of America, 1994.

———. *Frederick Douglass: Selected Speeches and Writings*. Ed. Philip S. Foner. Abr. Yuval Taylor. Chicago: Lawrence Hill, 1999.

Dowling, David. *The Business of Literary Circles in Nineteenth-Century America*. New York: Palgrave Macmillan, 2011.

———. *Capital Letters: Authorship in the Antebellum Literary Market*. Iowa City: University of Iowa Press, 2009.

Dyer, Richard. *Heavenly Bodies: Film Stars and Society*. 2nd ed. London: Routledge, 2004.

———. *The Matter of Images: Essays on Representation*. 2nd ed. London: Routledge, 2000.

———. "Stars as Images." In Marshall, *Celebrity Culture Reader*, 153–76.

Eddy, T. M. "Barnum." *The Ladies' Repository* 15, no. 3 (March 1855): 170–75.

Elmer, Jonathan. *Reading at the Social Limit: Affect, Mass Culture, and Edgar Allan Poe*. Stanford, Calif.: Stanford University Press, 2000.

Emerson, Ralph Waldo. *Collected Works of Ralph Waldo Emerson*. Ed. Robert Spiller et al. 10 vols. Cambridge, Mass.: Harvard University Press, 1971–2013.

———. *The Journals and Miscellaneous Notebooks of Ralph Waldo Emerson*. Ed. William H. Gilman et al. 16 vols. Cambridge, Mass.: Belknap, 1960–82.

———. *The Later Lectures of Ralph Waldo Emerson: 1843–1871*. Vol. 1. Ed. Ron Bosco and Joel Myerson. Athens: University of Georgia Press, 2001.

———. *The Letters of Ralph Waldo Emerson*. Ed. Ralph L. Rusk and Eleanor M. Tilton. 10 vols. New York: Columbia University Press, 1939–95.

Erkkila, Betsy. *Whitman the Political Poet*. New York: Oxford University Press, 1989.

Erkkila, Betsy, and Jay Grossman, eds. *Breaking Bounds: Whitman and American Cultural Studies*. New York: Oxford University Press, 1996.

Ernest, John. *Liberation Historiography: African American Writers and the Challenge of History, 1794–1861*. Chapel Hill: University of North Carolina Press, 2004.

———. *Resistance and Reformation in Nineteenth-Century African American Literature: Brown, Wilson, Jacobs, Delaney, Douglass, and Harper*. Jackson: University Press of Mississippi, 1995.

Fanuzzi, Robert. *Abolition's Public Sphere*. Minneapolis: University of Minnesota Press, 2003.

———. "The Trouble with Douglass's Body." *ATQ* 13, no. 1 (March 1999): 27–49.

Felluga, Dino Franco. *The Perversity of Poetry: Romantic Ideology and the Male Poet of Genius*. Albany: State University of New York Press, 2005.

Fern, Fanny [Sara Willis Parton]. *Ruth Hall and Other Writings*. Ed. Joyce Warren. New Brunswick, N.J.: Rutgers University Press, 1986.

Fishkin, Shelly Fisher. *From Fact to Fiction: Journalism and Imaginative Writing in America*. Baltimore: Johns Hopkins University, 1985.

Fliegelman, Jay. *Declaring Independence: Jefferson, Natural Language, and the Culture of Performance*. Stanford, Calif.: Stanford University Press, 1993.

Folsom, Ed. *Walt Whitman's Native Representations*. Cambridge: Cambridge University Press, 1994.

Francis, Sean. "'Outbidding at the Start the Old Cautious Hucksters': Promotional Discourse and Whitman's 'Free' Verse." *Nineteenth-Century Literature* 57, no. 3 (December 2002): 381–406.

Fretz, Eric. "P. T. Barnum's Theatrical Selfhood and the Nineteenth-Century Culture of Exhibition." In Thomson, *Freakery*, 97–107.

Frost, Linda. *Never One Nation: Freaks, Savages, and Whiteness in U.S. Popular Culture, 1850–1877*. Minneapolis: University of Minnesota Press, 2005.

Garvey, T. Gregory. *Creating the Culture of Reform in Antebellum America*. Athens: University of Georgia Press, 2006.

Gaul, Theresa Strouth, ed. *To Marry an Indian: The Marriage of Harriett Gold and Eliza Boudinot in Letters, 1823–1839*. Chapel Hill: University of North Carolina Press, 2005.

Geary, Susan. "The Domestic Novel as a Commercial Commodity: The Making of a Best Seller in the 1850s." *Papers of the Bibliographical Society of America* 70 (1976): 365–93.

Gilroy, Amanda, and W. M. Verhoeven. *Epistolary Histories: Letters, Fiction, Culture*. Charlottesville: University of Virginia Press, 2000.

Gleason, William A. *The Leisure Ethic: Work and Play in American Literature, 1840–1940*. Stanford, Calif.: Stanford University Press, 1999.

Glymph, Thavolia. *Out of the House of Bondage: The Transformation of the Plantation Household*. Cambridge: Cambridge University Press, 2008.

Goldsmith, Jason. "Celebrity and the Spectacle of Nation." In Mole, *Romanticism and Celebrity Culture*, 21–40.

Greenspan, Ezra. *Walt Whitman and the American Reader*. Cambridge: Cambridge University Press, 1990.

Greiman, Jennifer. *Democracy's Spectacle: Sovereignty and Public Life in Antebellum American Writing*. New York: Fordham University Press, 2010.

Gunn, Robert. "'How I Look': Fanny Fern and the Strategy of Pseudonymity." *Legacy* 27, no. 1 (2010): 23–42.

Gustafson, Sandra M. *Eloquence Is Power: Performance and Oratory in Early America*. Chapel Hill, N.C.: Omohundro Institute of Early American History and Culture, 2000.

Habermas, Jürgen. *The Structural Transformation of the Public Sphere: An Inquiry into a Category of Bourgeois Society*. Trans. Thomas Burger. Cambridge, Mass.: MIT Press, 1991.

Halttunen, Karen. *Confidence Men and Painted Women: A Study of Middle-Class Culture in America, 1830–1870*. New Haven, Conn.: Yale University Press, 1982.

Hamilton, Sheryl N. *Impersonations: Troubling the Person in Law and Culture*. Toronto: University of Toronto Press, 2009.

Harris, Jennifer. "Marketplace Transactions and Sentimental Currencies in Fanny Fern's *Ruth Hall*." *ATQ* 20, no. 1 (March 2006): 343–59.

Harris, Neil. *Humbug: The Art of P. T. Barnum*. Boston: Little, Brown, 1973.

Harris, Susan K. *19th-Century American Women's Novels: Interpretive Strategies*. Cambridge: Cambridge University Press, 1990.

Hayes, Kevin J. "Visual Culture and the Word in Edgar Allan Poe's 'The Man of the Crowd.'" *Nineteenth-Century Literature* 56, no. 4 (March 2002): 445–65.

Hendler, Glenn. *Public Sentiments: Structures of Feeling in Nineteenth-Century American Literature*. Chapel Hill: University of North Carolina Press, 2001.

Henkin, David M. *City Reading: Written Words and Public Spaces in Antebellum New York*. New York: Columbia University Press, 1998.

Hewitt, Elizabeth. *Correspondence and American Literature, 1770–1865*. Cambridge: Cambridge University Press, 2004.

Hoig, Stan. *The Kiowas and the Legend of Kicking Bird*. Boulder: University Press of Colorado, 2000.

Holmes, Oliver Wendell. *Ralph Waldo Emerson*. Boston: Houghton Mifflin, 1884, 1912.

Holzer, Harold. *Lincoln Seen and Heard*. Lawrence: University of Kansas Press, 2000.

Holzer, Harold, Gabor S. Boritt, and Mark E. Neely Jr. *The Lincoln Image: Abraham Lincoln and the Popular Print*. New York: Scribner, 1984.

Homestead, Melissa. "'Every Body Sees the Theft': Fanny Fern and Literary Proprietorship in Antebellum America." *New England Quarterly* 74, no. 2 (June 2001): 210–37.

Hudson, Frederic. *Journalism in the United States, from 1690–1872*. New York: Harper & Brothers, 1873.

James, Henry. *Partial Portraits*. Ann Arbor: University of Michigan Press, 1970.

Jefferson, Thomas. *The Papers of Thomas Jefferson, Volume 33: 16 February to 30 April 1801*. Princeton: Princeton University Press, 2006. https://jefferson papers.princeton.edu/seected-documents/first-inaugural-address-0.

Jenkins, Henry. *Convergence Culture: Where Old and New Media Collide*. New York: New York University Press, 2006.

Kateb, George. *Emerson and Self-Reliance*. Lanham, Md.: Rowman & Littlefield, 2000.

Kelley, Mary. *Private Woman, Public Stage: Literary Domesticity in Nineteenth-Century America*. 1984. Chapel Hill: University of North Carolina Press, 2002.

Kerber, Linda. "Separate Spheres, Female Worlds, and Woman's Place: The Rhetoric of Women's History." In *Toward an Intellectual History of Women: Essays by Linda Kerber*. Chapel Hill: University of North Carolina Press, 1997. 159–99.

Krieg, Joann P. *Whitman and the Irish*. Iowa City: University of Iowa Press, 2000.

Kunhardt, Philip B., Jr., Philip B. Kunhardt III, and Peter W. Kunhardt. *P. T. Barnum: America's Greatest Showman*. New York: Knopf, 1995.

Lacan, Jacques. *The Four Fundamental Concepts of Psychoanalysis*. Ed. Jacques-Alain Miller. Trans. Alan Sheridan. New York: Norton, 1998.

Laffrado, Laura. "'I Thought from the Way You *Writ*, That You Were a Great Six-Footer of a Woman': Gender and the Public Voice in Fanny Fern's Newspaper Essays." In *In Her Own Voice: Nineteenth-Century American Woman Essayists*. Ed. Sherry Lee Linkon. New York: Garland, 1997.

Lampe, Gregory P. *Frederick Douglass: Freedom's Voice*. East Lansing: Michigan State University Press, 1998.

Langer, John. "Television's 'Personality System.'" In Marshall, *Celebrity Culture Reader*, 181–95.

Larkin, Edward. "Inventing an American Public: Thomas Paine, The *Pennsylvania Magazine*, and American Revolutionary Political Discourse." *EAL* 33, no. 3 (1998): 250–76.

Larson, Kerry C. *Whitman's Drama of Consensus*. Chicago: University of Chicago Press, 1988.

Lehuu, Isabelle. *Carnival on the Page: Popular Print Media in Antebellum America*. Chapel Hill: University of North Carolina Press, 2000.

Lemire, Elise. *"Miscegenation": Making Race in America*. Philadelphia: University of Pennsylvania Press, 2002.

Leverenz, David. *Manhood and the American Renaissance*. Ithaca, N.Y.: Cornell University Press, 1989.

Levine, Morton H. "Privacy in the Tradition of the Western World." In *Privacy: A Vanishing Value?* Ed. William C. Bier. New York: Fordham University Press, 1980.

Levine, Robert S. "The Slave Narrative and the Revolutionary Tradition of American Autobiography." *The Cambridge Companion to African American Slave Narrative*. Ed. Audrey A. Fisch. Cambridge: Cambridge University Press, 2007.

Lincoln, Abraham. *Speeches and Writings, 1859–1865*. New York: Library of America, 1989.

Lindberg, Gary. *The Confidence Man in American Literature*. New York: Oxford University Press, 1982.

Locall, Ernest J., Jr., ed. *Conversations of Lord Byron*. Princeton, N.J.: Princeton University Press, 1969.

Locke, John. *An Essay concerning Human Understanding*. 2 vols. Ed. Alexander Campbell Fraser. New York: Dover, 1959.

Looby, Christopher. *Voicing America: Language, Literary Form, and the Origins of the United States*. Chicago: University of Chicago Press, 1996.

Loughran, Trish. *The Republic in Print: Print Culture in the Age of U.S. Nation Building, 1770–1870*. New York: Columbia University Press, 2007.

Loving, Jerome. "The Political Roots of *Leaves of Grass*." *A Historical Guide to Walt Whitman*. Ed. David Reynolds. New York: Oxford University Press, 2000.

———. *Walt Whitman: The Song of Himself*. Berkeley: University of California Press, 1999.

Lowell, James Russell. *My Study Windows*. 1871. New York: AMS Press, 1971.

Marshall, P. David. *Celebrity and Power: Fame in Contemporary Culture*. Minneapolis: University of Minnesota Press, 1997.

———, ed. *The Celebrity Culture Reader*. New York: Routledge, 2006.

Martin, Waldo. *The Mind of Frederick Douglass*. Chapel Hill: University of North Carolina Press, 1984.

Marwick, Alice, and danah boyd. "To See and Be Seen: Celebrity Practice on Twitter." *Convergence* 17, no. 2 (May 2011): 139–58.

Mayhall, Mildred. *The Kiowas*. Norman: University of Oklahoma Press, 1962.

McConachie, Bruce. "Museum Theater and the Problem of Respectability for Mid-Century Urban Americans." In *The American Stage: Social and Economic Issues from the Colonial Period to the Present*. Ed. Ron Engle and Tice L. Miller. Cambridge: Cambridge University Press, 1993. 65–80.

McFeely, William S. *Frederick Douglass*. New York: Norton, 1991.
McGiffert, Arthur Cushman, Jr., ed. *Young Emerson Speaks: Unpublished Discourses on Many Subjects*. Boston: Houghton Mifflin, 1938.
McGill, Meredith. *American Literature and the Culture of Reprinting*. Philadelphia: University of Pennsylvania Press, 2003.
Mead, David. *Yankee Eloquence in the Middle West: The Ohio Lyceum, 1850–1870*. East Lansing: Michigan State College Press, 1951.
Milder, Robert. "A Radical Emerson?" In *The Cambridge Companion to Ralph Waldo Emerson*. Ed. Joel Porte and Saundra Morris. Cambridge: Cambridge University Press, 1999. 49–75.
Mole, Tom. *Byron's Romantic Celebrity: Industrial Culture and the Hermeneutic of Intimacy*. Basingstoke: Palgrave Macmillan, 2007.
———. *Romanticism and Celebrity Culture, 1750–1850*. Cambridge: Cambridge University Press, 2009.
Moon, Michael. *Disseminating Whitman: Revision and Corporeality in Leaves of Grass*. Cambridge, Mass.: Harvard University Press, 1991.
Moses, Carole. "The Domestic Transcendentalism of Fanny Fern." *TSLL* 50, no. 1 (Spring 2008): 90–119.
Moses, Wilson J. "Writing Freely? Frederick Douglass and the Constraints of Racialized Writing." In *Frederick Douglass: New Literary and Historical Essays*. Ed. Eric J. Sundquist. Cambridge: Cambridge University Press, 1990.
Mott, Frank Luther. *The Golden Multitudes: The Story of Best Sellers in the United States*. New York: Macmillan, 1947.
Mouffe, Chantal. *The Democratic Paradox*. London: Verso, 2000, 2009.
Moulton, William U. *The Life and Beauties of Fanny Fern*. Philadelphia: T. B. Peterson, 1855.
Mulvey, Laura. "Visual Pleasure and Narrative Cinema." *Screen* 16, no. 3 (Autumn 1975): 6–18.
Myerson, Joel, ed. *Emerson and Thoreau: The Contemporary Reviews*. Cambridge: Cambridge University Press, 1992.
Nasaw, David. *Going Out: The Rise and Fall of Public Amusements*. New York: Basic Books, 1993.
Nelson, Dana D. *National Manhood: Capitalist Citizenship and the Imagined Fraternity of White Men*. Durham, N.C.: Duke University Press, 1998.
Newbury, Michael. "Eaten Alive: Slavery and Celebrity in Antebellum America." In Michael Newbury, *Figuring Authorship in Antebellum America*. Stanford, Calif.: Stanford University Press, 1997. 79–118.
Newfield, Christopher. *The Emerson Effect: Individualism and Submission in America*. Chicago: University of Chicago Press, 1996.
Newman, Simon P. *Parades and the Politics of the Street: Festive Culture in the Early American Republic*. Philadelphia: University of Pennsylvania Press, 1997.
Noble, Marianne. *The Masochistic Pleasures of Sentimental Literature*. Princeton, N.J.: Princeton University Press, 2000.

Nord, David Paul. *Communities of Journalism: A History of American Newspapers and Their Readers*. Urbana: University of Illinois Press, 2001.

Noverr, Douglas A. "Journalism." In *A Companion to Walt Whitman*. Ed. Donald D. Kummings. Malden, Mass.: Blackwell, 2006. 29–41.

Nussbaum, Martha. "Democratic Desire." In Seery, *Political Companion to Walt Whitman*, 96–130.

Olive Branch. Boston. American Antiquarian Society, Worcester, Mass.

Packer, Barbara. "Historical Introduction." *The Collected Works of Ralph Waldo Emerson: The Conduct of Life*. Cambridge, Mass.: Belknap, 2005. il–l.

———. *The Transcendentalists*. Athens: University of Georgia Press, 2007.

Page, Ruth. "The Linguistics of Self-Branding and Micro-Celebrity in Twitter: The Use of Hashtags." *Discourse and Communication* 6, no. 2 (May 2012): 181–201.

Panzer, Mary. *Mathew Brady and the Image of History*. Washington, D.C.: Smithsonian Institution, 1997.

Peer, Larry H., ed. *Inventing the Individual: Romanticism and the Idea of Individualism*. Provo, Utah: International Conference on Romanticism, 2002.

Pollak, Vivian R. *The Erotic Whitman*. Berkeley: University of California Press, 2000.

Railton, Stephen. "'Seeing and Saying': The Dialectic of Emerson's Eloquence." *Emerson and His Legacy: Essays in Honor of Quentin Anderson*. Ed. Stephen Danadio, Stephen Railton, and Ormond Seavey. Carbondale: Southern Illinois University Press, 1986. 48–65.

Ramsey, Colin. "Cannibalism and Infant Killing: A System of 'Demonizing' Motifs in Indian Captivity Narratives." *CLIO* 24, no. 55 (1994): 55–68.

Ray, Angela G. *The Lyceum and Public Culture in the Nineteenth-Century United States*. East Lansing: Michigan State University Press, 2005.

Reese, David Meredith. *Humbugs of New-York*. New York: John S. Taylor, 1838.

Reiss, Benjamin. *The Showman and the Slave: Race, Death, and Memory in Barnum's America*. Cambridge, Mass.: Harvard University Press, 2001.

Reynolds, David S. *Walt Whitman's America: A Cultural Biography*. New York: Vintage/Random House, 1995.

"The Right to Privacy in Nineteenth-Century America." *Harvard Law Review* 94, no. 8 (1981): 1892–1910.

Roberts, Heather. "'The Public Heart': Urban Life and the Politics of Sympathy in Lydia Maria Child's *Letters from New York*." *American Literature* 76, no. 4 (December 2004): 749–75.

Robinson, David. *Apostle of Culture: Emerson as Preacher and Lecturer*. Philadelphia: University of Pennsylvania Press, 1982.

———, ed. *William Ellery Channing: Selected Writings*. New York: Paulist Press, 1985.

Rockwell, Stephen J. *Indian Affairs and the Administrative State in the Nineteenth Century*. New York: Cambridge University Press, 2010.

Rojek, Chris. *Celebrity*. London: Reaktion, 2001.

Rourke, Constance M. *Trumpets of Jubilee: Henry Ward Beecher, Harriet Beecher Stowe, Lyman Beecher, Horace Greeley, P. T. Barnum*. New York: Harcourt, 1927.

Rubin, Joseph Jay, and Charles H. Brown. *Walt Whitman of the New York Aurora: Editor at Twenty-Two*. State College, Penn.: Bald Eagle Press, 1950.

Ryan, Mary P. *Civic Wars: Democracy and Public Life in the American City during the Nineteenth Century*. Berkeley: University of California Press, 1997.

———. "Gender and Public Access: Women's Politics in Nineteenth-Century America," in Calhoun, *Habermas and the Public Sphere*, 259–88.

———. *Women in Public: Between Banners and Ballots, 1825–1880*. Baltimore: Johns Hopkins University Press, 1990.

Sanchez-Eppler, Karen. *Touching Liberty: Abolition, Feminism, and the Politics of the Body*. Berkeley: University of California Press, 1999.

Santayana, George. *Essays in Literary Criticism of George Santayana*. Ed. Irving Singer. New York: Scribner's, 1956.

Saxon, A. H. *P. T. Barnum: The Legend and the Man*. New York: Columbia University Press, 1989.

Schickel, Richard. *Intimate Strangers: The Culture of Celebrity*. Garden City, N.Y.: Doubleday, 1985.

Schiller, Dan. *Objectivity and the News: The Public and the Rise of Commercial Journalism*. Philadelphia: University of Pennsylvania Press, 1981.

Schudson, Michael. *Discovering the News: A Social History of American Newspapers*. New York: Basic Books, 1978.

Seery, John E. *A Political Companion to Walt Whitman*. Lexington: University Press of Kentucky, 2011.

Sekora, John. "Black Message/White Envelope: Genre, Authenticity, and Authority in the Antebellum Slave Narrative." *Callaloo* 32 (Summer 1987): 482–515.

Sellers, Charles. *The Market Revolution: Jacksonian America, 1815–1846*. New York: Oxford University Press, 1991.

Shamir, Milette. *Inexpressible Privacy: The Interior Life of Antebellum American Literature*. Philadelphia: University of Pennsylvania Press, 2006.

Sloan, John H. "'The Miraculous Uplifting': Emerson's Relationship with His Audience." *Quarterly Journal of Speech* 52 (1966): 10–15.

Smith, Sidonie. "Resisting the Gaze of Embodiment: Women's Autobiography in the Nineteenth Century." In *American Women's Autobiography: Fea(s)ts of Memory*. Ed. Margo Culley. Madison: University of Wisconsin Press, 1992. 75–110.

Sorisio, Carolyn. *Fleshing Out America: Race, Gender, and the Politics of the Body in American Literature, 1833–1879*. Athens: University of Georgia Press, 2002.

Stadler, Gustavus. *Troubling Minds: The Cultural Politics of Genius in the United States, 1840–1890*. Minneapolis: University of Minnesota Press, 2006.

Stallybrass, Peter, and Allon White. *The Politics and Poetics of Transgression*. Ithaca, N.Y.: Cornell University Press, 1986.

Stansell, Christine. *City of Women: Sex and Class in New York, 1789–1860*. New York: Knopf, 1986.

Stauffer, John. *The Black Hearts of Men: Radical Abolitionists and the Transformation of Race*. Cambridge, Mass.: Harvard University Press, 2002.
Strong, George Templeton. *The Diary of George Templeton Strong*. Vol. 3. New York: Macmillan, 1952.
Sundquist, Eric J. *To Wake the Nations: Race in the Making of American Literature*. Cambridge, Mass.: Belknap, 1993.
Thomson, Rosemarie Garland. *Extraordinary Bodies: Figuring Physical Disability in American Culture and Literature*. New York: Columbia University Press, 1997.
———, ed. *Freakery: Cultural Spectacles of the Extraordinary Body*. New York: New York University Press, 1996.
———. *Staring: How We Look*. Oxford: Oxford University Press, 2009.
Thoreau, Henry David. *Walden and Resistance to Civil Government*. Ed. William Rossi. New York: Norton, 1992.
Tocqueville, Alexis de. *Democracy in America*. Vol. 1. New York: Vintage, 1990.
Tompkins, Jane, ed. *Reader-Response Criticism: From Formalism to Post-Structuralism*. Baltimore: Johns Hopkins University Press, 1980.
———. *Sensational Designs: The Cultural Work of American Fiction, 1790–1860*. New York: Oxford University Press, 1985.
Vendler, Helen. *Invisible Listeners: Lyric Intimacy in Herbert, Whitman, and Ashbery*. Princeton, N.J.: Princeton University Press, 2005.
———. "Whitman's 'When Lilacs Last in the Dooryard Bloomed.'" In *Textual Analysis: Some Readers Reading*. Ed. Mary Ann Caws. New York: Modern Language Association, 1986.
Von Frank, Albert. *The Trials of Anthony Burns: Freedom and Slavery in Emerson's Boston*. Cambridge, Mass.: Harvard University Press, 1998.
Wald, Priscilla. *Constituting Americans: Cultural Anxiety and Narrative Form*. Durham, N.C.: Duke University Press, 1995.
Waldron, Karen E. "No Separations in the City: The Public-Private Novel and Private Public Authorship." In *Separate Spheres No More: Gender Convergence in American Literature, 1830–1930*. Ed. Monika M. Elbert. Tuscaloosa: University of Alabama Press, 2000.
Waldstreicher, David. *In the Midst of Perpetual Fetes: The Making of American Nationalism, 1776–1820*. Chapel Hill, N.C.: University of North Carolina Press, 1997.
Walker, Peter. *Moral Choices: Memory, Desire, and Imagination in Nineteenth-Century American Abolition*. Baton Rouge: Louisiana State University Press, 1978.
Wallace, Irving. *The Fabulous Showman: The Life and Times of P. T. Barnum*. New York: Knopf, 1959.
Warner, Michael. *Letters of the Republic: Publication and the Public Sphere in Eighteenth-Century America*. Cambridge, Mass.: Harvard University Press, 1990.
———. "The Mass Public and the Mass Subject." In Calhoun, *Habermas and the Public Sphere*, 377–401.
———. *Publics and Counterpublics*. New York: Zone, 2002.

Warren, Joyce. *Fanny Fern: An Independent Woman*. New Brunswick, N.J.: Rutgers University Press, 1994.

———. "Uncommon Discourse: Fanny Fern and the *New York Ledger*." In *Social Texts: Nineteenth-Century American Literature in Periodical Contexts*. Ed. Susan Belasco Smith and Kenneth Price. Charlottesville: University of Virginia Press, 1995. 51–68.

Warren, Samuel D., and Louis D. Brandeis. "The Right to Privacy." *Harvard Law Review* 4, no. 5 (December 15, 1890): 193–220.

Weber, Brenda R. *Women and Literary Celebrity in the Nineteenth Century: The Transatlantic Production of Fame and Gender*. London: Ashgate, 2012.

Welter, Barbara. "The Cult of True Womanhood: 1820–1860." *American Quarterly* 18 (Summer 1966): 151–74.

Whitman, Walt. *Drum Taps and Sequel to Drum-Taps*. Ed. F. DeWolfe Miller. Gainesville, Fla.: Scholars' Facsimiles & Reprints, 1959.

———. *Franklin Evans; or, The Inebriate*. Ed. Christopher Castiglia and Glenn Hendler. Durham, N.C.: Duke University Press, 2007.

———. *The Journalism*. Ed. Herbert Bergman. Vol. 1. New York: Peter Lang, 1998.

———. *Leaves of Grass: The First (1855) Edition*. Ed. Malcolm Cowley. New York: Penguin, 1959.

———. *Leaves of Grass 1860: The 150th Anniversary Facsimile Edition*. Ed. Jason Stacy. Iowa City: University of Iowa Press, 2009.

———. *Prose Works 1892*. 2 vols. Ed. Floyd Stovall. New York: New York University Press, 1963, 1964.

Wicke, Jennifer. *Advertising Fictions: Literature, Advertisement, and Social Reading*. New York: Columbia University Press, 1988.

Wider, Sarah. "What Did the Minister Mean: Emerson's Sermons and Their Audience." *ESQ* 34 (1988): 1–21.

Wilentz, Sean. *Chants Democratic: New York City and the Rise of the American Working Class, 1788–1850*. 2nd ed. New York: Oxford University Press, 2004.

Wilhelm, Julie. "An Expenditure Saved Is an Expenditure Earned: Fanny Fern's Humoring of the Capitalist Ethos." *Legacy* 29, no. 2 (2012): 201–21.

Williams, Raymond. *Keywords*. New York: Oxford University Press, 1976, 1983.

Willis, Nathaniel Parker. *Hurry-Graphs; or, Sketches of Scenery, Celebrities, and Society, Taken from Life*. New York: Scribner, 1851.

Wilson, Eric. *Emerson's Sublime Science*. New York: St. Martin's, 1999.

Wilson, Frances, ed. *Byromania: Portraits of the Artist in Nineteenth- and Twentieth-Century Culture*. New York: St. Martin's, 1999.

Yingling, Thomas. "Homosexuality and Utopian Discourse in American Poetry." In Erkkila and Grossman, *Breaking Bounds*, 135–46.

Zafar, Rafia. *We Wear the Mask: African Americans Write American Literature, 1760–1870*. New York: Columbia University Press, 1997.

Zboray, Ronald J. *A Fictive People: Antebellum Economic Development and the American Reading Public*. New York: Oxford University Press, 1993.

Žižek, Slavoj. *Looking Awry: An Introduction to Jacques Lacan through Popular Culture*. Cambridge, Mass.: MIT Press, 1994.

Zwarg, Christina. *Feminist Conversations: Fuller, Emerson, and the Play of Reading*. Ithaca, N.Y.: Cornell University Press, 1995.

INDEX

Adams, Bluford, 22, 24, 35, 45, 195n4, 198n69
Adams, John Quincy, 8
advertising, 6, 70, 161, 208n22; Barnum and, 21–23, 26, 29, 43, 195n1; Whitman and, 198n3. *See also* Barnum, P. T.: promotional strategies of; publicity
affect, 11, 16–17, 58, 73, 85–86, 98, 109, 160, 186, 189; affective expression, 11, 170, 189; celebrity culture and, 19; as commodity, 23; Dickens and, 115; feminine, 171; irony and, 165; public, 51, 85; public sphere and, 18. *See also* desire; pleasure
agency, 9, 13, 27, 95, 140
agonism, 20, 165
American Anti-Slavery Society (AASS), 118–19, 132, 143
amusement, 23, 65, 96, 135; Barnum and, 23, 26, 28–29, 42, 45, 48–50; paid, 15, 24; popular, 92, 103–4, 117, 119
Anderson, Benedict, 12
Arendt, Hannah, 124, 165
audience, 15, 81, 194n22; American, 198n57; authority of, 2–4, 35, 42, 117; Barnum's, 15–16, 22–29, 34–44, 48–50, 131, 195n4; celebrities and, 8, 13, 17; Douglass's, 131, 139, 147; Emerson's, 17, 88, 91, 97–98, 100–102, 105–6, 108, 110–12, 116; Fern's, 166, 170, 179; hype and, 29; interpretation, 2–5; popular, 203n33; print culture and, 8; slaves as, 127; white, 35, 40, 50, 137, 139; Whitman's, 51, 62, 67, 76, 78. *See also* mass audience
Augst, Thomas, 92, 95
Auld family, 129, 147–49, 152
Auld, Hugh, 124, 129

Auld, Thomas, 18, 133, 139, 148, 150–52, 205n28
Aurora. See *New York Aurora*
authority, 1, 14–15, 52, 60–61, 69, 72, 79, 102, 112, 162–64, 168, 170, 199n29, 200n40; and audience, 3–4, 35, 42, 117; of authorship, 2; blackness and, 119; celebrity and, 61–62; celebrity culture and, 2; editorial, 16; emotional, 19; gender and, 209n56; impersonal, 56–57, 111, 117; intellectual, 25, 35, 100, 117, 174; interpretive, 24, 64, 66–68, 80, 85, 93; male, 117, 176; moral, 107; patriarchal, 46; personal, 57–60; political, 9, 57, 59; popular, 90; of print, 8; slavery and, 137; social, 7, 57, 59, 61, 67, 117, 174, 176, 181; spectatorship and, 22–23, 43; state, 55; white, 40, 119, 138–39. *See also* cultural authority
authorship, 2, 6–7, 69, 156, 161, 174, 186, 193n15, 195n1, 200n42, 205n31; authority of, 2; as self-making, 23
autobiography, 158; Barnum's, 18, 21, 23–24, 27, 29, 38, 46–47, 49; Douglass's, 119–20, 122–23, 125, 127, 142–45, 149–50, 208n38; Fern and, 178; *Ruth Hall* and, 157–58, 178–79, 180, 192; women's, 157–58, 178, 207n7. *See also* authorship; public sphere

Baker, Houston A., 129, 145
Barnum, P. T., 15–16, 18, 63, 70–71, 123, 174, 177, 191, 196n23, 197n62, 198n69; advertising and, 15, 21–22, 25–27, 29, 35, 42, 44, 195n1; audiences, 15–16, 22–29, 34–44, 48–50, 131, 195n4; autobiography of, 24, 27, 47; celebrity of, 16, 24, 42–44, 47, 88;

225

Barnum, P. T. (*continued*)
  Emerson on, 87, 90; experience as editor, 42; fraudulence and, 21, 25–27, 32, 35–36, 42, 64, 87; human exhibits of, 15, 21, 23, 25–26, 34–35, 42, 44, 49–50, 130–31, 170, 173, 191; humbug and, 15, 22–23, 26–36, 39–42, 46, 50, 103; *Humbugs of the World*, 30–33, 196n26; hype and, 29–30, 39, 42, 196n18; and Indians, exhibitions of, 21, 34, 36–42, 191, 196n41; and Iraniston, 16, 44–47; Lecture Room, 35, 39–40; lectures of, 202n9; *The Life of P. T. Barnum, Written by Himself*, 27–29; on miscegenation, 32–34, 196n26; operational aesthetic of, 15, 25, 27, 41–42, 49; popular culture and, 15, 23–24, 33, 49, 90; populism of, 45; private life of, 43, 45–50, 178; promotional strategies of, 16, 22, 24–27, 29, 37; publicity and, 26, 43, 45, 47–50, 51; public life of, 46, 48, 198n67; racial exhibits of, 15, 23, 34–36, 42, 49, 191; on slavery, 26, 32–33, 48–49, 198n69; *Struggles and Triumphs*, 21, 29, 36–37, 39, 41, 47, 195n4; true womanhood and, 196n20; Universalism of, 47–48; whiteness and, 33, 49–50; as a writer, 23. *See also* freaks; freak shows; "What Is It?"
Barnum's American Museum, 21, 34, 36, 45, 95, 174, 195n4; Whitman and, 63
Bennett, James Gordon, 26, 57
Benstock, Shari, 157, 178
Berlant, Lauren, 167
best-seller, rise of, 6–7, 159, 193n16
black Americans, 152; privacy and, 122
blackness, 36, 137, 143–44, 153
Blake, David H., 62, 70–72, 77, 195n1
body (bodies), 8–9, 11, 16, 49, 91, 104–6, 108, 114–15, 117, 167, 204n59; black, 119, 125, 139–41, 143–44, 147, 152; of celebrities, 5; celebrity and, 88; civic, 26, 42; as commodity, 51; Douglass's, 143–44; Emerson's, 91–92, 97, 100, 111–13, 116; exhibited, 139; of Lincoln, 11, 84; male, 181; meaning of, 99; national, 12; nature as, 101; nonnormative, 10; nonwhite, 15, 34, 36, 42; as persons, 18, 25, 88–89, 92, 97, 132, 141, 143, 204n4; and physiognomy, 92, 188, 203n42;

preserved, 29; as prison, 136; of slaves, 119; social, 66; as spectacle, 26, 107; Whitman and, 77, 83; women's, 155, 158. *See also* identity; objectification; selfhood
Bonner, Robert, 154, 159, 180, 207n1
Bosco, Ronald A., 92, 100, 109
Boston, 15, 19, 157, 202n19; Douglass and, 117, 140; Emerson and, 94, 99, 117; Fern and, 161, 168, 178–79
Brandeis, Louis D., 123–24
Brook Farm, 2, 89
Brooklyn Daily Eagle, 64, 199n26
Brown, John, 35, 149
Bunker, Gary L., 78–79

Cabot, James Eliot, 1–2
Calvinism, 46, 161, 183, 188
capitalism, 6, 9, 17, 38, 55–57, 89–90, 96, 115, 159, 161, 187–89
Cassuto, Leonard, 130–31, 173
Castiglia, Christopher, 10
Castronovo, Russ, 84, 193n9
Catholicism, 58–59; anti-Catholicism, 52, 59, 199n31
Cayton, Mary Kupiec, 93, 202n9
celebrities, 7, 9, 11–14, 144, 181, 193n9, 194n23; audience interpretation of, 3–5, 53; emergence of, 2; images of, 159; modern, 98; objectification of, 44; physical presence of, 92; representations of, 3
celebrity culture, 2–9, 11–17, 19–20, 23–24, 43, 49, 51, 61, 73, 193n23; Barnum and, 42; desire and, 159; Douglass and, 120, 122, 141, 144, 157; Emerson and, 88–90, 101, 108–9, 111, 116, 157; Fern and, 154, 156, 170, 181, 192; newspapers and, 53; personal public sphere and, 88; publicity and, 47; religion and, 108; selfhood and, 48, 88; Whitman and, 67, 70–72, 77–78, 81, 85
celebrity image, 3–4, 6, 9, 42, 73, 88, 155
Channing, William Ellery, 96
Child, Lydia Maria, 188
citizenship, 5, 9–11, 46, 48, 84, 105; Douglass and, 117, 145; slaves and, 133; whiteness and, 119
Civil War, 36, 56, 78, 146, 153, 195n4

coffeehouse culture, 55–56, 161
Cohen, Lara Langer, 179, 207n12
Colley, Samuel G., 37–39, 41
community, 45, 66, 191; activist, 149; Barnum and, 48; desire for, 53; Emerson and, 117; imagined, 56, 84; national, 189; nationalistic, 59; slave, 135; sympathetic, 67, 190; white, 135; Whitman and, 67, 78. *See also* nationalism; public sphere
consumerism, 89, 192
consumers, 11, 13, 27, 41, 156, 159, 189
consumption, 9, 131, 156, 158–59; of the celebrity, 43, 51, 73, 120, 159; cultural, 65; visual, 23, 26
Cook, James W., 27, 36, 191, 195n4
correspondence, 165, 169–70, 174, 198n14, 208n25; authoritative claims and, 174, 199n29; Barnum's, 37–38, 47; of Fern, with readers, 19, 155, 164–65, 168, 170, 175–77, 187, 191; of readers, 55, 59–60; in *Ruth Hall*, 187–90; and Whitman, of readers, 16, 55, 59–60
Croly, David G., 32–34, 196n26
cultural authority, 5, 7, 50, 117, 163, 181–82; celebrity culture and, 14, 20; Emerson and, 90; fame and, 5; personal public sphere and, 4; public figure and, 17; Whitman and, 52, 62, 70. *See also* audience: authority of; authority
culture industry, 9, 45, 93, 95

death, 25, 83–86, 136; Emerson's, 1, 90, 98, 102; Heth's, 25; Lincoln's, 17, 84–85; objectification and, 81; slavery as social death, 121, 126, 142
DeLombard, Jeannine, 143–44, 205n31, 206n32
democracy, 5, 9, 12, 103, 139, 193n9; celebrity culture and, 11–12, 48, 62; Emerson and, 90; material culture of, 4; Whitman and, 61, 64, 67, 70
desire, 11, 17, 19, 29, 34, 51, 105; abstract, 73, 159; celebrity and, 157, 159; for community, 53; Douglass and, 122, 127–29; Emerson and, 109, 114; erotic, 8, 29, 155; Fern and, 155, 160, 190; homosexual, 171; Lacanian theory of, 73–74, 76; Whitman and, 70–72, 74–76, 78, 84–86. *See also* affect; body (bodies); consumption
Dickens, Charles, 8, 115
Douglass, Frederick, 15, 18, 27, 88, 92, 155, 157, 205n19, 205n28, 206n33; Auld family and, 18, 124, 129–30, 133, 139, 147–52, 205n28, 206n54; authorial photography and, 204n4; as autobiographical writer, 153, 206n38; black readers and, 140; celebrity and, 117, 120–23, 141–47, 152–53; education and, 129, 133–34; Emerson and, 117; escape attempt of, 136, 139; as lecturer, 118; letter to Thomas Auld, 148; *Life and Times of Frederick Douglass*, 120, 130, 144–45, 147, 149, 151–52; manhood and, 117, 131–33, 146–47; marriages of, 125, 147–48, 152; *My Bondage and My Freedom*, 131–36, 139–41, 144; Nantucket speech, 118, 133; *Narrative of the Life of Frederick Douglass, an American Slave*, 118, 120, 123–27, 129, 131–35, 148, 150–51, 204n5; performance and, 147; physical appearance/presence, 118, 132, 143, 204n4; as preacher, 204n1; as public figure, 18, 118, 120, 135, 144, 147; public image of, 119, 123; publicity and, 118, 121–23, 129, 133–34, 144–45, 152; public sphere and, 18, 119–20, 122, 131–33, 137, 140–43, 153; revolutionary figures and, 122, 205n11; Sears, Amanda, and, 149–50; selfhood and, 121, 124, 126, 129–30, 136, 141, 144; "Self-Made Men," 122; self-reliance and, 131; slave narrative and, 204n5; violent resistance and, 206n46; as witness to slavery, 205n31; writing and, 119
Dyer, Richard, 3–4, 201n58

Elmer, Jonathan, 8, 13, 73
Elssler, Fanny, 105–6, 112
emancipation, 32, 49, 146–48, 150, 152. *See also* slavery
Emerson, Ellen Tucker, 98, 112
Emerson, Ralph Waldo, 1–3, 15, 17–19, 45; "The American Scholar," 88–89, 113; betrays women's rights, 188; celebrity and, 1, 17, 116, 118; charisma of, 88, 108,

Emerson, Ralph Waldo (*continued*) 111; children of, 98, 104, 112; difficulty of, 93–95, 100; Divinity School "Address," 94, 108–9, 202n13; on domestic life, 204n55; Douglass and, 117; "Fate," 104; genius of, 17, 87, 90–91, 95, 97–99, 101–2, 113–17, 119; genuineness and, 17, 105, 110–11, 115–16; on great men, 89, 94, 106, 147, 204n59; impersonal philosophy of, 17, 90, 97, 103, 105, 107, 110–12, 114–15, 117; lectures of, 65, 75, 87–89, 91–100, 106–10, 112, 116; legacy of, 1, 91, 102; masculine power and, 100–102, 112, 117; *Nature*, 94, 104, 114; "The Over-Soul," 111; personality and, 90, 97, 103, 107, 109, 111, 115–17; physical appearance/person of, 92, 97; self and, 88–90, 95–96, 104–5, 107, 109–10, 113–17; "Self-Reliance," 87, 90, 103, 106; on self-reliance, 17, 89–91, 93, 102, 104, 106, 108–9, 114, 116–17; on solitude, 106, 113–15, 117; "The Times," 66, 106, 108–9; Unitarianism and, 108, 112; "The Uses of Great Men," 106–7; voice of, 88, 97, 99–102, 111; "Wealth," 93, 202n9; Whitman and, 65–66, 75. *See also* self-reliance
epistolarity. *See* correspondence
Ernest, John, 120–21, 146

fame, 5–7, 11, 48, 62; celebrity and, 5, 43, 81; Emerson and, 1; Fern and, 155
Farrington, Samuel, 156, 179–80
femininity, 166–67, 173. *See also* gender; woman (women)
feminism, 55, 127, 192, 208n23
Fern, Fanny (Sara Willis Parton), 15, 19, 154, 161; autobiography and, 157–58; celebrity culture and, 7, 154, 156, 170, 181, 192; celebrity of, 155, 158–60, 177–78, 180–82, 207n1; changeability of, 169–70, 172, 179; complaint and, 167; critique of publishing, 158, 178, 189; epigraphs and, 163; epistolary form and, 165–66, 176–77; first-person style and, 154, 164, 171; gender and, 92, 155–57, 159, 163–64, 175–76, 181–83; "How I Look," 181–82; identity and, 155, 166, 168–71, 176–77; imitations of, 171, 177, 190, 209n40; on *Leaves of Grass*, 207–208n19; on marriage, 156, 163–64; "The Model Husband," 161; "Mr. Punch Mistaken," 163; newspaper writing of, 162–63, 191; as novelist, 159; *The Olive Branch*, writings in, 159–77; pseudonym of, 7, 155–58, 165–67, 169, 177–80, 191; public sphere and, 18, 155–56, 174, 180, 191–92; reader correspondence of, 19, 155, 164–65, 168, 170, 175–77, 187, 191; *Ruth Hall*, 19, 156–57, 159, 179–80, 182–92, 207n12, 207n17, 209n56; satire and, 158, 163, 166–67, 173, 207n12; selfhood and, 156, 165; sentiment and, 156, 158, 166, 191, 207n12; "Sunshine and Young Mothers," 163–64; vernacular style of, 160, 165; Whitman and, 160, 178, 181, 207–208n19; writing strategies of, 154. *See also New York Ledger*; *Olive Branch*
flâneur, 188, 200n36; Whitman as, 52, 63, 69, 76–77, 80, 199n36
Folsom, Ed, 75, 81
Forbes, Edith Emerson, 98, 112
Franklin, Benjamin, 5, 43, 205n11
freaks, 36; Barnum and, 21, 34–35, 174; as nondescript, 35–36, 190–91
freak shows, 15, 26, 92, 130, 139, 174, 181, 197n62; Barnum and, 34, 49. *See also* objectification; spectacle
freedom, 33, 60, 64, 94, 121–22, 132; Douglass and, 119–25, 129–31, 136, 205n31; Emerson's individualist definition of, 115; Fern and, 158, 170; gender and, 164; intellectual, 116; masculine, 182; sexual, 179, 188; slavery and, 128, 134, 142, 152; women and, 184, 192
Frost, Linda, 34, 38
Fugitive Slave Act, 140, 206n46
Fuller, Margaret, 2, 113, 162, 204n57

Garrison, William Lloyd, 118, 132–33
Garrisonian movement, 119, 133, 204n1
Garvey, T. Gregory, 10
gaze, the, 18, 37, 141, 178, 181; black, 140; Lacan's theory of, 16, 52, 74, 76; male, 179–81, 186; objectifying, 42, 144, 180;

popular, 85; public, 43, 49, 86, 153; white, 23, 34, 49, 119, 138–39, 147, 196n19; Whitman and, 74, 76, 80. *See also* objectification
gender, 11, 15, 19, 30, 34, 204n58; Fern and, 163–65, 167–70, 172, 174–79, 181, 183; hierarchies, 161; identity, 21, 92, 165; ideologies, 155, 158, 186; language and, 132; roles, 55, 125, 157; in *Ruth Hall*, 187–88, 191, 209n56; separate spheres and, 125; Whitman and, 64. *See also* femininity; feminism; masculinity; woman (women)
genius, 17, 97, 105, 115, 204n56; Douglass as, 147; Emerson as, 17, 87, 90–91, 95, 97–99, 101–2, 113–17, 119
Glymph, Thavolia, 126–27
Goldsmith, Jason, 11
gossip, 184–85, 209n41. *See also* women: surveillance of
Great Moon Hoax of 1835, 25–26, 33
Greeley, Horace, 33, 57, 65–66, 75, 100
Greiman, Jennifer, 12, 42, 139

Habermas, Jürgen, 9, 55, 127, 208n23. *See also* public sphere
Harris, Jennifer, 186, 190
Harris, Neil, 15, 25, 27, 31
Harris, Susan K., 159, 185
Henkin, David M., 56, 199n19
heroism, 5, 113, 122, 131–32, 136–37, 140
Heth, Joice, 15, 23, 25–28, 42
Holmes, Oliver Wendell, 101
home architecture, 46, 197n65
honor, 5, 28
Hughes, John, 52, 58–62, 69, 85

identity, 5, 13, 16, 35, 74, 84, 165; Barnum's, 47; black, 120, 141; collective, 67; cultural, 18–19, 21, 26, 59; Douglass and, 131, 145, 204n4, 206n38; Fern's, 19, 154–56, 164, 166–71, 174, 176–78, 191–92; gender, 92, 168, 170, 173, 175, 178; individual, 5, 13; national, 5, 10–12, 15, 36, 41–42, 64, 85, 200n40; performative, 122; public, 6, 15, 75, 110, 119–20, 123, 176–77, 184; race and, 147; racial, 23, 34; rhetorical, 24; of the Union, 66; women writers and, 158. *See also* nationalism; personality; personhood; selfhood
Indians, 49, 197n52; Barnum exhibits, 21, 34, 36–42, 191, 196n41; delegation of leaders, 37–39, 196n41, 197n47, 197n50, 197n53; as Other, 41. *See also* Yellow Bear; Yellow Buffalo
individualism, 6, 12, 17, 30, 36, 43, 52–53, 64; Channing's, 96; Douglass and, 121, 123; Emerson and, 89–90, 110, 115; Fern and, 167–70; Jacksonian, 15, 60, 89. *See also* self-reliance
intimacy, 42, 88, 97, 102, 127, 183, 186; public, 15, 181; Whitman and, 71–78, 82–83, 85–86

Jackson, Andrew, 8
James, Henry, 1
Jim Crow, 141–42

Kimball's Theater (Boston), 96, 202n19
knowledge, 201n58; Barnum and, 25, 29–30; celebrity and, 3, 9, 24, 177, 179; Douglass and, 123, 128, 130, 133; impersonal, 114; production of, 15

Lacan, Jacques, 16, 73–74, 76
Laffrado, Laura, 157
Larson, Kerry C., 67, 71
Leaves of Grass. *See under* Whitman
Leverenz, David, 133, 204n55, 206n32
Lincoln, Abraham, 8, 16, 33, 40, 123; death of, 17; Douglass and, 144–45; Indian delegation and, 37, 197n53; portraits and, 79–80, 201n69; Whitman and, 3, 52, 78–85
Lind, Jenny, 21, 28–29, 34, 195n4, 196n20
literacy, 95, 99, 120, 123, 129, 133
Loughran, Trish, 56, 199n28
Loving, Jerome, 80–81, 199n31, 201n52
Lowell, James Russell, 101–2
lyceums, 92, 95–96, 115, 162

Marshall, P. David, 4, 13, 43, 61, 89
masculinity, 64, 80, 125, 131–33, 143, 146, 175; and black manhood, 140; as manliness,

masculinity (*continued*)
101, 132; middle-class, 22; and national manhood, 10, 41, 117, 147; white, 10, 39, 119. *See also* gaze: male; gender; identity

mass audience, 1, 3, 8, 12–13, 17, 61–62, 88; Barnum and, 42, 49; Emerson and, 90, 100, 102, 113, 116; Fern and, 180; Whitman and, 51, 53. *See also* audience

mass culture, 5–9, 12–14, 16–17, 19, 36, 51, 53, 88, 96; Child and, 188; Emerson and, 89–90, 99, 106–7, 115, 117; Frankfurt School and, 93; newspaper revolution and, 68; Whitman and, 71, 73

mass media, 3, 24, 55, 109

Massachusetts Anti-Slavery Society, 118

McGill, Meredith, 7

media image, 4, 24

miscegenation, 32–34, 36, 196n30

Mole, Tom, 6

Moses, Wilson J. 122–23

Mouffe, Chantal, 14

Moulton, William U., 15, 19, 157, 178–81; *The Life and Beauties of Fanny Fern*, 19, 178, 180

Murray, Anna, 124–25

Myerson, Joel, 92, 100, 109

nationalism, 10–12, 59, 85, 95, 175, 200n39; white, 118. *See also* community: national

nativism, 58, 66, 68; of Whitman, 53, 57, 199–200n31

Nelson, Dana D., 10–11, 41, 193n9

New York Aurora, 16, 52–53, 57–63, 65–66, 68, 199n24, 199n31; Whitman's writings in, 58–66

New York City, 15

New York Ledger, 154, 168, 181

New-York Tribune, 37, 65–66, 163

newspaper puffs, 22, 25, 29, 33, 37, 42, 66

newspaper revolution, 54, 56, 68

Norris, Thomas, 166, 168–69, 175–77

notoriety, 159, 168

objectification, 13, 24, 26; Barnum and, 41, 44, 50; Douglass and, 120, 130, 138; of femininity, 167; Fern and, 181; of nonwhite bodies, 15, 34; Whitman and, 52, 64, 81; of women, 155, 160, 182. *See also* gaze, the

Olive Branch (newspaper), 19, 154–55, 161, 168, 170, 183, 187, 207n11, 208n24, 209n40; Fern's writings in, 161, 163–67; readers' correspondence in, 171–78

orality, 53, 57, 163

oratory, 8, 54, 87–88, 112, 162, 203n46; Douglass and, 144; Emerson and, 87, 93, 97, 101, 109–10, 115

Other, 130; Indian as, 41; racial, 10; woman as, 9

ownership, 11, 57, 124

Packer, Barbara, 132, 203n42

Paine, Thomas, 59, 69, 199n28

Parton, James, 180, 208n19

penny press, 7, 53, 55–57, 67, 161–62, 198n7, 198n11, 199n19

personality, 5, 13, 16; Barnum and, 23; Emerson and, 2, 19, 90, 97, 103, 107, 109, 111, 115–17; Fern and, 154–55; marketplace for, 81; Whitman and, 70

personhood, 140–41; Barnum and, 16, 48; Douglass and, 18, 119, 121, 126, 132, 143, 145, 148, 155; Emerson and, 18; slaves and, 140. *See also* identity; selfhood

physiognomy, 92, 188; racial, 203n42

Pitts, Helen, 147–48

pleasure, 8, 15, 26–27, 41–42, 49, 73, 77, 83, 167; commodification of, 9, 15, 21–22, 29; erotic, 29; regulation of, 105; secular, 108. *See also* affect; desire; sentiment

pluralism, 12, 14, 50, 58, 66, 101, 180, 207n12

polygenesis, 34–35

popular culture, 49, 89, 93, 201n58; Barnum and, 15, 23–24, 33, 49, 90; Emerson and, 90; Whitman and, 85–86. *See also* amusement: popular; celebrity culture; mass culture

popular discourse, 4, 15, 34

print culture, 4, 6, 8, 42, 54–57, 157, 160

privacy, 8, 123–25, 56, 164, 182; Barnum and, 16, 45, 47–50; black, 18, 122; celebrity and, 157; Douglass and, 119, 122–23, 125, 129–30, 134–35, 139, 145, 148; Emerson and, 113,

118; Fern and, 178, 185, 190; gender and, 155; Lincoln and, 84; slavery and, 121–26, 128–29, 131, 135, 152; white, 126; Whitman and, 70, 72; women and, 184–85

private sphere, 23, 29, 186, 189; black, 126, 135, 140–41; Douglass and, 119–20, 122, 147; master's, 126–27, 145; slaves and, 128–29; women and, 156–57, 162, 179, 182. *See also* public sphere; separate spheres; women: surveillance of

promotional strategies, 6, 22–23, 43. *See also* Barnum, P. T.

public, the, 8–10, 50, 58, 99, 121, 180, 191, 205n22; Barnum and, 38–40; celebrity culture and, 62, 67, 157, 159; desire for amusement of, 29; Douglass and, 133, 149; Fern and, 160, 180; women writers and, 158

public figure(s), 2–8, 12–14, 50–51, 61–62, 81, 92, 108–9, 154, 157, 181; access to, 48; Barnum as, 23; black, 121–22, 142; Douglass as, 18, 118, 120, 135, 144, 147; Fern and, 160; images of, 116; impersonalization of, 98; judgment of, 43; love for, 16–17, 19, 85; personalization of, 67, 78; representations of, 53; ubiquity of, 88; white, 121–22

publicity, 2–3, 12, 18, 47–48, 50, 140; Barnum and, 26, 43, 45, 47, 49, 51; Bonner and, 154; Douglass and, 118, 121–23, 129, 133–34, 144–45, 152; Emerson and, 94, 104, 113; as exposure, 8, 119, 130, 132, 145, 169, 180; Fern and, 157, 159–60, 168, 170, 178–79; as hype, 29–30, 39, 42, 62, 70, 77, 196n18; mass, 15, 159 (*see also* notoriety); penny press and, 55–56; as public exposure, 23, 157, 178; as self-exposure, 70; slavery and, 139, 152; sorrow songs and, 128; Whitman and, 52–53, 59, 70, 72, 81; women and, 157, 180, 185. *See also* advertising; consumption

public opinion, 12, 32, 42, 89, 102–3, 116, 136, 188

public sphere, 4, 6, 9–10, 12, 19–20, 117, 165; Barnum and, 23, 29, 44, 48; black Americans in, 119, 122, 140–43, 153; celebrity culture and, 14, 51, 87; of civic debate/exchange, 14, 122; classical, 8; of commerce, 162; dialogic, 55; Douglass and, 18, 119–20,

122, 131–33, 137, 140–43, 153; Emerson and, 88–90, 95, 102, 110, 113; Fern and, 155–56, 174, 180, 191–92; Habermas on, 55–56, 127; impersonal, 8; intimacy and, 181; masculine, 158, 160, 162, 182; newspapers and, 53, 61, 67–68; patriarchal, 167; personal, 4, 8, 14–18, 34, 42, 52–53, 61–62, 65, 67–68, 73, 76–77, 88, 90–91, 95, 116, 154, 160, 180–82, 191; of print, 182; queer, 70; scholarship of, 4; slaves and, 152; white, 123, 135, 137; Whitman and, 52, 67, 71–74, 76–77, 79, 199–200n49; women and, 56, 153, 155–56, 159, 181, 183, 208n23. *See also* Habermas, Jürgen; private sphere; separate spheres

race, 141, 174; Barnum and, 15–16, 21, 23, 26, 30–31, 33–35, 49; celebrity culture and, 11; difference and, 23, 36, 119, 143; Douglass and, 117, 122, 137, 141–42, 144–47, 149; Emerson and, 107; nonwhites and, 10, 15, 42, 49, 56, 121; and racism, 33, 35–36, 129, 141, 144, 147, 149, 153; relations, 152; savages and, 131, 196n32; and whiteness, 33, 49–50, 119. *See also* gaze: white; identity; objectification; spectacle; whiteness

Reconstruction, 18, 146, 148, 152
Reese, David Meredith, 32
Rojek, Chris, 11, 108, 159
romanticism, 6, 86, 169–70, 177, 204n56, 206n33
Ruffin, George L., 145

Santayana, George, 101–2
satire, 33–34, 104; Fern and, 158, 163, 166–67, 173, 207n12
Saxon, A. H., 47, 196n23, 196n37
scandal, 6, 94, 116, 156, 209n41
secrecy, 134–35
selfhood, 5–6, 11, 36, 44, 50, 192; abstract, 5, 11, 18, 43, 88–89, 141, 145, 156, 182, 189; black, 18, 120–21, 141, 153; celebrity culture and, 47–48, 89, 170; Douglass and, 121, 124, 126, 129–30, 136, 141, 144; female, 9; Fern and, 19, 155, 158–59, 165, 168, 170, 177, 182, 192; Iranistan and, 16; masculine,

INDEX   231

selfhood (*continued*)
46; public persons and, 116; transcendent, 117, 132; whiteness and, 119; Whitman and, 53; women's, 156, 158, 160, 173. *See also* identity; individualism; personality; personhood
self-making, 6, 19, 24, 96, 136, 145
self-reliance, 17, 31, 89–91, 102–4, 106, 114, 116–17, 131; black, 146; and Douglass, 122–23, 136; Emersonian, 93, 108–10, 122–23, 136. *See also* individualism
sentiment, 14, 16, 66, 114, 153; and Fern, 156, 158, 166, 191, 207n12; public, 79; in *Ruth Hall*, 156, 191, 207n12; sentimental ideology, 156, 161. *See also* affect; Fern, Fanny
sentimentality, 54, 62, 64, 160–61, 163, 170–71, 182, 200n39, 209n45; blackness and, 143; celebrity and, 7; Fern and, 166, 175, 177, 183, 209n41; gender and, 161, 186; language and, 19; melodrama and, 202n19; personal public sphere and, 14; womanhood and, 18, 156, 163, 171, 183, 188, 191
separate spheres, 125, 157, 160, 162, 165, 176, 182–83. *See also* private sphere; public sphere
slave narratives, 119
slavery, 26; as social death, 126; surveillance and, 126–27. *See also* Douglass, Frederick; emancipation
Smith, Sidonie, 9, 158
Sorisio, Carolyn, 9
sorrow songs, 128, 140
sovereignty, 42, 58; popular, 12, 42; self, 137
spectacle, 12, 92, 96, 139, 191; anti-spectacle, Altieri's concept of, 200n40; Barnum and, 17, 42, 45, 49, 177; blackness and, 137, 139, 144; body as, 26; celebrities as, 13; democratic, 139; Douglass and, 138, 147; Emerson and, 90, 100, 103–7, 109; Fern and, 18–19; Whitman and, 65, 82
spectatorship, 13, 22–23, 42, 101, 119, 174, 178
Stadler, Gustavus, 92, 98, 204n59
Strong, George Templeton, 35–36
subject, 8–9, 13, 73–74, 78, 81, 109, 139, 206n35; Barnum as, 23; Douglass as, 143;

Fern as, 157, 179; male, 47, 117; observer as, 181; political, 80; visual, 79; white, 10, 42
Sullivan, John, 15
Sundquist, Eric J., 132, 136, 205n11
sympathy, 8, 78, 110, 185–90; communities of, 57; Douglass and, 140; Emerson and, 98, 112; Fern and, 19, 156, 173, 181–82, 191; race and, 33; Whitman and, 80

Thomson, Rosemarie Garland, 26, 36
Thoreau, Henry David, 31, 97, 196n23
Tocqueville, Alexis de, 12, 103
Tompkins, Jane, 4, 193n7
transcendentalism, 1, 31, 88, 96, 188
True Flag (Boston), 157, 161, 178
Turner, Nat, 134–35, 205n11

Unitarianism, 96, 108, 112, 136, 203n49

Vendler, Helen, 71, 74, 81
vernacular, 4, 8, 13, 18, 53–54, 56, 59, 67, 78, 162, 199n28; and Fern's style, 160, 165
virtue, 5, 48, 53, 62, 105, 131, 155; democratic, 160; women's, 173, 179, 183

Waldron, Karen, 185–86
Warner, Michael, 8–10, 57
Warren, Joyce, 160, 168, 178, 180, 192
Warren, Samuel D., 123–24
Weber, Brenda, 154–55, 207n9
"What Is It?" (Barnum exhibition), 34–36, 42, 119, 131, 191
whiteness, 33, 49–50, 119. *See also* race
Whitman, Walt, 3, 15–16, 78, 86; Americanism of, 58, 63, 67; anti-Irish sentiments of, 61, 199n31; and *The Aurora*, writings in, 58–66; "A Backward Glance o'er Travel'd Roads," 51; on Barnum, 64; "Behold This Swarthy Face," 75–76; "Calamus" poems, 16, 52, 70–78, 81, 84–86, 181, 201n52; celebrity and, 51, 53, 61, 67–72, 77–78, 81, 85; "City of My Walks and Joys," 52; editorial style of, 53, 57–59, 61, 63, 67, 199n31; Emerson and, 100; "Enfans d'Adam," 70; on fashion, 64; Fern and, 160, 178, 181,

207–208n19; first-person style and, 54, 63, 67; as flâneur, 52, 63, 69, 76–77, 80, 199n36; "A Glimpse," 72–73; and homosexuality, representations of, 71, 200–201n49; individualism of, 52–53; "In Paths Untrodden," 70; intimacy and, 71–78, 82–83, 85–86; journalism of, 16–17, 51–54, 56–57, 61–68, 71, 85, 199n24, 199n26, 200n42; *Leaves of Grass*, 16, 51, 63, 66, 70, 75, 80–81; —, first edition (1855), 68, 69, 70, 75, 208n19; —, third edition (1860) 52, 70–78; Lincoln and, 78–85; on love, 16, 19; on masculinity, 64, 80; nativism of, 53, 57, 199–200n31; on newspapers, 52–53; "Of the Terrible Doubt of Appearances," 84; Paine and, 59, 69, 199n28; panorama and, 64, 200n37; pluralism of, 66; publicity and, 51, 53; readers' letters and, 16, 55, 59–60; "Recorders Ages Hence," 74; "Scented Herbage of My Breast," 85; and the self, 51, 69; self-promotion of, 198n3; sex and, 155; "Song of Myself," 68, 69, 70, 75; *Specimen Days*, 79–80; "Sun-Down Papers from the Desk of a Schoolmaster," 54, 63; "To a Stranger," 77; "To the East and To the West" ["To You of New England"], 78; "When I Heard at the Close of the Day," 74; "When Lilacs Last in the Dooryard Bloom'd," 17, 52, 81–86; "Whoever You Are Holding Me Now in Hand," 76–77. See also *Brooklyn Daily Eagle*; *New York Aurora*

Willis, Nathaniel Parker, 65, 99–102

woman (women), 2, 10, 33, 40, 45, 127, 132, 155, 158, 163, 166–68, 170; authors, 7; autobiography and, 158–59, 178, 207n7; Barnum and, 195n4; domesticity and, 162, 164, 182–83; experiences of, 18–19, 157, 178, 191; expression of, 18; and the female complaint, 172–74, 184 (*see also* Berlant, Lauren); Fern and, 171–77, 188–92, 209n41, 209n56; as generic type, 178; literary marketplace and, 187; male discipline and, 209n45; marginalization of, 49; Native American, 196n41; as newspaper readers, 161; as Other, 9; power and, 176; and privacy, 184–85; private sphere and, 124, 156–57, 162, 179, 182; in public, 105, 108, 157, 178–79, 182–83, 194n33; publicity and, 175; public sphere and, 56, 119, 140, 153, 155–56, 159, 181, 183, 208n23; rights of, 119, 207n8; selfhood and, 155; stereotypes of, 25; surveillance of, 155, 157, 183–84 (*see also* gossip); white, 124; writers, 157, 165–66, 189, 208n25. *See also* femininity; feminism; Fern, Fanny; Fuller, Margaret; gender; identity: gender; selfhood; sentimentality

womanhood, 159, 165, 174, 180, 183, 188, 191–92; ideology of true, 29, 167, 170, 181, 196n20, 208n33; sentimental, 18, 156, 184

Woodbury, Charles Johnson, 91, 93

Yellow Bear, 37, 39–40, 196n41
Yellow Buffalo, 37–38, 196n41
Yingling, Thomas, 71, 73–74, 200n48

Zafar, Rafia, 125, 205n11

www.ingramcontent.com/pod-product-compliance
Lightning Source LLC
Chambersburg PA
CBHW032213230426
43672CB00011B/2543